The Journal of Christopher Columbus (During His First Voyage, 1492-93) and Documents Relating the Voyages of John Cabot and Gaspar Corte Real

WORKS ISSUED BY

The Hakluyt Society.

—o—

THE JOURNAL

OF

CHRISTOPHER COLUMBUS.

ETC.

No. LXXXVI.

A gran admiracion a gran espanto
Pensando sus grandezas me provoco
Y su mayor loor en qualquier canto
No se podrá decir escesco loco:

Pues Castilla y Leon le debe tanto
Que cuanto puedo yo decir es poco
No procuro deleites ni gasajos
Mas sufridor fue grande de trabajos.

JUAN DE CASTELLANOS, *Elegia IV.*

THE JOURNAL

OF

CHRISTOPHER COLUMBUS

(DURING HIS FIRST VOYAGE, 1492-93),

AND

DOCUMENTS RELATING TO THE VOYAGES

OF

JOHN CABOT

AND

GASPAR CORTE REAL.

Translated, with Notes and an Introduction,

BY

CLEMENTS R. MARKHAM, C.B., F.R.S.,

PRESIDENT OF THE HAKLUYT SOCIETY.

LONDON:

PRINTED FOR THE HAKLUYT SOCIETY,
4, LINCOLN'S INN FIELDS, W.C.

M.DCCC.XCIII.

1893

· LONDON :
PRINTED BY CHAS. J. CLARK, 4, LINCOLN'S INN FIELDS, W.C.

COUNCIL

OF

THE HAKLUYT SOCIETY.

107245

CONTENTS.

CONTENTS.

ILLUSTRATIONS.

INTRODUCTION.

I.—JOURNAL OF COLUMBUS.

HE Council of the Hakluyt So-
ciety has decided upon issuing
a translation of the Journal of
the First Voyage of Columbus on
the four hundredth anniversary
of that momentous expedition. It has also been
arranged that translations of the documents relating
to the voyages of John Cabot and Gaspar Corte
Real shall be included in the same volume. Those
voyages were direct consequences of the great discovery of Columbus. The Society has to thank Mr.
Harrisse, whose exhaustive works on the Cabots
and Corte Reals leave little but translation to be
done, for his kindness in giving permission for the
translation from his texts of some important documents,[1] the originals of which are difficult of access :
and also for permission to reproduce portions of the

---

[1] Specified in their places.

Cantino and La Cosa maps from his impressions. The thanks of the Society are also due to Mr. H. Welter, the publisher of Mr. Harrisse's last work, for permission to make use of the plates of the maps of Juan de la Cosa and Cantino.

Our late Secretary, Mr. R. H. Major, by his production of the *Select Letters of Columbus* (1847; 2nd ed., 1870), brought within the reach of members of this Society all the letters written by the Admiral himself on the subject of his four voyages, as well as some other original documents. There remains for the Council to furnish the members with a translation of the Journal of the first voyage, the only one that has been preserved, and this in a mutilated form. Our series will then contain all the contributions of the great discoverer himself, that have escaped destruction, to the history of his mighty achievements.

It is necessary, for the proper understanding of the Journal, that it should be preceded by the Toscanelli correspondence, because constant allusion is made to it by the Admiral; the places mentioned by Toscanelli were anxiously sought for at every turn; and the letters of Toscanelli were practically the sailing directions of Columbus. The famous Florentine astronomer, Paolo Toscanelli, was looked upon as the highest authority on cosmography and navigation in that age. King Affonso V of Portugal, through the Canon Fernam Martins, made an application to Toscanelli for information respecting the voyage westward to India. The astronomer replied fully on June 25th, 1474, enclosing a map. Soon afterwards Columbus, who was then at Lisbon, and had long pondered over these questions, resolved to make a similar application to the Florentine philosopher. He sent a letter, together with a small globe embodying his ideas, to Toscanelli, entrusting them to the care of an Italian named Lorenzo Birardi, who was going to Florence.[1] The reply was satisfactory.[2] Toscanelli sent his correspondent a copy of his letter to Martins, and a copy of the map, with some additional remarks. It was that letter and that map that were destined to play so important a part in the conduct of the first voyage. Columbus replied, and received a second briefer but equally cordial letter from Toscanelli. The Toscanelli correspondence is given in Italian in the *Vita dell Ammiraglio*,[3] and in Spanish in the *History* of Las Casas.[4] Both these translations are inaccurate, and several passages are inserted that are not in the original, which was in Latin. This original Latin text was discovered in 1860, in the Columbine Library at Seville, by the librarian, Don José Maria Fernandez de Velasco. He found it in the Admiral's own handwriting, on a fly-leaf of one of the books which belonged to Columbus.[5]

---

[1] *Las Casas*, i, p. 92.

[2] The date of the letter to Columbus is discussed in a note at pages 3 and 4.　　　　　　　　　　　[3] Cap. xiii.

[4] *Las Casas*, i, 92-96. Las Casas, by mistake, calls Toscanelli *Marco* Paulo, instead of Paulo, in two places.

[5] The book is *Historia rerum ubique gestarum*, by Eneas Silvio Piccolomini (Venice, 1477, small folio, 105 leaves).

I have translated from the Latin text, as given in his life of Columbus by Don José Maria Asensio.[1] The Toscanelli map is lost. It was in possession of Las Casas when he wrote his history, and that is the last trace we have of it. But it is so minutely described in the letter that its restoration, with help from the globe of Martin Behaim, is not difficult. This has been well done in *Das Ausland* (1867, p. 5), and the restoration there given has been repeated to illustrate this volume.[2]

With the letter and map of Toscanelli as his sailing directions and chart, Columbus began to make entries in his Journal of Navigation, morning and evening, from the day he left Palos. He gives no special description of his three vessels, but it is believed that sketches of them, drawn by his own hand, have been preserved. In the Columbine Library at Seville, in the edition of the first decade of Peter Martyr, which belonged to the Admiral's son Fernando, there is a map of Española drawn with a pen, and showing the earliest Spanish forts and settlements. In two places on the map there are outline sketches of the three caravels, and in the opinion of competent persons these sketches are by Columbus himself. If so, they are the only authentic representations of the first vessels that ever crossed

---

[1] *Cristobal Colon*, por D. José Maria Asensio (Barcelona, 1890), i, p. 250.

[2] The *Ausland* restoration is given by Winsor in his *Narrative and Critical History of America*, ii, p. 103, and in his *Columbus*, p. 110.

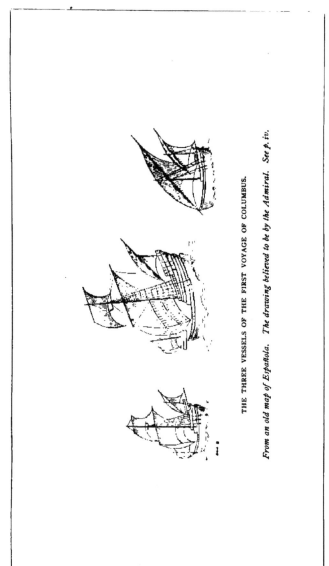

THE THREE VESSELS OF THE FIRST VOYAGE OF COLUMBUS.

From an old map of Española. The drawing believed to be by the Admiral. See p. iv.

the Atlantic. One of them has been reproduced to illustrate this volume.[1]

The Admiral diligently wrote his Journal until the day of his return to Palos. It was forwarded to Ferdinand and Isabella; but it is now lost. Las Casas had access to it when he wrote his history, and gives a very full abstract,[2] which was condensed by Herrera.[3] It was also used by Fernando Columbus in the *Vita dell Ammiraglio*.[4] In one place, where the Admiral describes his proceedings in the storm, when he threw a brief account of the voyage overboard in a barrel, the version of Fernando is much more full than that of Las Casas, and appears to be copied word for word. I have noticed the differences in their place. It is probable that Bernaldez also had access to the Journal, but made no great use of it,[5] and Oviedo never appears to have seen it.[6]

In the archives of the Duke of Infantado there was, in the end of the last century, a small folio volume in a parchment cover, consisting of seventy-six leaves closely written. It is in the handwriting of Las Casas. There is another old volume, but somewhat later than that of Las Casas, also in folio, and with a similar cover, consisting of 140 leaves. These are duplicate copies of a full abstract of the

---

[1] *Asensio*, i, p. 276.

[2] Lib. I, caps. xxxv to lxxv. The *History* by Las Casas was printed for the first time in 1875.

[3] Dec. I, Lib. I, caps. ix to xx, and Lib. II, caps. i to iii.

[4] Cap. xxxvi.

[5] *Historia de los Reyes Catolicos*, first printed in 1856.

[6] *Historia General de las Indias*.

Journal of Columbus. They were carefully collated by Don Juan Bautista Muñoz, the learned cosmographer of the Indies, and by Don Martin Fernandez Navarrete at Madrid, in February 1791. The abstract of the Journal, in the handwriting of Las Casas, was printed by Navarrete in the first volume of his *Coleccion de los viages y descubrimientos que hicieron por mar los Españoles*, and published in 1825. The present translation is made from the text of Navarrete.[1]

The Prologue, which is in fact the covering letter to Ferdinand and Isabella, is given in full. The rest is an abstract of the entries of each day, but there are long and frequent quotations, word for word, which are shown by the phrases " the Admiral says", or "these are the Admiral's words". In more than one place Las Casas complains of the illegible character of the handwriting of the original document from which he is making his abstract, but the mistakes appear to be chiefly with regard to figures. The substitution of leagues for miles occurs several times; and there are other blunders of the same kind, due to inaccurate transcription.

The Journal, even in the mutilated condition in which it has come down to us, is a document of

---

[1] Sixty-six years ago a translation was made in America, at the suggestion of Mr. Ticknor: *Personal Narrative of the First Voyage of Columbus*, translated by Samuel Kettell (Boston, 1827). A portion was also translated by Admiral Becher (12th Oct. to 28th Oct.), for the purposes of his book, the *Landfall of Columbus* (Potter, 1856).

immense value. Our sympathy and interest are excited in every page. We observe the conscientious
care with which the great discoverer recorded his proceedings, and with what intelligence he noted the
natural objects that surrounded him in the New
World. All were new to him; but he compared
them with analogous products seen in other parts of
the world, and drew useful inferences. The fulness
of his entries was due to the rapid working of
a vivid imagination, as one thought followed another
in rapid succession through his well-stored brain.
Even the frequent repetitions are not tedious, because
they give such life and reality to the document,
reminding us of the anxious and overwrought hero
jotting down his thoughts whenever he could find
a spare moment amidst the press of work. It has
been said that his sole aim appeared to be the
acquisition of gold. This unfair criticism is made
in ignorance. It must be remembered that the
letter of Toscanelli was his guide; and that the
gold, pearls, and spices were the marks by which he
was to know the provinces of the great Kaan; so
that he was bound to make constant inquiries for
these commodities. The eagerness with which he
pushed his inquiries, and his repeated disappoint-
ments, are touching. He seeks to find the places
mentioned by his guide, by fancied resemblance of
names, as when he would identify Cipangu with
Cibao in Española. This search, however, only
occupied part of his thoughts. Nothing seems to
escape his observation, and he frequently regrets

his ignorance of botany, because it prevented him from being able to report more exactly on the new species of plants that surrounded him. But the feature in his remarks which comes out most prominently is his enthusiastic admiration of scenery, and of the natural beauties of the strange land. The Journal is a mirror of the man. It shows his failings and his virtues. It records his lofty aims, his unswerving loyalty, his deep religious feeling, his kindliness and gratitude. It impresses us with his knowledge and genius as a leader, with his watchful care of his people, and with the richness of his imagination. Few will read the Journal without a feeling of admiration for the marvellous ability and simple faith of the great genius whose mission it was to reveal the mighty secret of the ages.

The Journal is the most important document in the whole range of the history of geographical discovery, because it is a record of the enterprise which changed the whole face, not only of that history, but of the history of mankind. Even during the fourteen remaining years of the Admiral's life its immediate result was the completed discovery of all the West Indian islands and of the coast of the New World from Cape San Agustin, 8° S. of the line, to the Gulf of Honduras, either by the Admiral himself, or by his followers and pupils.

The Admiral's achievement aroused a feeling of emulation in other countries. There is a direct connection between the ideas and labours of the illustrious Genoese and the voyages of his countryman John Cabot. From rather a different point of view the undertakings of Gaspar Corte Real had its origin in the discovery of Columbus. The work of these two worthies, Cabot and Corte Real, therefore, finds its proper place in the same volume with the Journal of the Admiral.

The foot-notes in the Journal marked with N. are by Navarrete. Interpolations by Las Casas are in brackets.

II.—JOHN CABOT.

A remarkable fatality has deprived posterity of any authentic record of the first English voyages to America. Not a single scrap of writing by John Cabot has been preserved. The map and globe of John Cabot no longer exist, and although a single copy of a map by his son Sebastian has survived, it was not prepared to illustrate his father's discoveries, but is a compilation drawn for the Spanish Government nearly half a century afterwards. The second-hand information fails satisfactorily to supplement the meagre official documents, which consist of two Letters Patent and a few entries in the Privy Purse Accounts of Henry VII and his son. There are two short letters from Spanish Ambassadors, three news-letters from Italians in London, the reports of what Sebastian is said to have dropped in conversation generally, written down years afterwards, the reports of his intrigues with the Venetian Government, and

a few brief notices of doubtful authenticity in
English chronicles and collections of voyages. Even
the principal entry in the Chronicles, said to be
copied from Fabyan's work, is not to be found in
any known edition of Fabyan ; while the unfortunate
habit of our greatest authority, Richard Hakluyt, of
making verbal alterations in the documents of which
he made use, further increases our difficulties.

These are the sources of information, such as they
are, from which we must derive our knowledge of
the first English voyages to America. By a careful
use of them, and an equally careful avoidance of
conjecture and hypothesis, we can piece together all
that can now be known of the earliest important
maritime enterprises in which England was concerned, and of the great navigator who conceived
and led them.

Mr. Charles Deane contributed an admirable
review of the materials forming our existing knowledge of the Cabot voyages to Winsor's *Narrative
and Critical History of America* (vol. iii, pp. 1-58),
in which he treats the various questions bearing on
the subject with sound judgment and great learning.

An exhaustive work on the Cabots, including the
original documents in their respective languages, and
valuable notes on the cartography, was published by
Mr. Harrisse, at Paris, in 1882.[1]

Desimoni has published a work on the Cabots at

---

[1] *Jean et Sébastien Cabot, leur Origine et leur Voyages*, par
Henry Harrisse (Paris, 1882).

Genoa,[1] and a considerable work, also including all the original documents, by Tarducci, has recently appeared at Venice.[2]

John Cabot was probably a Genoese[3] who, after having resided in Venice for fifteen years, from 1461 to 1476, was admitted to the rights of citizenship in the latter year.[4] He was married to a Venetian woman, and had three sons, named Luigi, Sebastian, and Sancio, all of whom must have been of age when the Letters Patent were granted to them in 1497; so that the youngest cannot have been born later than 1475. As this was within the period during which John Cabot was qualifying for citizenship by residence at Venice, his sons must have been born there.

During the next twenty years the story of John Cabot is an almost entire blank. The Genoese was usually called a Venetian because he had acquired Venetian citizenship. He became an experienced

---

[1] C. Desimoni, *Intorno a Giovanni Caboto* (Genoa).

[2] *Di Giovanni e Sebastiano Caboto, Memorie Raccolte e Documentate da F. Tarducci* (Venezia, 1892).

[3] "Another Genoese like Columbus" (Puebla, Spanish Ambassador, July 1498; also Ayala). "Sebastian Gaboto, a Genoa's son" (Stow from Fabyan; also Languet, Grafton, Holinshed). These statements are, to a certain extent, confirmed by the fact that John Cabot required to be naturalised in Venice, which proves that he was not a Venetian born. On the other hand, Tarducci puts forward arguments to establish his Venetian birth (*Di G. e S. Caboto, Memorie*, cap. i).

[4] "1476, March 28th. That the privilege of citizenship, within and without, be granted to John Caboto for having resided 15 years according to custom." (*Archivo di Stato Venezia, Libro Privilegi*, t. ii, p. 53; *Tarducci*, p. 339.)

navigator, and had commercial transactions along the
Arabian coast, even visiting Mecca, or its port,[1]
where he witnessed the arrival of caravans with
spices from the distant East, and speculated on the
distance they had come, and on the difficulties of the
route.[2]

When the news of the great discovery of Columbus became known, John Cabot eagerly sought for
information, and was aroused to a spirit of emulation.
He went to Seville and Lisbon to seek for help in
the enterprise he contemplated[3]; and adopted all the
ideas of his great countryman respecting Antilla and
the seven cities, the Isle of Cipango, and the kingdom of the great Kaan.   He then came to settle in
London as a merchant,[4] with his wife and three sons.
Of good address and an expert navigator,[5] John
Cabot presented himself at the Court of Henry VII

---

[1] Soncino (see p. 204).   He could not have actually visited
Mecca, as stated by Soncino, for Christians were not allowed to
approach within several leagues of that city.   He may have been
at Jiddah.

[2] Despatch of Raimondo di Soncino to the Duke of Milan,
dated London, 18th Dec. 1497 (*Annuario scientifico*, Milan, 1866,
p. 700; *Archiv d'Etat Milan; Harrisse*, p. 324).

[3] "Pedro de Ayala to the Catholic Sovereigns, 25 July 1498."
In *Calendar of State Papers* (Spain), i, p. 176, No. 210.

[4] *The Anonymous Guest in Ramusio*, i, f. 414 (ed. Ven., 1550):
"Nella citta di Londra."   Sebastian told this witness that he was
then very young, yet old enough to have already learnt the
humanities and the sphere: "Che gli era assai giovane non gia
peroche non avesse imparato et lettere d'humanità et la sphera."
There is no evidence that the Cabots were at Bristol previous to
the voyage in 1497.

[5] Soncino, 18th Dec. 1497 (see p. 203).

at the right moment. The great discovery of
Columbus was being much discussed, and the
courtiers were declaring that it was a thing more
divine than human to have found that way, never
before known, of going to the east where the spices
grow.[1] In the midst of this excitement, John Cabot,
a navigator, "who had made himself very expert
and cunning in the knowledge of the circuit of the
worlde and islands of the same", was presented to the
King, and made his proposal to do for England what
Columbus had done for Spain. He would show a
new route to Cipango and the land of the great
Kaan, and would bring back his ships laden with
spices. He demonstrated his arguments by a chart,
and eventually gained the ear of the wary usurper.
Henry resolved to let the adventurer attempt the
discovery of new isles, and granted him and his sons
Letters Patent, as well as material assistance.

The Letters Patent, dated March 5th, 1496,[2] grant
to John Cabot, Citizen of Venice, and to his sons
Lewis,[3] Sebastian, and Sancio, the right to navigate
in any direction they please, under the King's flag,
and at their own costs and charges, to seek out and
discover unknown lands and islands. They were

---

[1] Eden's *Decades*, f. 255; *Ramusio*, i, f. 415: "Dicendosi che
era stata cosa piu tosta divina che humana" (see p. 213).

[2] Old style.

[3] Mr. Deane, quoting from the *Armorial de la Noblesse de
Languedoc* (Paris, 1860, vol. ii, p. 163), mentions that Lewis Cabot
is said to have settled at Saint-Paul-le-Coste, in the Cevennes, and
that a family is traced from him to the present time. The arms
are: *Azure*, 3 chabots (fish) *or*.

authorised to become governors of the new territories, a fifth of all profits and revenues being reserved for the King ; and merchandise coming from
the new lands was exempted from customs duties.
All British subjects were prohibited from visiting
the new lands without a licence from the Cabots, on
pain of forfeiture of ship and cargo ; and the King's
lieges were enjoined to afford all necessary assistance
to the adventurers.

John Cabot selected the port of Bristol for the
equipment of his expedition, and there he embarked
in a ship believed to have been called the *Matthew*,[1]
with a crew of eighteen men, nearly all Englishmen,
and natives of Bristol.[2] His young son Sebastian,
then aged twenty-two at least, probably accompanied
him[3] ; but the other two sons are nowhere mentioned, except in the Letters Patent. The *Matthew*
is said to have been manned and victualled at the
King's cost,[4] which is unlikely ; and she was accom-

---

[1] "In the year 1497, the 24th of June, on St. John's Day, was
Newfoundland found by Bristol men in a ship called the *Matthew*."
History and Antiquities of Bristol, Wm. Barrett (Bristol, 1789,
p. 172), quoting from an old document, which, however, has not
since been seen.

[2] Soncino : "Quasi tutti Inglesi et de Bristo."

[3] On legend No. 8 of the map of Sebastian Cabot is the statement : "This land, formerly unknown to us, was discovered by
Joan Caboto, Veneciano, and Sebastian Caboto, his son." This
is the only evidence that Sebastian accompanied his father on his
first voyage. On the other hand, the Drapers' Company, in 1521,
represented that it was then the belief that Sebastian never was
there himself.

[4] Stow, quoting from Fabyan, followed by Hakluyt.

panied by three or four small vessels laden with
merchandise,[1] being the ventures of London merchants. But it does not appear whether more than
one ship actually crossed the Atlantic.[2]

The expedition sailed in the beginning of May[3]
1497, and, after a voyage of fifty days, it reached
land at five o'clock in the morning of Saturday, the
24th of June, being St. John's Day,[4] which was
called "Prima terra vista". The name of St. John
was given to another large island that was sighted.[5]
We know, from the map of Sebastian Cabot, that
the "Prima terra vista" is the northern end of the
island of Cape Breton, and "St. John" is in the
position of the Magdalen Islands. This is just the
landfall that John Cabot would have naturally made.
His course is clearly pointed out by the object of
his voyage, which was, like that of Columbus, to
reach the territory of the Great Kaan. The course
of Columbus was west, and that of John Cabot
must also have been west.[6] The distance is 2,300

---

[1] Stow, quoting from Fabyan, followed by Hakluyt.

[2] Pasqualigo only speaks of one ship ("ando con uno naviglio"),
and Soncino speaks of one ship with eighteen men ("uno piccolo
naviglio e xviii persone si pose ala fortuna"). The letters patent
authorised five ships.

[3] Hakluyt quoting Fabyan (see p. 200).

[4] Legend No. 8 on the map of Sebastian Cabot. The Latin
version gives the *hour* in the morning, the Spanish only says
in the morning.   [5] *Ibid.*

[6] Soncino, in his despatch from London to the Duke of Milan,
of December 18th, 1497, says: "Partitosi da Bristo, et passato
Ibernia piu occidentale e poi alzatosi verso el septentrione, co-
mencò ad navigare ale parte orientale, lassandosi (fra qualche

miles[1] in a voyage of fifty days, or forty-six miles a day. Working her way slowly westward during many days, a vessel like the *Matthew* would have made a great deal of leeway, and during the latter part of the voyage the current would have set her two hundred or more miles to the south.[2] The south coast of Newfoundland being obscured by mist, the north end of Cape Breton is exactly the landfall the *Matthew* might be expected to make under the above circumstances. Cabot hoisted the English standard on the newly-discovered land, and side by side with it he planted the lion of St. Mark, the flag of his adopted country. He did not see any inhabitants, but brought back some snares for game, and a needle for making nets.

As he was back in the end of July, he had no time to spare, and must have started at once on his voyage home.[3] Sailing from the north coast of

---

giorni) la tramontana ad mano drita"—"He departed from Bristol, and having passed Ireland, which is further west, and then turned towards the north, he began to navigate towards the eastern part, leaving (for some days) the pole on the right hand." This is not very clear. If Cabot had his ship's head north, or north of west, after passing Ireland, it would be owing to contrary winds which prevented him from laying his course. Soncino has evidently written east for west, because he says that the Pole was on the right hand, which could only be when steering west.

[1] Pasqualigo gives 700 leagues, which is nearly right. Soncino very much under-estimates the distance at 400 leagues.

[2] The course actually made good would be half a point south of west.

[3] Pasqualigo says: "Andato per la costa lige 300"—"He went along the coast 300 leagues." This is impossible. Such a cruise

Cape Breton on June 26th, with a southerly set, on the next day, after proceeding about seventy miles, he appears to have sighted land, on his starboard hand, near Sydney[1]; but he was short of provisions, and could not afford to lose time by stopping. As might be expected in going eastward, Cabot made a better voyage than when he was outward bound. It only occupied him about thirty-five days, and he arrived at Bristol in the last days of July or the first week of August.[2]

John Cabot was received on his return with great honour. The King granted him money for his personal expenses. Pasqualigo wrote to his brothers at Venice to report how the great discoverer was dressed in silk and styled the Grand Admiral, was residing at Bristol with his family, and preparing for

---

in the *Matthew* would have occupied three weeks at least from June 25th, or until the middle of July. As Cabot was back in Bristol in the end of July, it is clear that this additional cruise cannot have taken place. Pasqualigo was merely repeating second-hand gossip.

[1] "Al tornar aldreto a visto do ixole ma non ha voluto desender per non perder tempo che la vituaria li mancava"—"On the return he saw two islands on the starboard side, but he would not land because he could not waste time, as the provisions were running short" (Pasqualigo). See p. 201.

[2] The date is fixed by Pasqualigo, who says that the expedition was absent three months; and also by a royal grant of £10 to Cabot on August 10th. Allowing for two or three days at Bristol on arrival, the journey to London to report himself, the audiences, and the time for the consummation of the penurious Henry's bounty, the ship must have arrived at Bristol at least ten days previous to the 10th of August. See extract from Privy Purse Accounts, Henry VII, *Biddle*, p. 80, *n.*

a second expedition on a larger scale. The Milanese envoy, Raimondo di Soncino, being personally acquainted with Cabot, wrote a more authoritative despatch on the subject for his master, Ludovico il Moro. Soncino, as well as the Spanish Ambassador, had seen the chart of his discoveries prepared by John Cabot, and also a solid sphere constructed by the great navigator. The Milanese envoy had the advantage of conversing with Cabot himself, and heard from him of the enormous supplies of fish to be obtained on the Newfoundland banks, which were considered likely to supersede the trade in stock-fish with Iceland; and of his design to reach the Spice Islands by way of Cipango, in imitation of Columbus. Soncino also spoke to several of the crew, including a Burgundian, and a Genoese barber from Castione,[1] both of whom anticipated great results from the second voyage.

New Letters Patent were issued on February 3rd, 1498, this time to John Cabot alone, without mention of his sons. The discoverer is authorised to equip six English ships in any port within the King's dominions, being of 200 tons burden or under, and to take them to the land and isles lately discovered by the said John. He is empowered to enter all men and boys who may volunteer for the service; and all officers and others, the King's subjects, are commanded to afford needful assistance.

The second expedition was also fitted out at

---

[1] Castiglione, near Chiavari, according to Desimoni.

Bristol. Sebastian probably accompanied his father again,[1] and it would appear that Thomas Bradley and Lancelot Thirkill, of London, commanded two of the other ships, having received royal loans of £30 for their equipment.[2] John Carter is also mentioned as receiving £2. The expedition consisted of five armed ships, victualled for a year, with 300 men, according to Peter Martyr and Gomara. They sailed in the summer of 1498, at some time before the 25th of July.[3] One was driven back by a storm.[4]

The few details respecting this second voyage of John Cabot are derived from the reports of statements made long afterwards by his son Sebastian, which appear in the works of Peter Martyr, Ramusio, Gomara, and Galvano. His actual discoveries were shown on his map, a copy of which was sent to Spain, and transferred to the famous map drawn by Juan de la Cosa in 1500. John Cabot first directed his course to the north, and went so far towards the

---

[1] The accounts given by Sebastian to Peter Martyr, and to the anonymous guest whose discourse is recorded by Ramusio, evidently refer to the second voyage of John Cabot, although the son takes all the credit to himself, and does not mention his father. It was the general belief, in 1521, according to the Drapers' Company, that Sebastian never went on these voyages. It may be assumed, however, that Sebastian was probably on board. His age would have been twenty-three, his father's over sixty.

[2] *Excerpta Historica*, Nicholas (1831), p. 116; also *Biddle*, p. 86.

[3] The date of the letters from the Spanish ambassadors, Puebla and Ayala, reporting their departure.

[4] Ayala to the Sovereigns, 25th July 1498 (*Harrisse*, p. 329).

Pole as to meet with icebergs, and to experience
almost constant daylight in July.[1]   Seeing so much
ice, he turned to the south, and came to the bank of
Newfoundland, where he met with enormous quantities of fish called *Bacallaos*.[2]   The people are
described as being covered with the skins of beasts,
and many bears were seen.   Continuing on a
southerly course along the North American coast,
he reached the latitude of Cape Hatteras,[3] whence
he was obliged to return home owing to want of
provisions.   The Spanish Ambassador had reported,
in July 1498, that Cabot was expected to return in
the following September.   We know nothing more
of John Cabot.   Neither the return of his expedition,
nor the date or place of his death, is recorded.

Juan de la Cosa was supplied, through the Spanish
Ambassador in London, with a chart, showing the
discoveries of John Cabot.   On his mappe-monde of
1500 he indicates the discoveries by English flags

---

[1] Peter Martyr does not mention any latitude for the farthest
north of Cabot.   The anonymous guest, whose discourse is recorded by Ramusio, says 56°; Gomara says 58°; Galvano, 60°.
Ramusio, writing from memory, says that Cabot had once written
to him, years before, when he gave 67° 30' as the latitude.   Sir
Humphrey Gilbert also has 67° 30', copying Ramusio.

[2] Peter Martyr makes the erroneous statement that Cabot gave
the country the name of Bacallaos.   It is really the Basque name
for cod.

[3] Peter Martyr says that the most southern point reached by
Cabot was the latitude of the Straits of Gibraltar.   The guest in
Ramusio says that he reached Florida.   Gomara gives his furthest
south at 38°; and Galvano has the same latitude; adding that
"some say he reached Florida".

Plate II.

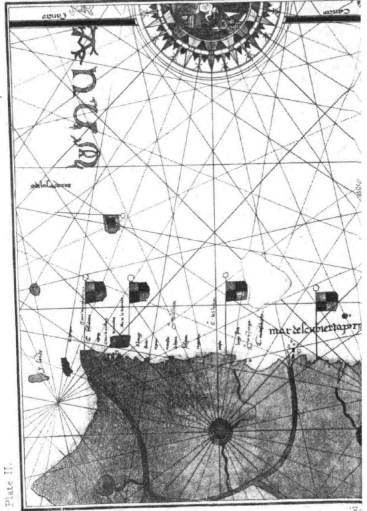

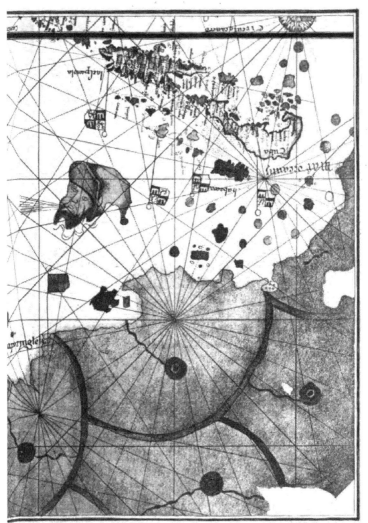

THE NORTH-EAST COAST IN THE MAP OF LA COSA

(1500)

along the coast of North America, with a number of names of capes and bays between them. This coast-line cannot be exactly identified, as there are no lines for latitude, and the West India Islands are placed north of the tropic; but it appears to be intended to extend from 50° to 30° N. from about Cape Breton to a little south of Cape Hatteras.[1] This would be in accordance with the statement of Peter Martyr.

John Cabot was the pioneer of English discovery and English colonisation. A long life of mercantile adventure had prepared him for the great work; and the experienced old navigator was at least sixty years of age when he offered his services to Henry VII. His great merit was that he at once appreciated the genius and prevision of Columbus, and understood the true significance of his magnificent achievement. He studied the theories and the methods of his illustrious countryman, and understood the great work that was left for others to achieve by following his lead. The results more than justified his representations. In his first voyage he showed the way across the Atlantic in high latitudes; and in the second he discovered the coast of North America, between the Arctic Circle and the Tropic of Cancer. We learn no more of his career, and nothing of the close of his life; but this

---

[1] The map drawn by Sebastian Cabot in 1542 affords little help with regard to his father's discoveries, except in the identification of the *Prima Tierra Vista*. It is a compilation including later work, but the coast of North America is represented very much as it is on the map of Juan de la Cosa.

is enough to secure a place for John Cabot among the greatest navigators of that age of discovery.

The work of John Cabot bore fruit in subsequent years, and the way he had shown across the Atlantic was not forgotten. On March 19th, 1501, Letters Patent were granted to three merchants of Bristol, named Warde, Ashurst, and Thomas, associated with three natives of the Azores.[1] They made a voyage across the Atlantic, and the isle discovered by John Cabot was again visited.[2] In the three following years other voyages were undertaken across the Atlantic.[3]

III.—Sebastian Cabot.

Since the results of recent researches have been known, the son can no longer be associated with the discoveries of the father. With regard to the place of Sebastian's birth, he told Peter Martyr, in 1519,

[1] *Biddle*, p. 312.

[2] 27th January 1502. "To men of Bristol that found the Ile, £5." (Privy Purse Expenses, Henry VII.)

[3] 1503. "To the merchants of Bristol that had been in Newfoundland, £20" (*Hakluyt*, i, 219). 1503, November 17th. "To one that brought hawkes from the Newfoundedland, £1" (*Exc. Hist.*). 1504, April 8th. "To a prieste that goeth to the new ilande, £2" (*Exc. Hist.*, p. 131). 1505. "To Portyngales that brought popyngais and catts of the mountaigne with other stuf to the King's grace, £5." "Wild catts and popyngays of the Newfound Island" (*Exc. Hist.*, p. 133).

that he was a Venetian born[1]; he told Contarini, in
1522, that he was born in Venice[2]; and he told
Richard Eden that he was born at Bristol.[3] His
own word can have no weight, for he made statements respecting the place of his birth just as it
happened to suit his convenience. But we know
from the Letters Patent that his younger brother
must have been of age when they were granted in
1497. Sebastian must have been at least a year
older. So he was born not later than 1474. His
father had his domicile in Venice from 1461 to 1476.
Sebastian was, therefore, born in Venice.

It is uncertain whether Sebastian Cabot accompanied his father on his voyages of discovery. He
is reported to have said that he was himself the
discoverer, ignoring his father; and, on the other
hand, the general belief in England was that he
never visited the new land himself.[4] On the whole,

---

[1] "Genere Venetus, sed a parentibus in Britanniam insulam
tendentibus . . . . transportatus pene infans." (*Dec. III*, Lib. vi.)

[2] "Per dirve il tuto io naqui a Venetia ma sum nutrito in
Ingelterra." (Letter from Contarini to the Council of Ten.)

[3] "Sebastian Cabote tould me that he was borne in Brystowe,
and that at iiii yeare ould he was carried with his father to Venice,
and so returned agayne into England with his father after certayne
years, whereby he was thought to have been born in Venice"
(margin of the translation of Peter Martyr, ed. 1555, fol. 255);
Tarducci, p. 89, *n*. Tarducci argues that Cabot cannot have
made this statement in the form given by Eden, and that Eden
must have misunderstood him (*Di G. e S. Caboto, Memorie*,
pp. 92, 93).

[4] In March 1521, when the great Livery Companies of London
were required to contribute towards the fitting out of the ships of
discovery to be commanded by Sebastian Cabot, the Drapers'

it seems most probable that John Cabot did take
his young son with him, who was then about twenty-
two years of age.   There is also reason for thinking
that he was employed by the Bristol merchants in
their voyage in 1502, for he is said to have brought
three men, taken in Newfoundland, to the King in
that year.[1]   During the next ten years we hear
nothing of Sebastian.   But he must have occupied
them in business connected with navigation and
cartography; for, when there was an agreement
between Henry VIII and Ferdinand V to undertake a combined expedition against the south of
France, in 1512, Sebastian Cabot was employed to
make a map of Gascony and Guienne.[2]   Lord
Willoughby de Broke had command of the troops
which were landed at Pasages in June 1512,[3] and
Sebastian accompanied him.[4]   By that time the

Company was their spokesman, and in excusing themselves they
said : "Sebastian, as we hear say, never was in that land himself,
but he makes reports of many things as he hath heard his father
and other men speke in tymes past." (*Warden's Account of the
Drapers' Company MSS.*, vol. vii, fo. 87, first made known by W.
Herbert in his *History of the Twelve Great Livery Companies of
London*, 1837, i, p. 410.) See *Harrisse*, p. 29.

[1] *Stow's Chronicle* (1580), p. 875, said to be quoted from
Fabyan.   But no such passage occurs in any printed edition
of Fabyan.   See also *Hakluyt's Divers Voyages* (Hakluyt
Society's ed., p. 23).

[2] *Calendar of State Papers, H. VIII (Dom. and For.)*, ii,
Pt. II, p. 1456.

[3] *Rymer*, xii, 297 ; *Herbert's Henry VIII*, p. 20.   For Lord
Willoughby, see *Dugdale's Baronage*, Pt. II, p. 88.

[4] *MSS. Munoz Coll.*, t. xc., fol. 109, *verso*, quoted by Harrisse,
p. 331.

younger Cabot must have become a draughtsman of some note, for King Ferdinand applied to Lord Willoughby for his services, and, on September 13th, 1512, gave him the appointment of a captain, with a salary of 50,000 marks.[1] In March 1514 it had been arranged that he should undertake a voyage of discovery in the Spanish service, and in 1515 he was appointed a pilot. He married a Spaniard named Catalina Medrano,[2] and it was at this time that he became acquainted with Peter Martyr, who wrote : " Familiarem habeo domi Cabottum ipsum, et contubernalem interdum"—"Cabot is my very frend whom I use familiarlye, and delyte to have hym sometymes keepe my company in my owne house."[3]

On the death of King Ferdinand in 1516, Sebastian Cabot went to England with his wife and daughter Elizabeth, and he appears to have remained there during the rule of Cardinal Cisneros, although he was still in the Spanish service. He is said to have been concerned in the equipment of an expedition for Henry VIII in 1517, which is alleged to have " taken none effect" owing to the " faint heart" of one Sir Thomas Perte.[4] But as Cabot was

---

[1] Herrera, _Dec. I_, Lib. ix, cap. 13; _Dec. II_, Lib. i, cap. 12.

[2] Letter cited by Navarrete, _Bib. Mar._, ii, 698.

[3] _De Rebus Oceanicis et Orbe Novo, Dec. III_, Lib. vi, p. 232 (ed. Paris, 1587); _Eden's trans._, Willes ed., f. 125.

[4] This circumstance is mentioned by Eden. The voyage of 1517 is not mentioned by any other writer. Eden's work, published in 1553, is entitled, _A treatyse of the Newe India after the description of Sebastian Munster in his book of Universal Cosmo-_

then in the Spanish service, and as he declined
similar employment in 1519 on that very ground,[1]
there must be some mistake. He may have given
advice, but nothing more ; and at this very time he
was engaged in an intrigue with a Venetian friar
named Stragliano Collona, proposing to leave both
Spain and England in the lurch, and to devise a
plan by which Venice should secure all the benefits
to be derived from the northern voyages.   His own
words are plain enough as regards England.   He
said: "As by serving the King of England I should
not be able to serve my country, I wrote to the
Cesarean Majesty that he should not, on any account,
give me permission to serve the King of England,
because there would be great injury to his service."[2]
In the face of all this it is not credible that Sebastian
Cabot undertook a voyage for the King of England
in 1517.   Indeed, the words of Eden, "the voyage
took none effect", can only be explained by the
assumption that the Atlantic was not crossed by
Perte's ship.   There was some intention of employ-

---

graphia, translated out of Latin into English by Richard Eden.
The passage is as follows : "At such time as our sovereigne Lord
of noble memory, King Henry the Eight, furnished and set forth
certen shippes under the governaunce of Sebastian Cabot, yet
living, and one Sir Thomas Perte, whose faynte heart was the
cause that the voyage took none effect" (in the *Dedication to the
Duke of Northumberland*; also *Hakluyt*, iii, 498).

[1] Contarini to the Senate of Venice, 31st December 1522 : "I
replied that, being in the service of His Majesty, I was not able
to undertake it without permission."

[2] Letter from Contarini, 31st December 1522. See p. 220.

ing Sebastian on a voyage from England in 1521, but it came to nothing, and he was all the time playing a double game with Spain and Venice.

Cabot returned to his employment at Seville in 1521, having previously received the appointment of Chief Pilot.[1] Yet, while in the service of Spain, and in possession of all the intentions and secrets of the Spanish Government, he engaged in an intrigue with the Venetian Senate to transfer his services to the Republic. He employed a native of Ragusa, named Hieronymo di Marin, to convey his proposals to the Council of Ten, under a vow of secrecy sworn on the sacrament. These proposals appear to have been no less than, by the use of knowledge acquired in the English and Spanish services, to transfer all the advantages and benefits of the contemplated northern voyage to Venice. The Council of Ten heard what the Ragusan had to say, rewarding him with a present of 20 ducats, and they considered the matter to be of such importance that the Venetian Ambassador in Spain, Gasparo Contarini, was instructed in a letter, dated September 27th, 1522, to have an interview with Sebastian Cabot and report the result.

Contarini's account was that his first step in the negotiation was successful. He quietly ascertained whether Sebastian was at Court, then at Valladolid, and sent his secretary to tell him that there was

---

[1] Herrera, *Dec. II*, Lib. iii, cap. 7. He was appointed Piloto Mayor on 5th February 1518.

a letter at the embassy which concerned his private affairs. This brought the Chief Pilot to the Venetian Ambassador's house, and Contarini dexterously succeeded in gaining his confidence. Cabot related the circumstances of his employment in England and Spain, but declared that his desire was to benefit his native country, by proceeding to Venice and laying the details of his proposal before the Council of Ten. He proposed to get permission to proceed to Venice, on the plea of recovering his mother's jointure, and other private affairs.

The Venetian Ambassador felt very doubtful whether the scheme of Cabot was feasible. Any expedition fitted out at Venice could easily be stopped by the King of Spain in passing through the Straits of Gibraltar. The only other plan would be to equip vessels outside the Mediterranean, on the shores of the Atlantic, or in the Red Sea. But the difficulties surrounding any such projects would render them impracticable. The cogency of the shrewd diplomatist's argument was admitted by Cabot ; but he maintained that his great knowledge and experience had suggested to him other means by which the end could be attained, which he would only divulge in person to the Venetian Council. Contarini shrugged his shoulders, and the interview ended. But after an interval Cabot again came to the Venetian embassy at Valladolid, on the 27th of December —St. John's Day. On this occasion he did all he could to impress Contarini with his great professional knowledge and skill, discussing many geographical points with him, and explaining a method he had invented of finding the longitude by means of the variation of the needle. Then, touching on the main business, he confidently asserted that the Council of Ten would be pleased with the plan he had devised, declaring that he was ready to go to Venice at his own expense. He entreated Contarini to keep the matter secret, as his life depended on it.

Four days afterwards, on the 31st of December 1522, the Venetian Ambassador, in a long and able despatch, reported the results of his interviews with Cabot; and on March 7th, 1523, he further reported that Cabot had delayed his visit to Venice because he was called to England on business, and would be absent for three months. This is explained by an entry respecting the funeral of Sir Thomas Lovell, K.G.,[1] from which it appears that Sebastian Cabot, Chief Pilot of Spain, came to London to attend at the obsequies of Sir Thomas in

---

[1] "Expense of the funeral of Sir Thomas Lovell, K.G., who died at his manor of Elsynge in Enfield, Middlesex, 25th May 1524, and was buried at Haliwell. Item, paide the 18th day of February, to John Godryk of Tory, in the county of Cornwall, drap., in full satysfaccon and recompenses of his charge, costis, and labour conductyng Sebastian Cabott, master of the Pylotes in Spayne, to London, at the request of the testator by Indenture of Covenauntes, 43s. 4d." (*Calendar of State Papers, Dom. and For., Henry VIII*, iv, Pt. I, p. 154, No. 366), quoted by Tarducci, p. 158, and Harrisse. Sir Thomas Lovell was made Chancellor of the Exchequer for life in 1485, Treasurer of the Household, 1502, Constable of the Tower, one of the executors of the will of Henry VII, and Steward and Marshal of the House of Henry VIII. He was knighted at the battle of Stoke, 1487.

1524, in compliance with a request in the will of the deceased. Cabot returned to Spain in the end of 1524.

Contarini received great praise from his Government for the way in which he had conducted the negotiations; but they fell to the ground, apparently owing to the important employment on which Cabot was soon afterwards engaged under the Spanish Government.

The Conference of Badajoz on the question of the right to Moluccas between Spain and Portugal was opened in 1524, and Sebastian Cabot was employed as an assessor. The decision in favour of Spain led to the equipment of an expedition for the discovery of the isles of Tarshish, Ophir, and the eastern Catay, of which Sebastian Cabot received the command.[1] It consisted of three vessels and 150 men; the two other ships being commanded by Francisco de Rojas and Martin Mendez, with whom the Captain-General disagreed. Miguel de Rodas embarked as a volunteer. The ships sailed in April 1526, and, in consequence of the quarrels between the leader of the expedition and his captains, Cabot adopted a very high-handed measure. He beached the two captains, Rojas and Mendez, and the volunteer Rodas, on the coast of Brazil. They were rescued by a Portuguese ship, and trouble was thus prepared for the Venetian on his return. Entering

---

[1] Cabot laid aside a portion of his pay for the maintenance of his wife, Catalina Medrano, during his absence. (*Munos MSS., Indios*, 1524-26, 77, Est 23 gr., fol. 165, *verso*, quoted by Harrisse, p. 355.)

the river Plate, Cabot explored the river Parana to
its junction with the Paraguay, and established two
forts.   But he was eventually attacked by an over-
whelming force of natives, one of his forts was carried
by assault, and he was obliged to abandon the
enterprise.[1]   He returned to Spain in August 1530,
and had to meet serious charges respecting his
treatment of Mendez and Rojas.   On February 1st,
1532, he was condemned to two years of exile at
Oran for excesses committed during the expedition[2];
but the Emperor pardoned him after a year, and he
was again at Seville in June 1533.[3]

Sebastian Cabot must have been a man of great
ability and address, while his knowledge and experience made his services very valuable.   It is evident,
from his restoration to favour, after returning from
his disastrous expedition, that the Government of
Charles V entertained a high opinion of his useful-
ness.   He remained Chief Pilot of Spain from 1533
to 1547, and it must have been at this time that the
guest, to whose conversation Ramusio listened at
the table of Hieronimus Fracastor, visited Cabot at
Seville.   Then the old navigator, who had reached

---

[1] Herrera, *Dec. III*, Lib. ix, cap. 3; *Dec. IV*, Lib. viii, cap.
11; *Gomara*, ch. lxxxix.

[2] Navarrete, *Bib. Mar.*, ii, 699.

[3] In June 1533, in a letter to Juan de Samano, the Emperor's
secretary, Cabot excused himself for not having finished a map,
owing to the death of his daughter and the illness of his wife
(*Munoz MSS.*, vol. lxxix, fo. 287, quoted by Harrisse; and *Tarducci*, p. 404).   In the will of William Mychell, chaplain, in 1516,
there is a legacy of 3s. 4d. to Cabot's daughter Elizabeth.

the age of seventy, professed to be anxious to rest
from active service, "after having instructed so many
practical and valiant young seamen, through whose
forwardness I do rejoice in the fruit of my labours.
So I rest with the charge of this office as you see."
The guest added that, among other things, Cabot
showed him a great mappe-monde, illustrating the
special navigations as well of the Portuguese as of
the Spaniards. If this was the mappe-monde that
was discovered lately, it bore the following title:
" Sebastian Cabot, Captain and Pilot Major to his
Cesarean and Catholic Majesty the Emperor Charles
V of that name, the King our Lord, made this
figure extended on a plane, in the year of the birth
of our Saviour Jesus Christ 1544." It is a coloured
map drawn on an ellipse, $4\frac{1}{4}$ feet long by $3\frac{1}{2}$ wide,
having a series of descriptive legends, in Latin and
Spanish, on the right and left. It is a compilation
showing the then recent discovery of the Gulf of
St. Lawrence by Jacques Cartier. Newfoundland
is represented as a group of islands. The work
done by John Cabot, in his first voyage, is indicated
by the *Prima Tierra Vista*, at the north end of
Cape Breton,[1] and the *I. de S. Juan* in the place of
the modern Magdalen Islands. Along the coast of

---

[1] On the map of Michael Lok, given in *Hakluyt's Divers
Voyages*, with the relation of Verazzano, the words "J. Gabot,
1497", are written over the land ending with the north point of
Cape Breton. But the island "S. Johan" is placed to the south,
and not in the position of the Magdalen Islands, as in the map of
Sebastian Cabot.

Labrador is written *Costa d el hues norueste*. San Brandon Isle retains its place in the middle of the Atlantic. From Cape Breton a coast-line is made to run west and south, resembling that shown as discovered by the English, on the map of Juan de la Cosa in 1500. But the names along the coast of North America do not agree with those on the map of Juan de la Cosa.

The great value of the 1544 map of Sebastian Cabot is that it fixes the landfall of his father's first voyage. On this point he is the highest authority, and his evidence is quite conclusive if it was given in good faith. Mr. Harrisse argues that it was not given in good faith, but not, I think, on sufficient grounds. He first endeavours to show that while Cabot was at the head of the Hydrographic Department at Seville, and responsible for the accuracy of the charts, the landfall in 48° was never shown, and the three maps of that period, that survive, all place the English discoveries between 56° and 60°. Mr. Harrisse therefore infers that Cabot did not then claim dis- coveries further south. But the answer to this is that he did make such claim. He told the guest in Ramusio, Peter Martyr, and everyone he met, that he discovered all the coast as far south as Florida. It is true that, after the map of La Cosa in 1500, where the English southern discoveries are fully portrayed, they do not appear on Spanish maps ; but the statements of Sebastian Cabot prove that this cannot have been with his willing concurrence.

d

The omission must have been due to some other cause. The coast shown in 60° N. on the Ribero and other maps of course refer to John Cabot's second, not to his first voyage, when he reached Cape Breton.

Mr. Harrisse then justifies his hypothesis that Sebastian Cabot placed his landfall at Cape Breton, knowing well that it was really several hundred miles further north, by pointing out his constant mendacity and treason, and that such underhand dealings were in keeping with his natural disposition. But this is not sufficient without a motive, and the motive suggested by Mr. Harrisse seems quite inadequate. He says that the explorations of Jacques Cartier, from 1534 to 1543, had brought to light a valuable region round Cape Breton, suitable for colonies; and that Sebastian placed the landfall there in 1544 as a suggestion of British claims, a declaration that the region of the Gulf of St. Lawrence belonged to England, and a bid for favour. He went to England three years afterwards. But it would have been useless and unnecessary, as well as dangerous, to falsify an official Spanish map with this object; for the English Government possessed his father's maps, and he had all along claimed the discovery, not only of this part, but of the whole coast as far as Florida. We may therefore conclude that, as Sebastian Cabot had no motive for falsifying his map, he did not do so; and that the "Prima Terra Vista", where he placed it, is the true landfall of John Cabot on his first voyage.[1]

On November 28th, 1545, Sebastian Cabot was charged, in conjunction with Pedro Mexia, Alonso Chaves, and Diego Gutierrez, to examine and report upon the new work on navigation by Pedro de Medina, entitled *Arte de Navegar*.[2] This is the last recorded duty performed by Cabot in Spain. Two years afterwards he left that country and arrived in England. The old man's action must have been secret, and in the nature of a flight, for he resigned neither his pension nor his appointment before his departure. It was a betrayal, for he took with him a knowledge of all the secret counsels and intentions of the Spanish Government, acquired during an official career extending over a period of more than

---

[1] The mappe monde of Sebastian Cabot is mentioned by Sanuto, Ortelius, Hukluyt, Purchas, and Sir Humphrey Gilbert. Hakluyt, Purchas, and Gilbert mention "the great map in Her Majesty's privy gallery at Whitehall, cut by Clement Adams"; and Hakluyt gives the legend No. 8 from it, referring to the voyage of John Cabot. The map of Adams must, therefore, have been a copy of the 1544 map of Sebastian. Willes mentions another copy, "Cabot's table which the Earl of Bedford hath at Cheynies" (*Eden*, 1577, f. 232). These maps have disappeared.

The only existing copy of the map by Sebastian Cabot was found in the house of a curate in Bavaria by Dr. Martius, Secretary of the Academy of Sciences at Munich. It was bought from M. de Heunin in 1844 for 400 francs, and is now in the Bibliothèque Nationale at Paris. Jomard has reproduced it, but without the legends.

[2] Lista de la Esposicion Americanista B. 52, referred to by Tarducci, p. 280, *n*.

thirty years. The actual cause for this flight and betrayal is unknown. That the flight was arranged in concert with the English Privy Council is made clear by a warrant of £100 paid to one Mr. Peckham, on October 9th, 1547, for transporting "one Cabot, a Pilot, to come out of Hispain, to serve and inhabit in England".

When Sebastian Cabot came to England, in the beginning of the reign of Edward VI, he was at least seventy-three years of age. On January 6th, 1548, he was granted a pension of £166 13s. 4d. (250 marks) a year,[1] with the duties, though not the title, of Chief Pilot of England. The Emperor Charles V, through the English Ambassadors at Brussels, Sir Thomas Cheyne and Sir Philip Hoby, requested that Cabot might be sent back, "forasmuch as he cannot stand the King your Master in any great stead, seeing he hath small practice in these seas, and is a very necessary man for the Emperor, whose servant he is, and hath a pension of him." The despatch containing this request was dated at Brussels on November 25th, 1549.[2] The reply, on April 21st, 1550, was that Sebastian Cabot refused to return to Spain, and that, being King Edward's subject, he could not be compelled to go against his will.[3] In the following year Cabot received £200 from Edward VI, by Council warrant, "by way of

---

[1] *Hakluyt.*

[2] Strype's *Ecclesiastical Memorials*, vol. ii, Pt. 1, p. 296 (Oxford, 1822).

[3] *Harleian MS.* 525, f. 9; quoted by Harrisse.

the King's Majesty's reward",[1] and was evidently in high favour. Charles V made one more effort to recover his Chief Pilot, by writing to his cousin Queen Mary on the subject, from Mons, on the 9th of September 1553, but without effect.[2]

Meanwhile, Cabot had again opened communications with the Venetian Government, through Giacomo Soranzo, their Ambassador in London. His proposal was to conduct a Venetian fleet to Cathay through the strait of which he pretended to have the secret[3]; and the same excuse for asking permission to go to Venice, on urgent private affairs, was to be adopted as had been proposed in the negotiation with Contarini in 1522. It completely deceived Dr. Peter Vannes, the English Ambassador at Venice, who, in a despatch dated September 12th, 1551, reported to the Council the steps that had been taken to further Cabot's business, and the goodwill of the Seigniory.[4] The contemporaries of the astute old pilot had no suspicion of the intrigues revealed to posterity by the publication of the Vene-

---

[1] Strype, *Ecc. Mem.*, ii, Pt. ii, pp. 76 and 217.

[2] *Calendar of State Papers* (Foreign), 1553-58, t. i, No. 31, p. 10. Edward VI died on July 6th, 1553.

[3] *Calendar of State Papers*, Rawdon Brown, t. v, No. 711, p. 264. The despatch of Soranzo does not exist, but we have the reply from the Council of Ten.

[4] *Calendar of State Papers* (Foreign), 1861, p. 171, No. 444. Dr. Vannes says that Ramusio, the Hakluyt of Italy, and then one of the secretaries of the Seigniory, was acting as Cabot's agent at this time.

tian State Papers ; but this second negotiation ended in nothing.[1]

Cabot was employed to draw up instructions for the voyage of Willoughby and Chancellor in May 1553,[2] and, when the Company of Merchant Adventurers was incorporated on February 26th, 1555, he was named Governor for life.[3]   In this capacity he superintended the equipment of the *Searchthrift*, under the command of Stephen Burrough, coming down to Gravesend to take leave of that gallant explorer on April 27th, 1556, and taking part in the feasting and dancing on that occasion.[4]

On the 27th of May 1557 Sebastian Cabot resigned his pension, and on the 29th one half of it was restored to him, and the other half was granted to one William Worthington, apparently as a colleague appointed in consequence of Cabot's great age.[5]   He was at least eighty-three.   This is the last official mention of Sebastian Cabot, who probably died the same year.

There is evidence that Sebastian Cabot gave close attention to questions relating to the variation of the compass.   In the geography of Livio Sanuto,

---

[1] Tarducci offers some excuses for the conduct of Cabot, in having entered upon these intrigues with Venice, while he was a servant of the Spanish and English Governments (*Tarducci*, p. 157 and p. 291), but they are not satisfactory.

[2] *Hakluyt*, i, 226.

[3] Strype, *Ecc. Mem.*, iii, Pt. I, p. 320 ; *Hakluyt*, i, p. 267.

[4] *Hakluyt*, i, p. 274.

[5] *Rymer*, xv, 466 ; *Biddle*, p. 217.   Philip arrived in London on May 20th, 1557.

that learned Italian says that, many years before the
period at which he wrote, Guido Gianetti da Fano
"informed him that Sebastian Cabot was the discoverer of that secret of the variation of the needle
which he then explained to the most serene King of
England (Edward VI), near to whom (but then engaged in other affairs) this Gianetti was most honourably employed ; and he also demonstrated how much
this variation was, and that it was not the same in
every place."[1]   In 1522, Cabot had told the Venetian Ambassador Contarini "of a method he had
observed of finding the distance between two places
east and west of each other by means of the needle,
a beautiful discovery, never observed by any one
else".[2] This fallacy, that the longitude could be
found by observing the variation at two places, was
subsequently adopted by Plancius, who even constructed an instrument for observing it. The idea
haunted the mind of Cabot to his dying day ; but it
was not original, being the conception of Jacob
Besson.[3] Eden mentions that Cabot continued to
talk of a divine revelation to him of a new and
infallible method of finding the longitude, which he
was not permitted to disclose to any mortal, even
on his death-bed. He adds : " I thinke the goode
old man, in that extreme age, somewhat doted, and
had not yet, even in the article of death, utterly

---

[1] *Geographia*, Livio Sanuto (Venezia, 1588), Lib. i, f. 2 ; *Biddle*,
p. 177, quoted by Harrisse.

[2] Contarini, *ubi sup*.

[3] Besson, *La Cosmolabe* (Paris, 4to), 1567, quoted by Harrisse.

shaken off all worldlye vayne glorie."[1]   Eden was
present at Cabot's death, but does not mention
when or where it took place, or where he was
buried.

On the death of Sebastian Cabot, all his maps
and papers came into the possession of his colleague,
William Worthington.   Hakluyt, writing in · 1582,[2]
said that "shortly, God willing, shall come out in
print all his (Sebastian Cabot's) own mappes and
discourses, drawne and written by himselfe, which
are in the custodie of the worshipful Master William
Worthington, one of Her Majesty's Pensioners, who
(because so worthie monuments should not be buried
in perpetual oblivion) is very willing to suffer them
to be overseene, and published in as good order as
may be, to the encouragement and benefite of our
countrymen."   But this was never done.[3]

---

[1] "Epistle Dedicatory.   A very necessarie and profitable book
concerning navigation, compiled in Latin by *Joannes Taisnerus*, a
publik Professor in Rome, Ferraria, and other Universities in
Italie, named a Treatise of continual motions.   Translated into
English by *Richard Eden*" (London, Rd. Jugge).   *Biddle*, p. 222.

[2] *Divers Voyages*, p. 26 (Hakluyt Society's ed.).   Worthington was one of the ordinary gentlemen and pensioners of
Edward VI, and "bailiff and collector of the rents and revenues
of all the manors, messuages, and hereditaments within the city of
London and county of Middlesex which did belong to colleges,
guilds, fraternities, or free chapels" (Strype, *Ecc. Mem.*, vol. ii,
Pt. II, p. 234).   A pardon was granted to him, being indebted to
the King £392 10s. 3d., his servant having run away with the
money.   He seems to have been employed in France and Scotland.

[3] Biddle suggested that Worthington handed over the papers of

The consideration of all the original documents relating to Sebastian Cabot do not leave a pleasant impression on the mind. His statements about his birth, made to suit his purpose at the moment, show that he was rather unscrupulous; while his recorded assertions that all the credit of his father's discoveries was due to himself, if correctly repeated, display an amount of vanity and an absence of filial affection, combined with a disregard for truth, which are repelling. He is said to have told the guest, quoted by Ramusio, that his father had died at the time when the news of the discovery of Columbus arrived; and that it was he, Sebastian, who made the proposal to Henry VII, and fitted out the ships in 1497! In the conversations repeated by Peter Martyr, by Ramusio, by Gomara, and Galvano, the father is never mentioned, and the reader is made to suppose that Sebastian alone was the discoverer. The same impression was received by writers in England. Fabyan, repeated by Stow, gives Sebastian, and not John, as the name of the explorer, and Sir Humphrey Gilbert was even more completely deceived, after a perusal of Ramusio. In his *Discourse of a New Passage to Cataia*, he writes as if John Cabot had never existed, and as if Sebastian had commanded the expeditions. This false impression was often repeated, and when Mr.

Cabot to Philip II, when he was in England in 1557. But this appears to be disproved by the fact that they were still in Worthington's possession in 1582.

Biddle[1] wrote his Memoir on Sebastian Cabot, he reached the climax of unintentional injustice by writing of the father as merely an old merchant, who never even went to sea. The truth was revealed by the discovery of the letters of the Italian news-writers, and of the Spanish despatches. It is true that on Legend No. 8 of his map Sebastian mentions his father coupled with himself—"this land was discovered by Joan Caboto, Venetian, and Sebastian Caboto his son"—but this rather confirms the painful impression caused by the silence respecting his father elsewhere. For John Cabot was a great navigator of long experience, advanced in years, and in sole command of the expeditions; while Sebastian, if he went with him at all, which is not certain, was then a lad of twenty-two. Fernando Columbus might as well have coupled his name with that of his illustrious father when he wrote the account of the fourth voyage. But that was the last thing Fernando would have done. The contrast is striking between the filial piety of the son of Columbus, and the absence of feeling for the memory and fame of his father on the part of the son of John Cabot.

---

[1] *A Memoir of Sebastian Cabot*, without author's name (London, 1831), p. 50. John Biddle was an eminent American jurist and statesman of Pittsburg, Pennsylvania. He was born in 1795, and died in 1847. He purchased the well-known portrait of Sebastian Cabot as an old man, which was burnt with his house at Pittsburg. But a good copy had been made, now belonging to the New York Historical Society.

It is fair, however, to bear in mind that we have the statements of Sebastian at second-hand. It is possible that he was not silent respecting the services of his father, and that those who repeated the conversations omitted to mention one who would not have the same interest for them as the living explorer with whom they were talking.

A still more unfavourable impression is caused by a perusal of the correspondence of Contarini and Soranzo. Sebastian Cabot, for his own ends, was ready to enter upon secret negotiations with another country at a time when he was in the pay and employment of Spain or England, and was trusted by his employers. There can be no doubt of his ability and knowledge. He would not have retained his employments so long, and his services would not have been so highly valued, both by Charles V and by the English Privy Council, if he had not possessed those qualities in an eminent degree. But the truth, as revealed by the documents that have been preserved, obliges us to add that Sebastian Cabot appears to have been wanting in filial affection, that his veracity is more than doubtful, that he had no feeling of loyalty to his employers, and that he was ready, without scruple, to sacrifice them for his own ends. There may be some mitigation in the fact that all his intrigues appear to have been for the benefit of his native country. His cunning and shrewdness secured his safety, and his double dealing was unknown. He reached an honoured and respected old age, after a long and prosperous career; but he owed his success to his good fortune and to the secrecy in which his dealings were shrouded, not to his probity and good faith. John Cabot was the great navigator, the explorer and pioneer who lighted English enterprise across the Atlantic. His son Sebastian tried to get the credit of his father's work, and for a time succeeded; but in the end the truth has prevailed. While the son of Columbus devoted his life to the pious work of preserving his father's fame, the son of Cabot so obscured the story of his father's discoveries that the merit of them was attributed to himself, and it has taken centuries of research to recover the truth, and to place John Cabot in his rightful position. He was second only to his illustrious countryman as a discoverer, and his place is in the forefront of the van of the long and glorious roll of leaders of English maritime enterprise.

IV.—GASPAR CORTE-REAL.

The voyages of Gaspar Corte-Real were the direct consequence of the first voyage of Columbus. But while John Cabot, fully imbued with the ideas of his great countryman, sailed in quest of the kingdom of the Grand Kaan and of Cipango, the Portuguese had the more practical object of discovering what unknown lands to the westward were within their sphere of action. By the Treaty of Tordesillas between Spain and Portugal, signed on June 7th,

1494, the Papal line of demarcation was extended to eleven hundred and thirteen miles (370 leagues) west of the Cape Verde Islands.[1] There might well be valuable unknown lands within those limits.

Gaspar Corte-Real, the third and youngest son of a good family in Algarve, was born in about 1450. His father, Joao Vaz Corte-Real, became Captain Donative of the islands of Terceira and St. George, in the Azores, in 1474, and died at Angra, in Terceira, in July 1496. Next to nothing is known of the early life of Gaspar, but he was Lieutenant for his family in Terceira in 1497 ; and in May 1500 he received letters patent from Manoel, King of Portugal, to lead an expedition of discovery.

He fitted out two ships at the joint expense of himself and his next brother, Miguel,[2] and sailed in the spring of 1500, from Lisbon, according to Damian de Goes, or from Terceira, according to Galvão.

The authorities for the voyages of Corte-Real are a passage in the Chronicle of King Manoel, by Damian de Goes ; another in the " Tratado" of Antonio Galvão ; three news-letters from Italians who were at Lisbon when the ships returned, and an important map prepared to show the new discoveries. Two of the letters are from Pietro Pasqualigo, the Ambassador from Venice, one to the

---

[1] The first line, by the Bull of May 4th, 1493, was drawn 100 leagues west from the Cape Verde Islands.

[2] Galvão says that it was at his own sole expense, but other documents prove that his brother shared the cost.

Seigneury, and the other to his brothers.[1]   The
other is from an Italian named Alberto Cantino to
Hercules d'Este, Duke of Ferrara.[2]   The Society
is indebted to the kindness of Mr. Henry Harrisse
for permission to have these letters translated from
the texts in his important work, *Les Corte-Real et
leurs voyages au Nouveau Monde.*   Cantino was
commissioned by the Duke of Ferrara to have a
map of the world drawn at Lisbon, to show the discoveries of Corte-Real.   It was executed during the
year 1502, with the title, "Nautical Chart for the
islands newly found in the region of India"; and was
duly transmitted to Ferrara.   Its subsequent history
is curious.   The Pope seized the duchy of Ferrara
in 1592, and the map was taken to Modena, where
one of the degenerate descendants of Duke Hercules
had it pasted on the folds of a common screen.
When the mob broke into the palace at Modena in
1859, this screen was stolen, and some years afterwards Signor Boni, the librarian of the D'Este
Library, found it in a pork butcher's shop.   He
bought it, and the precious map is now preserved in
that library at Modena.   Mr. Harrisse, to whom
geographical science is deeply indebted for so many

---

[1] The letter of Pasqualigo to his brothers has long been known,
as it was published in the *Paesi novamente retrovati* in 1507.
The one to the Seigneury is from a manuscript in the Marcian
Library at Venice, published in the *Diarii di Marino Sanuto*
in 1880-81.

[2] From the State Archives at Modena; and first published in
the work of Mr. Harrisse on the Corte-Reales, p. 204.

other things, published a fine facsimile of the Cantino
map in 1883.

The Cantino map is drawn on vellum, richly
coloured and gilt, and measures 3 feet 2 inches long
by 3 feet 5 inches.   It is a plane chart, the lengths
of degrees of latitude and longitude being equal
throughout. The draughtsman employed by Cantino,
in order to execute his commission, must have applied to the pilots who returned in the ships of the
Corte-Real expedition, and must have received their
rough "cards" showing the coast-lines discovered,
with some details. He alone would be responsible
for the positions he selected for these new coast-lines
on his map of the world.   They are represented by
the southern point of Greenland, a coast with a forest
of trees just to the east of the Papal dividing line
(which is traced across the map), and evidently
intended for the east coast of Newfoundland, and a
coast-line drawn due north and south, from the
latitude of Lisbon for about 700 miles north, and
just to the west of the longitude of Cuba, which is
shown to the south of it, but much too far north.
This can be nothing else than the coast of North
America.   These three coast-lines are the new
features of the map, and, therefore, represent the
discoveries of Corte-Real.

The Cantino map is the most important authority
for these discoveries, supplemented by the letters of
the Italians and the brief notices of the chronicles.
There are also two legends on the map referring to
Greenland and Newfoundland.

Following these guides, we find that, after a long voyage northwards, Corte-Real sighted the lofty mountains of Greenland near Cape Farewell, but did not land. Greenland is called " Punta d'Asia", and we learn, from the legend on the map, that the cosmographers at Lisbon believed it to be a part of the Asiatic Continent.[1] Proceeding northwards, they came among icebergs, and sent boats to fill up with fresh water from the rills flowing down their sides. Next day they reached the edge of the ice.[2] This obliged them to alter course, and they eventually sighted land in 50° N.,[3] being the eastern coast of Newfoundland. It was so covered with trees, suitable for masts and yards of ships, that Corte-Real gave it the name of "Terra Verde".[4] Thence he returned to Lisbon.

The second expedition was fitted out by Gaspar Corte-Real at Lisbon in the spring of 1501 ; and he

---

[1] See page 240. Legend on the map. This view was adopted by Ruysch, who was the first to separate Greenland from Europe, and connect it with Asia.

[2] Cantino's letter (see p. 233). Cantino mixed up the first and second voyages. The first part of his account, about icebergs and the frozen sea, refers to the first voyage. This is quite clear, for he says that it occupied four months to reach the icebergs (*quatro mesi continui*), and three more months to arrive at the land. Allowing another month at least for the return voyage, that makes -eight months. Now the second voyage occupied less than five months, consequently he cannot possibly be writing of that. We do not know the duration of the first voyage, except roughly from these *data* of Cantino. The rest of the letter doubtless refers to the second voyage.

[3] Galvão.   [4] Damian de Goes.

sailed on the 15th of May,[1] to complete his discoveries of the previous year, shaping a course
west and north.

The key to an understanding of the course taken
by Corte-Real on his second voyage is to be found
in the letters of Pasqualigo. The Italian envoy
says that at a distance of 1,800 miles (Cantino gives
more correctly 2,800 miles) they came to land, that
they coasted along it for 600 or 700 miles, but that
they failed to reach the land discovered in the first
voyage, by reason of the ice. Now they cannot
possibly have coasted for 700 miles from north to
south after leaving Lisbon, consequently they must
have coasted from south to north, and this is twice
distinctly stated by Pasqualigo. An explanation of
the other new coast-line on the Cantino map, placed
south to north, and beginning in the latitude of
Lisbon, is thus supplied. At the south end this
land turns west,[2] and there are some islands.

---

[1] Cantino says the ships had been absent nine months in
October, and consequently they must have sailed in January, according to him. He had mixed up the first voyage with the
second. Damian de Goes gives the date of May 15th for their
sailing : which is probably right. Mr. Harrisse has published
documents showing that the supply of biscuit was received on board
on April 21st.

[2] It has been conjectured that this turn of the coast is intended
to represent Florida. But Florida was unknown until 1513, and
the turn of the coast is in the latitude of Lisbon. It may perhaps
be argued that as Cuba and Española are placed so far north of
their real latitude on this map, so may the turn of the coast be.
But there is no such analogy. Cantino's draughtsman was de-
pendent on Spanish cartographers, such as Juan de la Cosa, for

e

Corte-Real, steering west from Lisbon for 2,800 (3,000) miles, always with fine weather, according to Cantino,[1] reached the entrance to Delaware Bay, or Chesapeake Bay, where the land is made to turn west, and this point is named the Cape of the end of April,[2] doubtless to commemorate some event which took place on that day, possibly a visit from the King, just before the expedition sailed. Altogether, there are twenty-two names written along the coast, all Portuguese, though the meaning of some is not quite clear, owing, perhaps, to damp or rubbing in the places where they were written on the original "card" of the pilot.

After reaching this bay, Corte-Real shaped a course to the north, wishing to connect his discovery with the land he had reached on the previous voyage. At first he was in a temperate region yielding delicious fruits. Proceeding northwards, he came to very large rivers, indicating the existence of a great continent. Next there was a region

---

the latitude of Cuba and Española, who misled him. Those islands are equally out, as regards latitude, on the map of La Cosa. For his new coast-line he had the original observations of the pilots of Corte-Real.

[1] " Sempre con bon tempo."

[2] *C. do fim do abrill.* Mr. Stevens, who thought that the west coast-line on the Cantino map was a duplicate Cuba turned the wrong way, stated that Columbus himself named the east point of Cuba *Cape Fundabrill,* because he started from there on the 30th of April (*Johann Schöner, a reproduction of his Globe of 1523,* by Henry Stevens, edited by C. H. Coote, p. xviii). Columbus never gave it that name. He named the east point of Cuba *Alpha et Omega,* on December 5th, 1492. See note at p. 97.

with large pine trees.[1] Then they came to a sea abounding in fish.[2] They had reached Nova Scotia or Cape Breton, having sailed along the coast for 700 miles. At some place, where they landed, a broken sword and two silver rings were found, relics of the second voyage of John Cabot.[3]

Still wishing to reach Newfoundland, the land discovered during the first voyage further north, Corte-Real left the coast, and pushed into the foggy, ice-encumbered sea. He and his vessel were never again heard of. In Portugal his east coast of Newfoundland received the name of the Land of Corte-Real.[4] The other two vessels made the best of their way to Lisbon, with several natives on board, arriving on the 9th and 11th of October, after a voyage of a month. The distance from Nova Scotia to Lisbon is 2,000 miles, so that the ships made good about seventy miles a day.

In due time the rough "cards" of the pilots were furnished to Cantino's draughtsman; and he had to deal with the materials supplied to him in construct-

---

[1] See the letter from Cantino at p. 233.
[2] See p. 238. [3] See p. 237.
[4] In the map of the Ptolemy of 1513, by Bernardus Sylvanus, the name Corte-Real is turned into Latin. There is an island named "Regalis Domus", and another to the east of it called "Terra Labora". But there is no reference to Labrador in any of the authorities for the voyages of Corte-Real. The King of Portugal is said to have hoped to derive good slave labour from the lands discovered by Corte-Real. That is all. The name "Labrador" is not Portuguese; and Corte-Real was never on the Labrador coast

f

ing his map of the world, drawn to show the recently found lands. He placed Newfoundland to the east of the Papal line, just bringing it within the Portuguese dominion. This, of course, causes serious distortion, for the 3,000 miles sailed west on the second voyage obliged him to place the North American coast much further to the west, and thus, drawing on a plane chart, there appears to be an inordinate distance between the two lands. He also made the mistake of putting the western coast on a north and south line, instead of giving it the proper trend to the east. If this had been done, with more easterly longitude to commence with, and Cuba with the other islands had been placed south of the tropic, the map would not have been amiss. The same draughtsman must have supplied materials for other maps. The Portuguese map by Canerio, recently discovered at Paris, but undated, copies the outlines and names from that of Cantino. The same western coast-line appears on the important map of the world by Johann Ruysch, engraved in 1508, with most of the names. But here the western coast of Cantino is turned into Cuba, while the real Cuba is omitted; and Newfoundland is made a part of the continent of Asia. The map of the world by Waldseemüller, for the Ptolemy of 1513, has an exact copy of the western coast-line on the Cantino map, but continues it, without any names, round to Venezuela. The blunder of placing Cuba and Española north of the tropic is here repeated.

The Cantino coast appears again on the Schöner globes of 1515 and 1520, where it is continued southwards to an extensive land called Parias, which is separated by a strait from South America. It is also traceable on the maps of Petrus Apianus (1520) and of Grynæus (Basle, 1532), which in this part are repetitions of the delineation on the Schöner globes. It will thus be seen that the work of the Cantino draughtsman, based on surveys by the pilots of Corte-Real, exercised a very decided influence on cartography for many years, almost until the appearance of the great map of Ortelius in 1570. Recent writers on the subject of the Cantino map have ignored the obvious fact that the western coast there delineated must be assumed to be a discovery by Corte-Real unless there is positive evidence to the contrary, because the map was drawn to show those discoveries. It was a *Carta da nauigar per le isole nouam^{te} tr(ovate)*. The consequence has been that several theories have been started to account for the appearance of such a coast-line.[1]

---

[1] Mr. Harrisse came to the conclusion that the coast did not represent the work of Corte-Real, because it was placed at such an immense distance west of Newfoundland. He thought that an experienced navigator like Corte-Real could not possibly have made such a blunder (*Les Corte-Real*, p. 149). But Corte-Real had nothing whatever to do with it. He never returned, and was dead long before the map was drawn. The draughtsman was alone responsible for the positions of the coast-lines on his *mappa-mundi*, and in placing Newfoundland so far east he was influenced by political motives, as has been explained. Mr. Harrisse sees that the west coast must be that of North America, but he sup-

When Gaspar Corte-Real did not return all through the winter, his brother Miguel fitted out two ships, and went in search of him in the spring of 1502. He, too, was never heard of more, although his consort returned safely. Then the eldest brother, Vasque Anes Corte-Real, the Captain-donative of Terceira and St. George, proposed to go in search of Gaspar and Miguel. But King Manoel felt that there had already been too many valuable lives lost, and refused his consent. Vasque Anes lived to the patriarchal age of ninety, and continued the line. His great-grandson, Manoel Corte-Real, fell fighting by the side of King Sebastian at the fatal battle of Kasr-el-Kebir, in 1578, when the male line of the Corte-Reals became extinct.

---

poses that it was discovered and mapped by a series of unknown navigators previous to the year 1502. The rejection of the obvious solution, that the draughtsman employed to draw the discoveries of Corte-Real did draw them, has given rise to various other untenable theories about this coast-line. Mr. Stevens thought the Cantino coast-line was a duplicate Cuba (p. xx), a "bogus" Cuba, as his editor calls it (p. xxxiii), (*Johann Schöner*, by Henry Stevens, edited by C. H. Coote, 1888); while Varnhagen conjectured that it was a discovery of Vespucci during his apocryphal first voyage! Others think it is Yucatan, or work done by the English. Varnhagen did not know the Cantino map, but argued from the map in the Ptolemy of 1513, which is copied from the same materials.

SAILING DIRECTIONS

OF

COLUMBUS.

BEING THE LETTERS FROM PAOLO TOSCANELLI.

B

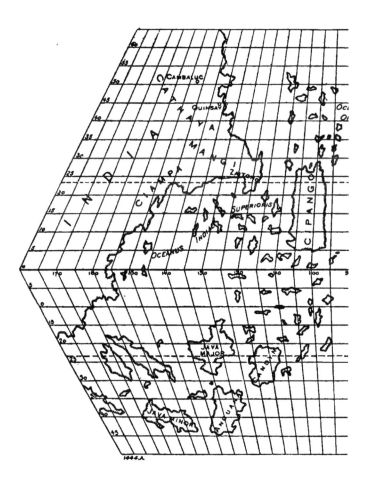

1444.A.

RESTORATION OF TI

FIRST LETTER

OF

PAOLO TOSCANELLI TO COLUMBUS.

(Enclosing a map and a copy of his letter to Martins.)

Prologue to Columbus.[1]

AUL, the Physician, to Cristobal Colombo greeting. I perceive your magnificent and great desire to find a way to where the spices grow, and in reply to your letter I send you the copy of another letter which I wrote, some days ago,[2] to a friend and favourite of the most serene King of Portugal before the wars of Castille,[3]

---

[1] The prologue, addressed to Columbus, is printed by Las Casas, i, 92-96, and in cap. viii of the *Vita del Ammiraglio*. The original Latin is lost.

[2] Las Casas has "*Ha dias*". In the *Vita*.—"*Alquanti giorni fa.*"

[3] Toscanelli means that his correspondent was a friend and favourite of the King before the wars of Castille in the reign of Henry IV, which began in 1465. He fixes the date of his letter to Columbus by the words " some days ago", that is, he wrote the first letter, a copy of which he sends, some days before the letter to Columbus. The date of the first letter is June 24th, 1474.

But Mr. Harrisse takes the words, "before the wars of Castille", as referring to the date of the first letter, and assumes that it is intended in reply to another which, by direction of his Highness, he wrote to me on the said subject, and I send you another sea chart[1] like the one I sent him, by which you will be satisfied respecting your enquiries: which copy is as follows:

A Copy of the letter to Martins.[2]

"Paul, the Physician, to Fernan Martins, Canon at Lisbon, greeting. It was pleasant to me to understand that your health was good, and that you are in the favour and intimacy with the most generous and most magnificent Prince, your King.[3] I have already spoken with you respecting a shorter way to the places of spices than that which you

---

to imply that the letter of Columbus was written after the wars of Castille, which he supposes to mean the war of succession with Portugal from 1475 to 1479. So he concludes that the letter to Columbus was not written before 1480. But, granting that the words "before the wars of Castille" refer to the date of the letter, it does not follow that the second letter was written after the war was over. The first letter may have been written in 1474 before the war began, and the second in 1475 after the war began.

The words "some days ago" are, however, conclusive evidence that the words "before the wars of Castille" do not refer to the date of the letter. If they did, the words "some days ago" would be unmeaning. The date of the letter to Martins being June 24th, 1474, that of the letter to Columbus was some days afterwards, in July 1474.

[1] This chart, after the death of the Admiral and his son Fernando, became the property of Las Casas (i, p. 96), but it is now lost.

[2] A copy of the original Latin letter from Toscanelli to Martins in the handwriting of Columbus himself, was found in the Columbine Library at Seville in 1860. It was in a fly-leaf of a book by Eneas Silvius, which formerly belonged to the Admiral. It is printed in Asensio's *Life of Columbus* (i, p. 250), and the above is translated from the text of Asensio. A Spanish version is given by Las Casas, i, p. 92, and an Italian version is in the *Vita del Ammiraglio*, cap. xiii.

[3] Affonso V, who was a nephew of Prince Henry the Navigator. He succeeded his father, King Duarte, in 1438, and died in 1481.

take by Guinea, by means of maritime navigation. The most serene King now seeks from me some statement, or rather a demonstration to the eye, by which the slightly learned may take in and understand that way. I know this can be shown from the spherical shape of the earth, yet, to make the comprehension of it easier, and to facilitate the work, I have determined to show that way by means of a sailing chart. I, therefore, send to his Majesty a chart made by my own hands, on which are delineated your coasts and islands, whence you must begin to make your journey always westward, and the places at which you should arrive, and how far from the pole or the equinoctial line you ought to keep, and through how much space or over how many miles you should arrive at those most fertile places full of all sorts of spices and jewels. You must not be surprised if I call the parts where the spices are west, when they usually call them east, because to those always sailing west, those parts are found by navigation on the under side[1] of the earth. But if by land and by the upper side,[2] they will always be found to the east. The straight lines shown lengthways on the map indicate the distance from east to west, and those that are drawn across show the spaces from south to north. I have also noted on the map several places at which you may arrive for the better information of navigators, if they should reach a place different from what was expected, by reason of the wind or any other cause ; and also that they may show some acquaintance with the country to the natives, which ought to be sufficiently agreeable to them. It is asserted that none but merchants live on the islands. For there the number of navigators with merchandize is so great that in all the rest

---

[1] " Per subterraneas navigationes."
[2] " Per superiora itinera."

of the world there are not so many as in one most noble port called Zaitun.[1] For they affirm that a hundred ships laden with pepper discharge their cargoes in that port in a single year, besides other ships bringing other spices. That country is very populous and very rich, with a multitude of provinces and kingdoms, and with cities without number, under one prince who is called Great Kan,[2] which name signifies *Rex Regum* in Latin, whose seat and residence is generally in the province Katay.[3] His ancestors desired intercourse with Christians now 200 years ago. They sent to the Pope and asked for several persons learned in the faith, that they might be enlightened, but those who were sent, being impeded in their journey, went

---

[1] "Zaitun (or Zayton) is believed to be Chwangchan-fu (often called in our charts Chinchew), a famous seaport of Fokien, in China, about 100 miles S.W. by S. of Fuchau" (Sir H. Yule's note, *Marco Polo*, ii, 219). Marco Polo calls it "the very great and noble city of Zayton". He says that "for one shipload of pepper that goes to Alexandria, or elsewhere, destined for Christendom, there come a hundred such, aye and more, too, to this haven of Zayton, for it is one of the two greatest havens in the world for commerce". Ibn Batuta pronounces it to be the greatest haven in the world. Marco Polo further says that "the haven of Zayton is frequented by all the ships of India, which bring thither spicery and all other kinds of costly wares, including precious stones and pearls".

[2] Sir H. Yule points out the distinction between Khan and Kaan (or Kan). The former may be rendered Lord, and was applied to chiefs, whether sovereigns or not. In Persia, Afghanistan, and Musulman India it has become a common affix to all names. But Kaan is a form of Khakan, the peculiar title of the supreme sovereign of the Mongols. Marco Polo always writes Kaan as applied to the Great Kaan. Toscanelli, followed by Columbus, writes Kan. In 1259, Kublai became sovereign of the Mongols, and the Grand Kaan was the Emperor of China of his dynasty.

[3] The name of Khitay, or Cathay, is derived from a people called Khitan, whose chief ruled over northern China for two hundred years, until 1123. Southern China remained under the native Sung dynasty, and was called Machin, or Mangi, with their capital at Hang-chau.

back.   Also in the time of Eugenius one of them came to
Eugenius,[1] who affirmed their great kindness towards
Christians, and I had a long conversation with him on
many subjects, about the magnitude of their rivers in
length and breadth, and on the multitude of cities on the
banks of the rivers.   He said that on one river there were
near 200 cities with marble bridges great in length and
breadth, and everywhere adorned with columns.   This
country is worth seeking by the Latins, not only because
great wealth may be obtained from it, gold and silver, all
sorts of gems, and spices, which never reach us ; but also
on account of its learned men, philosophers, and expert astro-
logers, and by what skill and art so powerful and magni
ficent a province is governed, as well as how their wars
are conducted.   This is for some satisfaction to his request, so far as the shortness of time and my occupations
admitted : being ready in future more fully to satisfy his
royal Majesty as far as he may wish.

"Given at Florence, June 24th, 1474."

---

[1] In 1260, Nicolo and Maffeo Polo left Constantinople, and reached
the court of the Great Kaan Kublai.   He determined to send them
back as his Ambassadors to the Pope, accompanied by an officer of
his own court.   His letters to the Pope were mainly to desire the
despatch of a large body of educated missionaries to convert his
people.   They returned in 1269, and found that no Pope existed, for
Clement IV died in 1268, and no new election had taken place.
There was a long interregnum ; and the Polos, tired of waiting, started
for the East again in 1271, taking their nephew Marco with them.   On
the coast of Syria they heard of the Pope's election as Gregory X, but
the new Pope only supplied them with two Dominicans, who lost
heart and drew back.   The Venetians returned to the court of Kublai
in 1275.

The second mission of which Toscanelli speaks was two hundred
years later.   Eugenius IV (the only Eugenius after 1153) was Pope
from 1431 to 1447 ; and it is to a mission in his time that the Florentine astronomer refers.

Letter to Columbus Resumed.[1]

From the city of Lisbon due west there are 26 spaces marked on the map, each of which has 250 miles, as far as the most noble and very great city of Quinsay.[2] For it is a hundred miles in circumference and has ten bridges, and its name signifies the city of Heaven; many wonders being related concerning it, touching the multitude of its handicrafts and resources. This space is almost a third part of the whole sphere. That city is in the province of Mangi,[3] or near the province Katay, in which land is the royal residence. But from the island Antilia, known to you,[4]

---

[1] In the *Vita del Ammiraglio* this is printed as if it was a part of the letter to Martins.

[2] Quinsay, or Kinsay, represents the Chinese term Kingaze, which means capital. The name of this capital city was then Lin-ggan, and is now Hang-chau-fu. Marco Polo gives an account of the great city of Kinsay in chapter lxxvi of his second book. He calls it "the most noble city of Kinsay, a name which is as much as to say in our tongue the city of Heaven". He also says that it was a hundred miles in circumference, and that there were in it 12,000 bridges of stone, which Toscanelli reduces to ten. "The Ocean Sea comes within 25 miles of the city at a place called Ganfu, where there is a town and an excellent Haven. The city of Kinsay is the head of all Mangi." (Yule's *Marco Polo*, ii; 69.)

[3] Mangi, or Manzi, was the name applied to China south of the Hwang-ho, held by the native Sung dynasty until 1176. Persian writers call it Machin.

[4] This proves that Columbus had referred to Antilia in his lost letter to Toscanelli. The fabulous island of Antilia or Antilla first appeared on a *portolano* of 1425. It is placed on the chart of Andrea Bianco of Venice, bearing date 1436, in longitude 25° 35′ W. Ruysch, in his map engraved after the death of Columbus, removed it to between 37° W. and 40° W., adding a legend to the effect that it was discovered long ago by Roderick, the last of the Gothic Kings of Spain, who took refuge there after his defeat by the Moors, but had since been searched for in vain. Another tale was that two archbishops and five bishops escaped to Antilia, after the death of Roderick, and that they built seven cities there. One of the beautiful

to the most noble island of Cippangue[1] there are ten
spaces. For that island is most fertile in gold, pearls, and
precious stones, and they cover the temples and palaces
with solid gold. Thus the spaces of sea to be crossed in
the unknown parts are not great. Many things might
perhaps have been declared more exactly, but a diligent
thinker will be able to clear up the rest for himself. Fare·
well, most excellent one.

---

portolani of Benincasa shows it, on the western edge, as a very large
oblong island, with the names of the seven cities all given.

The name Antilles was first applied to the West Indian Islands on
the Portuguese map drawn for Cantino in 1500.

[1] Marco Polo says : " Chipangu is an island towards the east in
the high seas, 1,500 miles distant from the continent, and a very great
island it is. The Lord of that island hath a great palace which is
entirely roofed with fine gold. Moreover, all the pavement of the
palace, and the floors of its chambers, are entirely of gold, in plates
like slabs of stone, a good two fingers thick ; and the windows are
also of gold, so that altogether the richness of this palace is past all
bounds and all belief. They have also pearls in abundance and
quantities of other precious stones." (Yule's *Marco Polo*, ii, p. 237.)

Sir H. Yule says that Chipangu represents the Chinese Zhi-pan-
kwe, the kingdom of Japan. The name Zhi-pan being the Mandarin
form of which the term Niphon, used in Japan, is a variation, both
meaning " the origin of the sun", or sun-rising. Our Japan was probably taken from the Malay " Japang". Kæmpfer repeats the fable of
the golden palace.

SECOND LETTER

OF

PAOLO TOSCANELLI TO COLUMBUS.[1]

PAUL, the Physician, to Cristoval Colombo greeting. I received your letters with the things you sent me, and with them I received great satisfaction. I perceive your magnificent and grand desire to navigate from the parts of the east to the west, in the way that was set forth in the letter that I sent you, and which will be demonstrated better on a round sphere. It pleases me much that I should be well understood; for the said voyage is not only possible, but it is true, and certain to be honorable and to yield incalculable profit, and very great fame among all Christians. But you cannot know this perfectly save through experience and practice, as I have had in the form of most copious and good and true information from distinguished men of great learning who have come from the said parts, here in the court of Rome, and from others being merchants who have had business for a long time in those parts, men of high authority. Thus when that voyage shall be made, it will be to powerful kingdoms and cities and most noble provinces, very rich in all manner of things in great abundance and very necessary to us, such as all sorts of spices in great quantity, and jewels in the greatest abundance.

It will also go to the said Kings and Princes who are very desirous, more than ourselves, to have intercourse and

---

[1] Given by Las Casas, i, p. 95.

speech with Christians of these our parts, because a great part of them are Christians, as well as to have speech and intercourse with men of learning and ingenuity here, as well in religion as in all the other sciences, by reason of the great fame of the empires and governments in these parts that has reached them. On account of all these things, and of many others that might be mentioned, I do not wonder that you, who have great courage, and all the Portuguese people who have always been men eager for all great undertakings, should be with a burning heart and feel a great desire to undertake the said voyage.

JOURNAL

OF THE

FIRST VOYAGE OF COLUMBUS.

JOURNAL

OF THE

FIRST VOYAGE OF COLUMBUS.

This is the first voyage and the routes

and direction taken by the Admiral Don Cristobal
Colon when he discovered the Indies, sum-
marized; except the prologue made for the
Sovereigns, which is given word for
word and commences in this
manner.

In the name of our Lord Jesus Christ.

ECAUSE, O most Christian, and very
high, very excellent, and puissant
Princes, King and Queen of the
Spains and of the islands of the
Sea, our Lords, in this present year
of 1492, after your Highnesses had
given an end to the war with the
Moors who reigned in Europe, and had finished it in the
very great city of Granada, where in this present year,
on the second day of the month of January, by force
of arms, I saw the royal banners of your Highnesses
placed on the towers of Alfambra, which is the fortress of
that city, and I saw the Moorish King come forth from
the gates of the city and kiss the royal hands of your
Highnesses, and of the Prince my Lord, and presently in.

that same month, acting on the information that I had given to your Highnesses touching the lands of India, and respecting a Prince who is called *Gran Can*, which means in our language King of Kings, how he and his ancestors had sent to Rome many times to ask for learned men of our holy faith to teach him, and how the Holy Father had never complied, insomuch that many people believing in idolatries were lost by receiving doctrine of perdition : YOUR HIGHNESSES, as Catholic Christians and Princes who love the holy Christian faith, and the propagation of it, and who are enemies to the sect of Mahoma and to all idolatries and heresies, resolved to send me, Cristobal Colon, to the said parts of India to see the said princes, and the cities and lands, and their disposition, with a view that they might be converted to our holy faith ; and ordered that I should not go by land to the eastward, as had been customary, but that I should go by way of the west, whither up to this day, we do not know for certain that any one has gone.

Thus, after having turned out all the Jews from all your kingdoms and lordships,[1] in the same month of January,

---

[1] The decree for the expulsion of the Jews was really dated March 20th, 1492. Dr. Don Fernando Belmonte, an officer employed in the archives of Seville, recently discovered a document which refers to the expulsion of the Jews from Palos while Columbus was equipping his expedition.   It is a process taken before the Corregidor of Moguer in January 1552, and one Juan de Aragon, a native of Moguer, then aged 70, gave evidence.   He said that 55 years before, more or less, he was a boy on board a vessel at Palos, and saw Cristobal de Colon ready to sail for the Indies with three ships.   This was in August or September.   He further deposed that, having returned from his voyage, after having left the Jews in the parts beyond, and in another year, coming by sea, he met the ship of Martin Alonso Pinzon returning from the discovery (*Asensio*, i, 264).   This boy was, therefore, in the ship which conveyed some of the banished Jews from Palos to Africa, at the very time that Columbus was fitting out his expedition. January, in the text, is a misprint.

your Highnesses gave orders to me that with a sufficient fleet I should go to the said parts of India, and for this they made great concessions to me, and ennobled me, so that henceforward I should be called Don, and should be Chief Admiral of the Ocean Sea, perpetual Viceroy and Governor of all the islands and continents that I should discover and gain, and that I might hereafter discover and gain in the Ocean Sea, and that my eldest son should succeed, and so on from generation to generation for ever.

I left the city of Granada on the 12th day of May, in the same year of 1492, being Saturday, and came to the town of Palos, which is a seaport; where I equipped three vessels[1] well suited for such service; and departed from that port, well supplied with provisions and with many sailors, on the 3d day of August of the same year, being Friday, half an hour before sunrise, taking the route to the islands of Canaria, belonging to your Highnesses, which are in the said Ocean Sea, that I might thence take my departure for navigating until I should arrive at the Indies, and give the letters of your Highnesses to those princes, so as to comply with my orders. As part of my duty I thought it well to write an account of all the voyage very punctually, noting from day to day all that I should do and see, and that should happen, as will be seen further on. Also, Lords Princes, I resolved to describe each night what passed in the day, and to note each day how I navigated

---

[1] Columbus never mentions the name of the ship in which he sailed. It was owned by Juan de la Cosa of Santoña. Oviedo calls it the *Gallega;* Herrera, the *Santa Maria*. It was the largest, about 100 tons. The others were two caravels of Palos, called the *Pinta* and *Niña*. The *Pinta* was commanded by Martin Alonso Pinzon, and owned by two sailors who served on board. The *Niña*, named after its owners, the Niño family, was commanded oy Vicente Yañez Pinzon, with three Niños on board, one as pilot, another as master, and a third as one of the seamen.

C

at night. I propose to construct a new chart for navigating, on which I shall delineate all the sea and lands of the
Ocean in their proper positions under their bearings ; and
further, I propose to prepare a book, and to put down all as
it were in a picture, by latitude from the equator, and
western longitude. Above all, I shall have accomplished
much, for I shall forget sleep, and shall work at the business of navigation, that so the service may be performed ;
all which will entail great labour.

Friday, 3d of August.

We departed on Friday, the 3d of August, in the year
1492, from the bar of Saltes,[1] at 8 o'clock, and proceeded
with a strong sea breeze until sunset, towards the south,
for 60 miles, equal to 15 leagues[2]; afterwards S.W. and
W.S.W., which was the course for the Canaries.

Saturday, 4th of August.

They steered S.W. ¼ S.

---

[1] Saltes is an island formed by two arms of the river Odiel, in front
of the town of Huelva. It was inhabited certainly until the twelfth
century, and as late as 1267 King Alonso the Wise fixed the boundary
between the towns of Saltes and Huelva.   It is unknown when it
ceased to be inhabited, but even in the *Suma de Geografia* of Martin
Fernandez de Enciso, printed in 1519, mention is made of that town
of Saltes, yet it is certain that, at that time, only the church remained,
attached to those of Huelva, which shows that there were no longer
any inhabited houses.   No length of time can have passed before the
church itself fell into ruins, for, in order to preserve some memory of it,
a hermitage was founded in Huelva with the title of " Our Lady of
Saltes", in which a cross was kept, being a relic of the old church.
Some traces of the church remain, and the district is divided into
arable lands, pastures, and woods preserved for the chase ; being the
property of the Marquis of Ayamonte, with the title of Count of Saltes.
(*Huelva Ilustrada del Lic D. Juan de Mora.*   Sevilla, 1762.)—N.

[2] Columbus used Italian miles, which are shorter than the Spanish ;
four Italian being equivalent to three Spanish, or a league.—N.

Sunday, 5th of August.

They continued their course day and night more than 40 leagues.

Monday, 6th of August.

The rudder of the caravel *Pinta* became unshipped, and Martin Alonso Pinzon, who was in command, believed or suspected that it was by contrivance of Gomes Rascon and Cristobal Quintero, to whom the caravel belonged, for they dreaded to go on that voyage. The Admiral says that, before they sailed, these men had been displaying a certain backwardness, so to speak. The Admiral was much disturbed at not being able to help the said caravel without danger, and he says that he was eased of some anxiety when he reflected that Martin Alonso Pinzon was a man of energy and ingenuity. They made, during the day and night, 29 leagues.

Tuesday, 7th of August.

The rudder of the *Pinta* was shipped and secured, and they proceeded on a course for the island of Lanzarote, one of the Canaries. They made, during the day and night, 25 leagues.

Wednesday, 8th of August.

Opinions respecting their position varied among the pilots of the three caravels; but that of the Admiral proved to be nearer the truth. He wished to go to Gran Canaria, to leave the caravel *Pinta*, because she was disabled by the faulty hanging of her rudder, and was making water. He intended to obtain another there if one could be found. They could not reach the place that day.

Thursday, 9th of August.

The Admiral was not able to reach Gomera until the night of Sunday, while Martin Alonso remained on that

C 2

coast of Gran Canaria by order of the Admiral, because his
vessel could not be navigated. Afterwards the Admiral
took her to Canaria, and they repaired the *Pinta* very
thoroughly through the pains and labour of the Admiral, of
Martin Alonso, and of the rest.[1] Finally they came to
Gomera. They saw a great fire issue from the mountain
of the island of Tenerife, which is of great height. They
rigged the *Pinta* with square sails, for she was lateen
rigged ; and the Admiral reached Gomera on Sunday, the
2nd of September, with the *Pinta* repaired.

The Admiral says that many honourable Spanish gentlemen who were at Gomera with Doña Ines Peraza, mother
of Guillen Peraza (who was afterwards the first Count of
Gomera), and who were natives of the island of Hierro, declared that every year they saw land to the west of the
Canaries ; and others, natives of Gomera, affirmed the same
on oath. The Admiral here says that he remembers, when
in Portugal in the year 1484, a man came to the King from
the island of Madeira, to beg for a caravel to go to this land
that was seen, who swore that it could be seen every year,
and always in the same way. He also says that he re-
collects the same thing being affirmed in the islands of the
Azores ; and all these lands were described as in the same
direction, and as being like each other, and of the same size.[2]

---

[1] Herrera says that the rig of the *Niña* was altered from lateen to
square sails, at this time; and the *Pinta* was supplied with a new
rudder. (*Dec. I*, Lib. I, cap. ix.)

[2] By the death of Fernan Peraza in 1452, the lordship of the
Canaries remained with his daughter Doña Ines, married to Diego de
Herrera, whose title was confirmed by the King, Don Enrique IV, on
the 28th of September 1454. Then, as the Admiral says, the inhabitants of Gomera and of Hierro saw land to the westward every year,
which they supposed to be the imaginary isle of San Borondon. Afterwards the illusions and vulgar belief in its existence continued in spite
of the ships sent to find it, which never were able to do so, although
the ablest mariners were employed on the service. Viera, in his

Having taken in water, wood, and meat, and all else that the men had who were left at Gomera by the Admiral when he went to the island of Canaria to repair the caravel *Pinta*, he finally made sail from the said island of Gomera, with his three caravels, on Thursday, the 6th day of September.

Thursday, 6th of September.

He departed on that day from the port of Gomera in the morning, and shaped a course to go on his voyage; having received tidings from a caravel that came from the island of Hierro that three Portuguese caravels were off that

---

history of the Canaries, refers to all these attempts in detail, with sincerity and critical judgment, and Feijoo refutes the stories as superstitions of the common people.

Pedro de Medina, in his *Grandezas de España*, says that at no great distance from the island of Madeira there was another island called Antilia, which is not now seen, but which is found figured on a very ancient sea-chart; and Viera affirms that some Portuguese and inhabitants of Madeira saw lands to the westward which they were never able to reach, although they tried. From this took its origin the representing on the charts, which were then drawn, of some new islands in those seas, especially Antilia and San Borondon. This is found on the globe which was drawn by Martin Behaim at Nuremberg in 1492, to the S.W. of Hierro, though the Cape Verde Isles are interposed between them.

From these groundless notions which prevailed for nearly four centuries, and particularly at the time of the discoveries at the end of the fifteenth and beginning of the sixteenth centuries, and from the malignant envy that strove to detract from the merit of the great Columbus, may have arisen the rumour that the new continent and islands had previously been discovered either by Alonso Sanchez de Huelva, or by some other Portuguese or Biscayan navigator, as several Spaniards wrote; or by Martin de Behaim, as even in modern times some foreigners have affirmed. But Oviedo, a contemporary author, said that in reality no one was able to declare this novelty which was current among the vulgar, and that he considered it to be false. Don Cristóbal Cladera, in his *Investigaciones Históricas*, refuted these pretensions of natives and foreigners with very solid reasoning, defending the merit and glory of the first Admiral of the Indies.—N.

island with the object of taking him. (This must have been the result of the King's annoyance that Colon should have gone to Castille.[1])   There was a calm all that day and night, and in the morning he found himself between Gomera and Tenerife.

Friday, 7th of September.

The calm continued all Friday and Saturday, until the third hour of the night.

Saturday, 8th of September.

At the third hour of Saturday night it began to blow from the N.E., and the Admiral shaped a course to the west.   He took in much sea over the bows, which retarded progress, and 9 leagues were made in that day and night.

Sunday, 9th of September.

This day the Admiral made 19 leagues, and he arranged to reckon less than the number run, because if the voyage was of long duration, the people would not be so terrified and disheartened.   In the night he made 120 miles, at the rate of 12 miles an hour, which are 30 leagues.   The sailors steered badly, letting the ship fall off to N.E., and even more, respecting which the Admiral complained many times.

Monday, 10th of September.

In this day and night he made 60 leagues, at the rate of 10 miles an hour, which are 2½ leagues; but he only counted 48 leagues, that the people might not be alarmed if the voyage should be long.

Tuesday, 11th of September.

That day they sailed on their course, which was west, and made 20 leagues and more.   They saw a large piece

---

[1] An interpolation by Las Casas.

of the mast of a ship of 120 tons, but were unable to get it. In the night they made nearly 20 leagues, but only counted 16, for the reason already given.

Wednesday, 12th of September.

That day, steering their course, they made 33 leagues during the day and night, counting less.

Thursday, 13th of September.

That day and night, steering their course, which was west, they made 33 leagues, counting 3 or 4 less. The currents were against them. On this day, at the commencement of the night, the needles turned a half point to north-west, and in the morning they turned somewhat more north-west.[1]

Friday, 14th of September.

That day they navigated, on their westerly course, day and night, 20 leagues, counting a little less. Here those of the caravel *Niña* reported that they had seen a tern[2] and a boatswain bird,[3] and these birds never go more than 25 leagues from the land.

Saturday, 15th of September.

That day and night they made 27 leagues and rather more on their west course; and in the early part of the night there fell from heaven into the sea a marvellous

---

[1] " From this", says Herrera, " the Admiral knew that the needle did not point to the North Star but to another fixed point that is invisible. To turn north-west is the same as to say that the *fleur-de-lys*, which denotes the north point, does not point directly to the north, but that it turns to the left hand." He adds that this variation had never been observed by anyone up to that time, and that it caused much astonishment. (*Dec. I*, Lib. 1, cap. ix.)

[2] Garjao.　　　　　　　　　　　　　　　[3] Rabo de junco.

flame of fire,[1] at a distance of about 4 or 5 leagues from them.

Sunday, 16th of September.

That day and night they steered their course west, making 39 leagues, but the Admiral only counted 36. There were some clouds and small rain. The Admiral says that on that day, and ever afterwards, they met with very temperate breezes, so that there was great pleasure in enjoying the mornings, nothing being wanted but the song of nightingales. He says that the weather was like April in Andalusia. Here they began to see many tufts of grass which were very green, and appeared to have been quite recently torn from the land. From this they judged that they were near some island, but not the main land, according to the Admiral, "because", as he says, "I make the main land to be more distant".

Monday, 17th of September.

They proceeded on their west course, and made over 50 leagues in the day. and night, but the Admiral only counted 47. They were aided by the current. They saw much very fine grass and herbs from rocks, which came from the west. They, therefore, considered that they were near land. The pilots observed the north point, and found that the needles turned a full point to the west of north. So the mariners were alarmed and dejected, and did not give their reason. But the Admiral knew, and ordered that the north should be again observed at dawn. They then found that the needles were true. The cause was that the star makes the movement, and not the needles.[2]

---

[1] "Ramo" in the Journal. Herrera has "Llama de fuego".

[2] The ingenious Columbus, who was the first observer of variation, succeeded in allaying the fears of his people, by explaining, in a

At dawn, on that Monday, they saw much more weed
appearing, like herbs from rivers, in which they found a
live crab, which the Admiral kept. He says that these
crabs are certain signs of land. The sea-water was found
to be less salt than it had been since leaving the Canaries.
The breezes were always soft. Everyone was pleased, and
the best sailers went ahead to sight the first land. They
saw many tunny-fish, and the crew of the *Niña* killed one.
The Admiral here says that these signs of land came from
the west, "in which direction I trust in that high God in
whose hands are all victories that very soon we shall sight
land". In that morning he says that a white bird was seen
which has not the habit of sleeping on the sea, called *rabo
de junco* (boatswain-bird).

Tuesday, 18th of September.

This day and night they made over 55 leagues, the
Admiral only counting 48. In all these days the sea was
very smooth, like the river at Seville. This day Martin
Alonso, with the *Pinta*, which was a fast sailer, did not
wait, for he said to the Admiral, from his caravel, that he
had seen a great multitude of birds flying westward, that
he hoped to see land that night, and that he therefore

---

specious manner, the cause of the phenomenon. The surprise and
anxiety of the pilots and sailors are decisive proofs that no one had
observed until then the variation of the needle.—N.

Columbus had crossed the point of no variation, which was then
near the meridian of Flores, in the Azores, and found the variation no
longer easterly, but more than a point westerly. His explanation that
the pole-star, by means of which the change was detected, was not
itself stationary, is very plausible. For the pole-star really does
describe a circle round the pole of the earth, equal in diameter to
about six times that of the sun ; but this not equal to the change
observed in the direction of the needle.

pressed onward. A great cloud appeared in the north, which is a sign of the proximity of land.[1]

Wednesday, 19th of September.

The Admiral continued on his course, and during the day and night he made but 25 leagues because it was calm. He counted 22. This day, at 10 o'clock, a booby[2] came to the ship, and in the afternoon another arrived, these birds not generally going more than 20 leagues from the land. There was also some drizzling rain without wind, which is a sure sign of land. The Admiral did not wish to cause delay by beating to windward to ascertain whether land was near, but he considered it certain that there were islands both to the north and south of his position, (as indeed there were, and he was passing through the middle of them[3]). For his desire was to press onwards to the Indies, the weather being fine. For on his return, God willing, he could see all. These are his own words. Here the pilots found their positions. He of the *Niña* made the Canaries 440 leagues distant, the *Pinta* 420. The pilot of the Admiral's ship made the distance exactly 400 leagues.[4]

Thursday, 20th of September.

This day the course was W. b. N., and as her head was all round the compass owing to the calm that prevailed, the ships made only 7 or 8 leagues. Two boobies came to the ship, and afterwards another, a sign of the proximity of land. They saw much weed, although none was seen

---

[1] For eleven days they had not had to trim sails so much as a *palmo*, the wind always aft, the Admiral constantly noting everything, and proceeding carefully with astrolabe and sounding-lead. (Herrera, *Dec. I*, Lib. i, cap. ix.)

[2] Alcatraz.   [3] Interpolation by Las Casas.

[4] The distance of the Admiral's pilot is exact.—N.

on the previous day. They caught a bird with the hand, which was like a tern.[1] But it was a river-bird, not a sea-bird, the feet being like those of a gull. At dawn two or three land-birds came singing to the ship, and they disappeared beforè sunset. Afterwards a booby came from W.N.W., and flew to the S.W., which was a sign that it left land in the W.N.W.; for these birds sleep on shore, and go to sea in the mornings in search of food, not extending their flight mo land.

Friday, 21st o,

Most of the day it was calm wind. During the day and ni more than 13 leagues. At da that the sea appeared to be c from the west. A booby wa smooth, like a river, and the They saw a whale, which is a land, because they always keep

Saturday, 22nd

They shaped a course W.N turning from one to the other Scarcely any weed was seen.

and another bird. Here the Admiral says : "This con-trary wind was very necessary for me, because my people were much excited at the thought that in these seas no wind ever blew in the direction of Spain." Part of the day there was no weed, and later it was very thick.

Sunday, 23rd of September.

They shaped a course N.W., and at times more northerly; occasionally they were on their course, which was west,

---

[1] Garjao.

and they made about 22 leagues. They saw a dove
and a booby, another river-bird, and some white birds.
There was a great deal of weed, and they found crabs in
it. The sea being smooth and calm, the crew began to
murmur, saying that here there was no great sea, and that
the wind would never blow so that they could return to
Spain. Afterwards the sea rose very much, without wind,
which astonished them. The Admiral here says: "Thus
the high sea was very necessary to me, such as had not
appeared but in the time of the Jews when they went out
of Egypt and murmured against Moses, who delivered
them out of captivity."

Monday, 24th of September.

The Admiral went on his west course all day and night,
making 14 leagues. He counted 12. A booby came to
the ship, and many sandpipers.

Tuesday, 25th of September.

This day began with a calm, and afterwards there was
wind. They were on their west course until night. The
Admiral conversed with Martin Alonso Pinzon, captain of
the other caravel *Pinta*, respecting a chart which he had
sent to the caravel three days before, on which, as it would
appear, the Admiral had certain islands depicted in that
sea.[1] Martin Alonso said that the ships were in the posi-

---

[1] This chart, drawn for the Admiral, must have been that which
Paulo Toscanelli, the celebrated Florentine astronomer, sent to Lisbon
in 1474. It included from the north of Ireland to the end of Guinea,
with all the islands situated on that route ; and towards the west it
showed the beginning of the Indies, and the islands and places whither
they were proceeding. Colon saw this chart and read the accounts of
travellers, especially Marco Polo, which confirmed him in the idea
of finding India by the west, though it had hitherto always been
approached by the east. The situations of coasts and islands fixed on

tion on which the islands were placed, and the Admiral
replied that so it appeared to him : but it might be that
they had not fallen in with them, owing to the currents
which had always set the ships to the N.E., and that they
had not made so much as the pilots reported. The
Admiral then asked for the chart to be returned, and it
was sent back on a line. The Admiral then began to plot
the position on it, with the pilot and mariners. At sunset
Martin Alonso went up on the poop of his ship, and with
much joy called to the Admiral, claiming the reward as he
had sighted land. When the Admiral heard this positively
declared, he says that he gave thanks to the Lord on his
knees, while Martin Alonso said the *Gloria in excelsis* with
his people. The Admiral's crew did the same. Those of
the *Niña* all went up on the mast and into the rigging, and
declared that it was land. It so seemed to the Admiral,
and that it was distant 25 leagues. They all continued to
declare it was land until night. The Admiral ordered the
course to be altered from W. to S.W., in which direction
the land had appeared. That day they made 4 leagues
on a west course, and 17 S.W. during the night, in all 21 ;
but the people were told that 13 was the distance made
good : for it was always feigned to them that the distances
were less, so that the voyage might not appear so long.
Thus two reckonings were kept on this voyage, the shorter
being feigned, and the longer being the true one. The sea
was very smooth, so that many sailors bathed alongside.
They saw many *dorados* and other fish.

---

such vague information must have been very inaccurate, as they were
on the globe of Martin Behaim, constructed in 1492.—N.

Mr. Harrisse has translated the words *segun parece tenia pintadas el
Almirante ciertas islas,* " in which the Admiral seemed to have painted
certain islands," and assumes that the Admiral had painted the islands
himself. But I think the correct rendering of the passage is that the
Admiral had a chart with certain islands depicted on it. (See *Discovery of North America,* p. 401.)

Wednesday, 26th of September.

The Admiral continued on the west course until after noon. Then he altered course to S.W., until he made out that what had been said to be land was only clouds. Day and night they made 31 leagues, counting 24 for the people. The sea was like a river, the air pleasant and very mild.

Thursday, 27th of September.

The course west, and distance made good during day and night 24 leagues, 20 being counted for the people. Many *dorados* came. One was killed. A boatswain-bird came.

Friday, 28th of September.

The course was west, and the distance, owing to calms, only 14 leagues in day and night, 13 leagues being counted. They met with little weed ; but caught two *dorados*, and more in the other ships.

Saturday, 29th of September.

The course was west, and they made 24 leagues, counting 21 for the people. Owing to calms, the distance made good during day and night was not much. They saw a bird called *rabiforcado* (man-o'-war bird), which makes the boobies vomit what they have swallowed, and eats it, maintaining itself on nothing else. It is a sea-bird, but does not sleep on the sea, and does not go more than 20 leagues from the land. There are many of them at the Cape Verde Islands. Afterwards they saw two boobies. The air was very mild and agreeable, and the Admiral says that nothing was wanting but to hear the nightingale. The sea smooth as a river. Later, three boobies and a man-o'-war bird were seen three times. There was much weed.

Sunday, 30th of September.

The western course was steered, and during the day and night, owing to calms, only 14 leagues were made, 11 being counted. Four boatswain-birds came to the ship, which is a great sign of land, for so many birds of this kind together is a sign that they are not straying or lost. They also twice saw four boobies. There was much weed. *Note* that the stars which are called *las guardias* (the Pointers), when night comes on, are near the western point, and when dawn breaks they are near the N.E. point; so that, during the whole night, they do not appear to move more than three lines or 9 hours, and this on each night. The Admiral says this, and also that at nightfall the needles vary a point westerly, while at dawn they agree exactly with the star. From this it would appear that the north star has a movement like the other stars, while the needles always point correctly.

Monday, 1st of October.

Course west, and 25 leagues made good, counted for the crew as 20 leagues. There was a heavy shower of rain. At dawn the Admiral's pilot made the distance from Hierro 578[1] leagues to the west. The reduced reckoning which the Admiral showed to the crew made it 584 leagues ; but the truth which the Admiral observed and kept secret was 707.

Tuesday, 2nd of October.

Course west, and during the day and night 39 leagues were made good, counted for the crew as 30. The sea always smooth. Many thanks be given to God, says the Admiral, that the weed is coming from east to west, con-

---

[1] Herrera says 588.

trary to its usual course. Many fish were seen, and one was killed. A white bird was also seen that appeared to be a gull.

Wednesday, 3rd of October.

They navigated on the usual course, and made good 47 leagues, counted as 40. Sandpipers appeared, and much weed, some of it very old and some quite fresh and having fruit. They saw no birds. The Admiral, therefore, thought that they had left the islands behind them which were depicted on the charts. The Admiral here says that he did not wish to keep the ships beating about during the last week, and in the last few days when there were so many signs of land, although he had information of certain islands in this region. For he wished to avoid delay, his object being to reach the Indies. He says that to delay would not be wise.

Thursday, 4th of October.

Course west, and 63 leagues made good during the day and night, counted as 46. More than forty sandpipers came to the ship in a flock, and two boobies, and a ship's boy hit one with a stone. There also came a man-o'-war bird and a white bird like a gull.

Friday, 5th of October.

The Admiral steered his course, going 11 miles an hour, and during the day and night they made good 57 leagues, as the wind increased somewhat during the night : 45 were counted. The sea was smooth and quiet. "To God", he says, "be many thanks given, the air being pleasant and temperate, with no weed, many sandpipers, and flying-fish coming on the deck in numbers."

Saturday, 6th of October.

'The Admiral continued his west course, and during day and night they made good 40 leagues, 33 being counted. This night Martin Alonso said that it would be well to steer south of west, and it appeared to the Admiral that Martin Alonso did not say this with respect to the island of Cipango. He saw that if an error was made the land would not be reached so quickly, and that consequently it would be better to go at once to the continent and afterwards to the islands.

Sunday, 7th of October.

The west course was continued; for two hours they went at the rate of 12 miles an hour, and afterwards 8 miles an hour. They made good 23 leagues, counting 18 for the people. This day, at sunrise, the caravel *Niña*, which went ahead, being the best sailer, and pushed forward as much as possible to sight the land first, so as to enjoy the reward which the Sovereigns had promised to whoever should see it first, hoisted a flag at the mast-head and fired a gun, as a signal that she had sighted land, for such was the Admiral's order. He had also ordered that, at sunrise and sunset, all the ships should join him; because those two times are most proper for seeing the greatest distance, the haze clearing away. No land was seen during the afternoon, as reported by the caravel *Niña*, and they passed a great number of birds flying from N. to S.W. This gave rise to the belief that the birds were either going to sleep on land, or were flying from the winter which might be supposed to be near in the land whence they were coming The Admiral was aware that most of the islands held by the Portuguese were discovered by the flight of birds. For this reason he resolved to give up the west course, and to shape a course W.S.W. for the two following days. He

D'

began the new course one hour before sunset. They made good, during the night, about 5 leagues, and 23 in the day, altogether 28 leagues.

Monday, 8th of October.

The course was W.S.W., and 11½ or 12 leagues were made good in the day and night ; and at times it appears that they went at the rate of 15 miles an hour during the night (if the handwriting is not deceptive).[1] The sea was like the river at Seville. " Thanks be to God", says the Admiral, " the air is very soft like the April at Seville ; and it is a pleasure to be here, so balmy are the breezes." The weed seemed to be very fresh. There were many land-birds, and they took one that was flying to the S.W. Terns, ducks, and a booby were also seen.

Tuesday, 9th of October.

The course was S.W., and they made 5 leagues. The wind then changed, and the Admiral steered W. by N. 4 leagues. Altogether, in day and night, they made 11 leagues by day and 20½ leagues by night ; counted as 17 leagues altogether. Throughout the night birds were heard passing.

Wednesday, 10th of October.

The course was W.S.W., and they went at the rate of 10 miles an hour, occasionally 12 miles, and sometimes 7. During the day and night they made 59 leagues, counted as no more than 44. Here the people could endure no longer. They complained of the length of the voyage. But the Admiral cheered them up in the best way he could, giving them good hopes of the advantages they might gain from it. He added that, however much they might

---

[1] The parenthesis is by Las Casas. These miles were four to a league (see note 2, p. 18); so that fifteen miles would not really be quite ten geographical miles an hour.

complain, he had to go to the Indies, and that he would go on until he found them, with the help of our Lord.

Thursday, 11th of October.

The course was W.S.W., and there was more sea than there had been during the whole of the voyage. They saw sandpipers, and a green reed near the ship. Those of the caravel *Pinta* saw a cane and a pole, and they took up another small pole which appeared to have been worked with iron; also another bit of cane, a land-plant, and a small board. The crew of the caravel *Niña* also saw signs of land, and a small branch covered with berries. Everyone breathed afresh and rejoiced at these signs. The run until sunset was 26 leagues.

After sunset the Admiral returned to his original west course, and they went along at the rate of 12 miles an hour. Up to two hours after midnight they had gone 90 miles, equal to 22½ leagues. As the caravel *Pinta* was a better sailer, and went ahead of the Admiral, she found the land, and made the signals ordered by the Admiral. The land was first seen by a sailor named Rodrigo de Triana.[1] But the Admiral, at ten in the previous night, being on the castle of the poop, saw a light, though it was so uncertain that he could not affirm it was land. He called Pero Gutierrez, a gentleman of the King's bed-chamber, and said that there seemed to be a light, and that he should look at it. He did so, and saw it.[2] The

---

[1] It was full moon on October 5th. On the night of the 11th the moon rose at 11 P.M., and at 2 A.M. on the morning of the 12th it was 39° above the horizon. It would be shining brightly on the sandy shores of an island some miles ahead, being in its third quarter, and a little behind Rodrigo de Triana, when he sighted land at 2 A.M.

[2] Oviedo says that, after the Admiral and Gutierrez saw the light, a sailor from Lepe called out from the forecastle that there was a light. He was told by Salcedo, the Admiral's servant, that it had already been seen. Oviedo adds that this man from Lepe was so disgusted

Admiral said the same to Rodrigo Sanchez of Segovia, whom the King and Queen had sent with the fleet as inspector, but he could see nothing, because he was not in a place whence anything could be seen. After the Admiral had spoken he saw the light once or twice, and it was like a wax candle rising and falling. It seemed to few to be an indication of land ; but the Admiral made certain that land was close. When they said the *Salve*, which all the sailors were accustomed to sing in their way, the Admiral asked and admonished the men to keep a good look-out on the forecastle, and to watch well for land ; and to him who should first cry out that he saw land, he would give a silk doublet, besides the other rewards promised by the Sovereigns, which were 10,000 maravedis to him who should first see it.[1] At two hours after midnight the land was sighted at a distance of two leagues. They shortened sail, and lay by under the mainsail without the bonnets. The vessels were hove to, waiting for daylight ; and on Friday they arrived at a small island of the Lucayos, called, in the language of the Indians, *Guanahani*.[2] Presently

----

at not getting the reward, that he went to Africa and became a renegade. (*Oviedo*, Lib. II, cap. v.)

Oviedo derived his information from the gossip of Vicente Yañez Pinzon and Hernan Perez Matheos. The latter is not in any of the lists of those who served in the expedition. Oviedo knew him as a pilot at St. Domingo, and he certainly alleged that he was with the Admiral in his first voyage.

Fernando Columbus, in the *Vita del Ammiraglio*, described the light as like a candle that went up and down, as if people on shore were passing with it from one house to another (cap. xxi). See also Herrera (*Dec. I*, Lib. I, cap. xii).

[1] The pension of 10,000 maravedis was secured on the dues derived from the shambles at Seville. The Sovereigns awarded it to the Admiral, because the light seen first by him was believed to have been on land. (*Herrera.*)

[2] Watling Island, S.E. point in Lat. 23° 55′ S., Long. 74° 28′ W. It was named San Salvador by Columbus. (See *Letter to Santangel*, Major's translation, p. 2.)

they saw naked people. The Admiral went on shore in
the armed boat, and Martin Alonso Pinzon, and Vicente
Yañez, his brother, who was captain of the *Niña.* The
Admiral took the royal standard, and the captains went with
two banners of the green cross, which the Admiral took in
all the ships as a sign, with an F and a Y[1] and a crown over
each letter, one on one side of the cross and the other on
the other. Having landed, they saw trees very green, and
much water, and fruits of diverse kinds. The Admiral
called to the two captains, and to the others who leaped
on shore, and to Rodrigo Escovedo, secretary of the whole
fleet, and to Rodrigo Sanchez of Segovia,[2] and said that
they should bear faithful testimony that he, in presence of
all, had taken, as he now took, possession of the said island
for the King and for the Queen, his Lords making the
declarations that are required, as is more largely set forth
in the testimonies which were then made in writing.

Presently many inhabitants of the island assembled.
What follows is in the actual words of the Admiral in his
book of the first navigation and discovery of the Indies.
"I," he says, "that we might form great friendship, for I
knew that they were a people who could be more easily
freed and converted to our holy faith by love than by
force, gave to some of them red caps, and glass beads to
put round their necks, and many other things of little
value, which gave them great pleasure, and made them so
much our friends that it was a marvel to see. They afterwards came to the ship's boats where we were, swimming
and bringing us parrots, cotton threads in skeins, darts,
and many other things; and we exchanged them for
other things that we gave them, such as glass beads and
small bells. In fine, they took all, and gave what they had
with good will. It appeared to me to be a race of people

---

[1] Fernando and Ysabel.   [2] The royal inspector.

very poor in everything. They go as naked as when their
mothers bore them, and so do the women, although I did
not see more than one young girl. All I saw were youths,
none more than thirty years of age. They are very well
made, with very handsome bodies, and very good countenances. Their hair is short and coarse, almost like the
hairs of a horse's tail. They wear the hairs brought down
to the eyebrows, except a few locks behind, which they
wear long and never cut. They paint themselves black,
and they are the colour of the Canarians, neither black
nor white. Some paint themselves white, others red, and
others of what colour they find. Some paint their faces,
others the whole body, some only round the eyes, others
only on the nose. They neither carry nor know anything
of arms, for I showed them swords, and they took them by
the blade and cut themselves through ignorance. They
have no iron, their darts being wands without iron, some
of them having a fish's tooth at the end, and others being
pointed in various ways. They are all of fair stature and
size, with good faces, and well made. I saw some with
marks of wounds on their bodies, and I made signs to ask
what it was, and they gave me to understand that people
from other adjacent islands came with the intention of
seizing them, and that they defended themselves. I believed, and still believe, that they come here from the mainland to take them prisoners. They should be good servants and intelligent, for I observed that they quickly took
in what was said to them, and I believe that they would
easily be made Christians, as it appeared to me that they
had no religion. I, our Lord being pleased, will take
hence, at the time of my departure, six natives for your
Highnesses, that they may learn to speak. I saw no beast
of any kind except parrots, on this island." The above is
in the words of the Admiral.

Saturday, 13th of October.

"As soon as dawn broke many of these people came to the beach, all youths, as I have said, and all of good stature, a very handsome people. Their hair is not curly, but loose and coarse, like horse hair. In all the forehead is broad, more so than in any other people I have hitherto seen. Their eyes are very beautiful and not small, and themselves far from black, but the colour of the Canarians. Nor should anything else be expected, as this island is in a line east and west from the island of Hierro in the Canaries. Their legs are very straight, all in one line,[1] and no belly, but very well formed. They came to the ship in small canoes, made out of the trunk of a tree like a long boat, and all of one piece, and wonderfully worked, considering the country. They are large, some of them holding 40 to 45 men, others smaller, and some only large enough to hold one man. They are propelled with a paddle like a baker's shovel, and go at a marvellous rate. If the canoe capsizes they all promptly begin to swim, and to bale it out with calabashes that they take with them. They brought skeins of cotton thread, parrots, darts, and other small things which it would be tedious to recount, and they give all in exchange for anything that may be given to them. I was attentive, and took trouble to ascertain if there was gold. I saw that some of them had a small piece fastened in a hole they have in the nose, and by signs I was able to make out that to the south, or going from the island to the south, there was a king who had great cups full, and who possessed a great quantity. I tried to get them to go there, but afterwards I saw that they had no inclination. I resolved to wait until to-morrow in the afternoon and then to depart, shaping a course to the S.W.,

---

[1] " Todos a una mano."

for, according to what many of them told me, there was
land to the S., to the S.W., and N.W., and that the natives
from the N.W. often came to attack them, and went on to
the S.W. in search of gold and precious stones.

"This island is rather large and very flat, with bright
green trees, much water, and a very large lake in the
centre, without any mountain, and the whole land so green
that it is a pleasure to look on it. The people are very
docile, and for the longing to possess our things, and not
having anything to give in return, they take what they can
get, and presently swim away. Still, they give away all
they have got, for whatever may be given to them, down
to broken bits of crockery and glass. I saw one give 16
skeins of cotton for three ceotis[1] of Portugal, equal to one
blanca of Spain, the skeins being as much as an arroba of
cotton thread. I shall keep it, and shall allow no one to
take it, preserving it all for your Highnesses, for it may be
obtained in abundance. It is grown in this island, though
the short time did not admit of my ascertaining this for
a certainty. Here also is found the gold they wear fastened in
their noses. But, in order not to lose time, I intend to go
and see if I can find the island of Cipango.[2] Now, as it is
night, all the natives have gone on shore with their canoes."

Sunday, 14th of October.

"At dawn I ordered the ship's boat and the boats of the
caravels to be got ready, and I went along the coast of the

---

[1] For ceuti, a coin current at Ceuta, then belonging to Portugal.
—N.

[2] Toscanelli said, in his letter, that Cipango was an island 225
leagues from Antilla, and that it so abounded in gems and gold that
the temples and palaces were covered with golden plates. Marco
Polo describes it (Book III, cap. ii), and also says that the quantity of
gold is endless, that the palace is roofed with gold, and that pearls are
abundant. Chipangu is derived from Zhi-pan, the Chinese form of
Japan. (Yule, ii, p. 238.)

island to the N.N.E., to see the other side, which was on the other side to the east, and also to see the villages. Presently I saw two or three, and the people all came to the shore, calling out and giving thanks to God. Some of them brought us water, others came with food, and when they saw that I did not want to land, they got into the sea, and came swimming to us. We understood that they asked us if we had come from heaven. One old man came into the boat, and others cried out, in loud voices, to all the men and women, to come and see the men who had come from heaven, and to bring them to eat and drink. Many came, including women, each bringing something, giving thanks to God, throwing themselves on the ground and shouting to us to come on shore. But I was afraid to land, seeing an extensive reef of rocks which surrounded the island, with deep water between it and the shore forming a port large enough for as many ships as there are in Christendom, but with a very narrow entrance. It is true that within this reef there are some sunken rocks, but the sea has no more motion than the water in a well. In order to see all this I went this morning, that I might be able to give a full account to your Highnesses, and also where a fortress might be established. I saw a piece of land which appeared like an island, although it is not one, and on it there were six houses. It might be converted into an island in two days, though I do not see that it would be necessary, for these people are very simple as regards the use of arms, as your Highnesses will see from the seven that I caused to be taken, to bring home and learn our language and return; unless your Highnesses should order them all to be brought to Castille, or to be kept as captives on the same island; for with fifty men they can all be subjugated and made to do what is required of them. Close to the above peninsula there are gardens of the most beautiful trees I ever saw, and with leaves as green as those of Castille in the month of April and May, and much water. I examined all that port, and afterwards I returned to the ship and made sail. I saw so many islands[1] that I hardly knew how to determine to which I should go first. Those natives I had with me said, by signs, that there were so many that they could not be numbered, and they gave the names of more than a hundred. At last I looked out for the largest, and resolved to shape a course for it, and so I did. It will be distant five leagues from this of *San Salvador*, and the others some more, some less. All are very flat, and all are inhabited. The natives make war on each other, although these are very simple-minded and handsomely-formed people."

Monday, 15*th of October.*

"I had laid by during the night, with the fear of reaching the land to anchor before daylight, not knowing whether the coast was clear of rocks, and at dawn I made sail. As the island was more than 5 leagues distant and nearer 7, and the tide checked my way, it was noon when we arrived at the said island. I found that side facing towards the island of San Salvador trended north and south with a length of 5 leagues,[2] and the other which I followed ran east and west for more than 10 leagues.[2] As from this island I saw another larger one to the west, I clued up the sails, after having run all that day until night, otherwise I could not have reached the western cape. I gave the name of *Santa Maria de la Concepcion*[3] to the island, and almost as the sun set I anchored near the said cape to ascertain if it contained gold. For the people I had

---

[1] Deceptive appearance of clouds on the horizon.

[2] A misprint for miles. This is a mistake which the transcriber has made in several other places.

[3] Island of Rum Cay. See *Letter to Santangel*, p. 2.

taken from the island of San Salvador told me that
here they wore very large rings of gold on their arms and
legs. I really believed that all they said was nonsense,
invented that they might escape. My desire was not to
pass any island without taking possession, so that, one
having been taken, the same may be said of all. I anchored,
and remained until to-day, Tuesday, when I went to the
shore with the boats armed, and landed. The people, who
were numerous, went naked, and were like those of the
other island of San Salvador. They let us go over the
island, and gave us what we required. As the wind
changed to the S.E., I did not like to stay, and returned to
the ship. A large canoe was alongside the *Niña*, and one
of the men of the island of San Salvador, who was on
board, jumped into the sea and got into the canoe. In
the middle of the night before, another swam away behind
the canoe, which fled,[1] for there never was boat that could
have overtaken her, seeing that in speed they have a great
advantage. So they reached the land and left the canoe.
Some of my people went on shore in chase of them, but
they all fled like fowls, and the canoe they had left was
brought alongside the caravel *Niña*, whither, from another
direction, another small canoe came, with a man who
wished to barter with skeins of cotton. Some sailors
jumped into the sea, because he would not come on board
the caravel, and seized him. I was on the poop of my
ship, and saw everything. So I sent for the man, gave
him a red cap, some small beads of green glass, which
I put on his arms, and small bells, which I put in his ears,
and ordered his canoe, which was also on board, to be
returned to him. I sent him on shore, and presently
made sail to go to the other large island which was in
sight to the westward. I also ordered the other large

---

[1] This is a doubtful sentence, with a word omitted.

canoe, which the caravel *Niña* was towing astern, to be
cast adrift ; and I soon saw that it reached the land at the
same time as the man to whom I had given the above
things. I had not wished to take the skein of cotton that
he offered me. All the others came round him and seemed
astonished, for it appeared clear to them that we were
good people. The other man who had fled might do us
some harm, because we had carried him off, and for that
reason I ordered this man to be set free and gave him the
above things, that he might think well of us, otherwise,
when your Highnesses again send an expedition, they
might not be friendly. All the presents I gave were not
worth four maravedis. At 10 we departed with the wind
S.W., and made for the south, to reach that other island,
which is very large, and respecting which all the men that
I bring from San Salvador make signs that there is much
gold, and that they wear it as bracelets on the arms, on
the legs, in the ears and nose, and round the neck. The
distance of this island from that of Santa Maria is 9 leagues
on a course east to west. All this part of the island trends
N.W. and S.E., and it appeared that this coast must have
a length of 28 leagues. It is very flat, without any mountain, like San Salvador and Santa Maria, all being beach
without rocks, except that there are some sunken rocks
near the land, whence it is necessary to keep a good look-
out when it is desired to anchor, and not to come to very
near the land ; but the water is always very clear, and the
bottom is visible. At a distance of two shots of a lombard,
there is, off all these islands, such a depth that the bottom
cannot be reached. These islands are very green and
fertile, the climate very mild. They may contain many
things of which I have no knowledge, for I do not wish to
stop, in discovering and visiting many islands, to find gold.
These people make signs that it is worn on the arms and
legs ; and it must be gold, for they point to some pieces

that I have. I cannot err, with the help of our Lord, in finding out where this gold has its origin. Being in the middle of the channel between these two islands, that is to say, that of Santa Maria and this large one, to which I give the name of *Fernandina*,[1] I came upon a man alone in a canoe going from Santa Maria to Fernandina. He had a little of their bread, about the size of a fist, a calabash of water, a piece of brown earth powdered and then kneaded, and some dried leaves, which must be a thing highly valued by them, for they bartered with it at San Salvador. He also had with him a native basket with a string of glass beads, and two *blancas*,[2] by which I knew that he had come from the island of San Salvador, and had been to Santa Maria, and thence to Fernandina. He came alongside the ship, and I made him come on board as he desired, also getting the canoe inboard, and taking care of all his property. I ordered him to be given to eat bread and treacle, and also to drink : and so I shall take him on to Fernandina, where I shall return everything to him, in order that he may give a good account of us, that, our Lord pleasing, when your Highnesses shall send here, those who come may receive honor, and that the natives may give them all they require."

Tuesday, 16th of October.

" I sailed from the island of Santa Maria de la Concepcion at about noon, to go to Fernandina island, which appeared very large to the westward, and I navigated all that day with light winds. I could not arrive in time to be able to see the bottom, so as to drop the anchor on a clear place, for it is necessary to be very careful not to lose the anchors. So I stood off and on all that night until day,

---

[1] Long Island. See *Letter to Santangel*, p. 2.
[2] A small piece of money. See p. 40.

when I came to an inhabited place where I anchored, and whence that man had come that I found yesterday in the canoe in mid channel. He had given such a good report of us that there was no want of canoes alongside the ship all that night, which brought us water and what they had to offer. I ordered each one to be given something, such as a few beads, ten or twelve of those made of glass on a thread, some timbrels made of brass such as are worth a maravedi in Spain, and some straps, all which they looked upon as most excellent. I also ordered them to be given treacle to eat when they came on board. At three o'clock I sent the ship's boat on shore for water, and the natives with good will showed my people where the water was, and they themselves brought the full casks down to the boat, and did all they could to please us.

"This island is very large, and I have determined to sail round it, because, so far as I can understand, there is a mine in or near it. The island is eight leagues from Santa Maria, nearly east and west; and this point I had reached, as well as all the coast, trends N.N.W. and S.S.E. I saw at least 20 leagues of it, and then it had not ended. Now, as I am writing this, I made sail with the wind at the south, to sail round the island, and to navigate until I find *Samaot*, which is the island or city where there is gold, as all the natives say who are on board, and as those of San Salvador and Santa Maria told us. These people resemble those of the said islands, with the same language and customs, except that these appear to me a rather more domestic and tractable people, yet also more subtle. For I observed that those who brought cotton and other trifles to the ship, knew better than the others how to make a bargain.[1] In this island I saw cotton cloths made like

---

[1] " Refetar el pagamento." Las Casas has : ' Regatear sobre los precios y paga (i, 307).

mantles. The people were better disposed, and the women wore in front of their bodies a small piece of cotton which scarcely covered them.

"It is a very green island, level and very fertile, and I have no doubt that they sow and gather corn all the year round, as well as other things. I saw many trees very unlike those of our country. Many of them have their branches growing in different ways and all from one trunk, and one twig is one form, and another in a different shape, and so unlike that it is the greatest wonder in the world to see the great diversity; thus one branch has leaves like those of a cane, and others like those of a mastick tree: and on a single tree there are five or six different kinds. Nor are these grafted, for it may be said that grafting is unknown, the trees being wild, and untended by these people. They do not know any religion, and I believe they could easily be converted to Christianity, for they are very intelligent. Here the fish are so unlike ours that it is wonderful. Some are the shape of dories,[1] and of the finest colours in the world, blue, yellow, red, and other tints, all painted in various ways, and the colours are so bright that there is not a man who would not be astonished, and would not take great delight in seeing them. There are also whales. I saw no beasts on the land of any kind, except parrots and lizards A boy told me that he saw a large serpent. I saw neither sheep, nor goats, nor any other quadruped. It is true I have been here a short time, since noon, yet I could not have failed to see some if there had been any. I will write respecting the circuit of this island after I have been round it."

[1] Gallos.

Wednesday, 17th of October.

" At noon I departed from the village off which I was
anchored, and where I took in water, to sail round this
island of Fernandina. The wind was S.W. and South.
My wish was to follow the coast of this island to the S.E.,
from where I was, the whole coast trending N.N.W. and
S.S.E.; because all the Indians I bring with me, and
others, made signs to this southern quarter, as the direction
of the island they call Samoet, where the gold is. Martin
Alonso Pinzon, captain of the caravel *Pinta*, on board of
which I had three of the Indians, came to me and said that
one of them had given him to understand very positively
that the island might be sailed round much quicker by
shaping a N.N.W. course. I saw that the wind would not
help me to take the course I desired, and that it was fair
for the other, so I made sail to the N.N.W. When I was
two leagues from the cape of the island, I discovered a very
wonderful harbour.[1] It has one mouth, or, rather, it may
be said to have two, for there is an islet in the middle.
Both are very narrow, and within it is wide enough for a
hundred ships, if there was depth and a clean bottom, and
the entrance was deep enough. It seemed desirable to
explore it and take soundings, so I anchored outside, and
went in with all the ship's boats, when we saw there was
insufficient depth. As I thought, when I first saw it, that
it was the mouth of some river, I ordered the water-casks
to be brought. On shore I found eight or ten men, who
presently came to us and showed us the village, whither I
sent the people for water, some with arms, and others with
the casks : and, as it was some little distance, I waited two
hours for them.

---

[1] Port Clarence, in Long Island.

"During that time I walked among the trees, which was the most beautiful thing I had ever seen, beholding as much verdure as in the month of May in Andalusia. The trees are as unlike ours as night from day, as are the fruits, the herbs, the stones, and everything. It is true that some of the trees bore some resemblance to those in Castille, but most of them are very different, and some were so unlike that no one could compare them to anything in Castille. The people were all like those already mentioned: like them naked, and the same size. They give what they possess in exchange for anything that may be given to them. I here saw some of the ship's boys bartering broken bits of glass and crockery for darts. The men who went for water told me that they had been in the houses of the natives, and that they were very plain and clean inside. Their beds and bags for holding things[1] were like nets of cotton.[2] The houses are like booths, and

---

[1] "Paramentos de cosas." Las Casas has : "Paramentos de casa" (i, 310).

[2] Hammocks. In Española they were called *Hamacas*. Las Casas describes them as "made in loops, not woven like nets, the threads crossed, but the threads loose in their lengths, so that the fingers and hands can be put between them, and from *palmo* to *palmo* (8.3 in.), a little more or less, then fastened to other twisted threads, like the very well-worked nets which are made at Seville of *esparto* grass, for harness. These *hamacas* are the length of a man, and at the ends the same threads are formed into numerous loops. Into each loop they pass very fine cords of another material, stronger than cotton, such as rushes, and these are each a *brazo* (6 ft.) long, and the ends are all united in a knot at each end ; the *hamaca* being hung by these knots to the posts of the houses. Thus the *hamaca* remains slung in the air. The best are 3 or 4 yards in width, and they open them when they get in, as we open a sling that is very large. They lie across it, and are thus on the *hamaca*, with which they cover themselves, and as it is never in the least cold, this suffices" (i, p. 310). Herrera says that their beds consisted of a net fastened from one post to another which they call *Amacas*. (*Dec. I*, Lib. I, cap. xiii.)

E

very high, with good chimneys.[1] But, among many villages that I saw, there was none that consisted of more than from twelve to fifteen houses. Here they found that the married women wore clouts of cotton, but not the young girls, except a few who were over eighteen years of age. They had dogs,[2] mastiffs and hounds[3]; and here they found a man who had a piece of gold in his nose, the size of half a *castellano*, on which they saw letters. I quarrelled with these people because they would not exchange or give what was required ; as I wished to see what and whose this money was ; and they replied that they were not accustomed to barter.

"After the water was taken I returned to the ship, made sail, and shaped a course N.W., until I had discovered all the part of the coast of the island which trends east to west. Then all the Indians turned round and said that this island was smaller than Samoet, and that it would be well to return back so as to reach it sooner. The wind presently went down, and then sprang up from W.N.W., which was contrary for us to continue on the previous course. So I turned back, and navigated all that night to E.S.E., sometimes to east and to S.E. This course was steered to keep me clear of the land, for there were very heavy clouds and thick weather, which did not admit of my approaching the land to anchor. On that night it rained very heavily from midnight until nearly dawn, and even afterwards the clouds threatened rain. We found ourselves at the S.W. end of the island, where I hoped to

---

[1] These were ornamental points with which the roofs terminated. (*Las Casas.*)

[2] Columbus did not see these dogs, but only heard of them from his men. Las Casas tells us that they were a kind of dog that never barks (i, p. 311). Herrera says : "Vieronse tambien algunos perrilos mudos pequeños."

[3] *Brachetes*, in English *brach*. (*King Lear*, Act I, Sc. 4.)

anchor until it cleared up, so as to see the other island whither I have to go. On all these days, since I arrived in these Indies, it has rained more or less. Your Highnesses may believe that this land is the best and most fertile, and with a good climate, level, and as good as there is in the world."

Thursday, 18th of October.

"After it had cleared up I went before the wind, approaching the island as near as I could, and anchored when it was no longer light enough to keep under sail. But I did not go on shore, and made sail at dawn. . . . ."

Friday, 19th of October.

"I weighed the anchors at daylight, sending the caravel *Pinta* on an E.S.E. course, the caravel *Niña* S.S.E., while I shaped a S.E. course, giving orders that these courses were to be steered until noon, and that then the two caravels should alter course so as to join company with me. Before we had sailed for three hours we saw an island to the east, for which we steered, and all three vessels arrived at the north point before noon. Here there is an islet,[1] and a reef of rocks to seaward of it, besides one between the islet and the large island. The men of San Salvador, whom I bring with me, called it *Saomete*, and I gave it the name of *Isabella*.[2] The wind was north, and the said islet bore from the island of Fernandina, whence I had taken my departure, east and west. Afterwards we ran along the coast of the island, westward from the islet, and found its length to be 12 leagues as far as a cape, which I named *Cabo Hermoso*, at the western end. The island is beautiful, and the coast very deep, without sunken rocks off it. Outside the shore

---

[1] Bird Rock.
[2] Crooked Island. See *Letter to Santangel*, p. 2.

E 2

is rocky, but further in there is a sandy beach, and here I
anchored on that Friday night until morning. This coast
and the part of the island I saw is almost flat, and the
island is very beautiful ; for if the other islands are lovely,
this is more so. It has many very green trees, which are
very large. The land is higher than in the other islands,
and in it there are some hills, which cannot be called
mountains ; and it appears that there is much water
inland. From this point to the N.E. the coast makes a
great angle, and there are many thick and extensive groves.
I wanted to go and anchor there, so as to go on shore and
see so much beauty ; but the water was shallow, and we
could only anchor at a distance from the land. The wind
also was fair for going to this cape, where I am now
anchored, to which I gave the name of *Cabo Hermoso*,
because it is so. Thus it was that I do not anchor in that
angle, but as I saw this cape so green and so beautiful,
like all the other lands of these islands, I scarcely knew
which to visit first ; for I can never tire my eyes in looking
at such lovely vegetation, so different from ours. I believe
that there are many herbs and many trees that are worth
much in Europe for dyes and for medicines ; but I do not
know, and this causes me great sorrow. Arriving at this
cape, I found the smell of the trees and flowers so delicious
that it seemed the pleasantest thing in the world.
To-morrow, before I leave this place, I shall go on shore
to see what there is at this cape. There are no people,
but there are villages in the interior, where, the Indians I
bring with me say, there is a king who has much gold.
To-morrow I intend to go so far inland as to find the
village, and see and have some speech with this king, who,
according to the signs they make, rules over all the neighbouring islands, goes about clothed, and wears much gold
on his person. I do not give much faith to what they say,
as well because I do not understand them as because they

are so poor in gold that even a little that this king may have would appear much to them. This cape, to which I have given the name of *Cabo Fermoso*, is, I believe, on an island separated from Saometo, and there is another small islet between them. I did not try to examine them in detail, because it could not be done in 50 years. For my desire is to see and discover as much as I can before returning to your Highnesses, our Lord willing, in April. It is true that in the event of finding places where there is gold or spices in quantity I should stop until I had collected as much as I could. I, therefore, proceed in the hope of coming across such places."

Saturday, 20th of October.

"To-day, at sunrise, I weighed the anchors from where I was with the ship, and anchored off the S.W. point of the island of Saometo, to which I gave the name of *Cabo de la Laguna*, and to the island *Isabella*. My intention was to navigate to the north-east and east from the south-east and south, where, I understood from the Indians I brought with me, was the village of the king. I found the sea so shallow that I could not enter nor navigate in it, and I saw that to follow a route by the south-east would be a great round. So I determined to return by the route that I had taken from the N.N.E. to the western part, and to sail round this island to . . . . .[1]

"I had so little wind that I never could sail along the coast, except during the night. As it was dangerous to anchor off these islands except in the day, when one can see where to let go the anchor: for the bottom is all in patches, some clear and some rocky: I lay to all this Sunday night. The caravels anchored because they found

[1] Word missing in the manuscript. Navarette suggests "reconocerla".—N.

themselves near the shore, and they thought that, owing to the signals that they were in the habit of making, I would come to anchor, but I did not wish to do so."

Sunday, 21st of October.

" At ten o'clock I arrived here, off this islet,[1] and anchored, as well as the caravels. After breakfast I went on shore, and found only one house, in which there was no one, and I supposed they had fled from fear, because all their property was left in the house. I would not allow anything to be touched, but set out with the captains and people to explore the island. If the others already seen are very beautiful, green, and fertile, this is much more so, with large trees and very green. Here there are large lagoons with wonderful vegetation on their banks. Throughout the island all is green, and the herbage like April in Andalusia. The songs of the birds were so pleasant that it seemed as if a man could never wish to leave the place. The flocks of parrots concealed the sun; and the birds were so numerous, and of so many different kinds, that it was wonderful. There are trees of a thousand sorts, and all have their several fruits; and I feel the most unhappy man in the world not to know them, for I am well assured that they are all valuable. I bring home specimens of them, and also of the land. Thus walking along round one of the lakes I saw a serpent,[2] which we killed, and I bring home the skin for your Highnesses. As soon as it saw us it went into the lagoon, and we followed, as the water was not very deep, until we killed it with lances. It is 7 *palmos* long, and I believe that there are many like it in these lagoons. Here I came upon some aloes, and I have determined to take ten quintals on board to-morrow,

---

[1] Bird Rock, where he was on the 19th.   [2] Iguana.

for they tell me that they are worth a good deal. Also, while in search of good water, we came to a village about half a league from our anchorage. The people, as soon as they heard us, all fled and left their houses, hiding their property in the wood. I would not allow a thing to be touched, even the value of a pin. Presently some men among them came to us, and one came quite close. I gave him some bells and glass beads, which made him very content and happy. That our friendship might be further increased, I resolved to ask him for something; I requested him to get some water. After I had gone on board, the natives came to the beach with calabashes full of water, and they delighted much in giving it to us. I ordered another string of glass beads to be presented to them, and they said they would come again to-morrow. I wished to fill up all the ships with water at this place, and, if there should be time, I intended to search the island until I had had speech with the king, and seen whether he had the gold of which I had heard. I shall then shape a course for another much larger island, which I believe to be Cipango, judging from the signs made by the Indians I bring with me. They call it *Cuba*, and they say that there are ships and many skilful sailors there. Beyond this island there is another called *Bosio*,[1] which they also say is very large, and others we shall see as we pass, lying between. According as I obtain tidings of gold or spices I shall settle what should be done. I am still resolved to go to the mainland and the city of Guisay,[2] and to deliver the letters of your Highnesses to the Gran Can, requesting a reply and returning with it."

---

[1] Bohio.—N.

[2] A flourishing port of China, mentioned in the letter of Toscanelli, and more fully described by Marco Polo, who calls it Kinsay (see p. 8).

Monday, 22nd of October.

" All last night and to-day I was here, waiting to see if the king or other person would bring gold or anything of value. Many of these people came, like those of the other islands, equally naked, and equally painted, some white, some red, some black, and others in many ways. They brought darts and skeins of cotton to barter, which they exchanged with the sailors for bits of glass, broken crockery, and pieces of earthenware. Some of them had pieces of gold fastened in their noses, which they willingly gave for a hawk's bell and glass beads. But there was so little that it counts for nothing. It is true that they looked upon any little thing that I gave them as a wonder, and they held our arrival to be a great marvel, believing that we came from heaven. We got water for the ships from a lagoon which is near the *Cabo del Isleo* (Cape of the Islet), as we named it. In the said lagoon Martin Alonso Pinzon, captain of the *Pinta*, killed another serpent 7 *palmos* long, like the one we got yesterday. I made them gather here as much of the aloe as they could find."

Tuesday, 23rd of October.

" I desired to set out to-day for the island of Cuba, which I think must be Cipango, according to the signs these people make, indicative of its size and riches, and I did not delay any more here nor .....[1] round this island to the residence of this King or Lord, and have speech with him, as I had intended. This would cause me much delay, and I see that there is no gold mine here. To sail round would need several winds, for it does not blow here as men may wish. It is better to go where there is great entertainment, so I say that it is not reasonable to wait,

---

[1] Gap in the MS.

but rather to continue the voyage and inspect much land, until some very profitable country is reached, my belief being that it will be rich in spices. That I have no personal knowledge of these products causes me the greatest sorrow in the world, for I see a thousand kinds of trees, each one with its own special fruit, all green now as in Spain during the months of May and June, as well as a thousand kinds of herbs with their flowers ; yet I know none of them except this aloe, of which I ordered a quantity to be brought on board to bring to your Highnesses. I have not made sail for Cuba because there is no wind, but a dead calm with much rain. It rained a great deal yesterday without causing any cold. On the contrary, the days are hot and the nights cool, like May in Andalusia."

Wednesday, 24th of October.

" At midnight I weighed the anchors and left the anchorage at Cabo del Isleo, in the island of Isabella. From the northern side, where I was, I intended to go to the island of Cuba, where I heard of the people who were very great, and had gold, spices, merchandise, and large ships. They showed me that the course thither would be W.S.W., and so I hold. For I believe that it is so, as all the Indians of these islands, as well as those I brought with me in the ships, told me by signs. I cannot understand their language, but I believe that it is of the island of Cipango that they recount these wonders. On the spheres[1] I saw, and on the delineations of the map of the world,[2] Cipango is in this region. So I shaped a course W.S.W. until daylight, but at dawn it fell calm and began to rain, and went on nearly all night. I remained thus, with little wind, until the afternoon, when it began to blow

---

[1] The globe of Martin Behaim, made in 1492.
[2] The map of Toscanelli.

fresh. I set all the sails in the ship, the mainsail with
two bonnets,[1] the foresail, spritsail, mizen, main topsail,
and the boat's sail on the poop. So I proceeded until
nightfall, when the *Cabo Verde* of the island of Fernandina,
which is at the S.W. end, bore N.W. distant 7 leagues.
As it was now blowing hard, and I did not know how far
it was to this island of Cuba, I resolved not to go in search
of it during the night ; all these islands being very steep-
to, with no bottom round them for a distance of two
shots of a lombard. The bottom is all in patches, one bit
of sand and another of rock, and for this reason it is not
safe to anchor without inspection with the eye. So I
determined to take in all the sails except the foresail, and
to go on under that reduced canvas. Soon the wind increased, while the route was doubtful, and there was very
thick weather, with rain. I ordered the foresail to be furled,
and we did not make two leagues during that night."

· Thursday, 25th of October.

" I steered W.S.W. from after sunset until 9 o'clock,
making 5 leagues. Afterwards I altered course to west,
and went 8 miles an hour until one in the afternoon ; and
from that time until three made good 44 miles. Then
land was sighted, consisting of 7 or 8 islands, the group
running north and south, distant from us 5 leagues."

Friday, 26th of October.

" The ship was on the south side of the islands, which
were all low, distant 5 or 6 leagues. I anchored there.
The Indians on board said that thence to Cuba was a
voyage in their canoes of a day and a half ; these being
small dug-outs without a sail. Such are their canoes. I
departed thence for Cuba, for by the signs the Indians

---

[1] Pieces of canvas laced to the leeches of the mainsail on both sides.

made of its greatness, and of its gold and pearls, I thought
that it must be Cipango."

Saturday, 27th of October.

" I weighed from these islands at sunrise, and gave them
the name of *Las Islas de Arena*,[1] owing to the little depth
the sea had for a distance of 6 leagues to the southward of
them. We went 8 miles an hour on a S.S.W. course until
one o'clock, having made 40 miles. Until night we had
run 28 miles on the same course, and before dark the land
was sighted. At night there was much rain. The vessels,
on Saturday until sunset, made 17 leagues on a S.S.W.
course."

Sunday, 28th of October.

" I went thence in search of the island of Cuba on
a S.S.W. coast, making for the nearest point of it, and
entered a very beautiful river without danger of sunken
rocks or other impediments. All the coast was clear of
dangers up to the shore. The mouth of the river was
12 *brazos* across, and it is wide enough for a vessel to beat
in. I anchored about a lombard-shot inside." The Admiral
says that " he never beheld such a beautiful place, with
trees bordering the river, handsome, green, and different
from ours, having fruits and flowers each one according to
its nature. There are many birds, which sing very sweetly.
There are a great number of palm trees of a different kind
from those in Guinea and from ours, of a middling height,
the trunks without that covering,[2] and the leaves very
large, with which they thatch their houses. The country
is very level." The Admiral jumped into his boat and
went on shore. He came to two houses, which he believed

---

[1] The Ragged Isles, north of Cuba.
[2] Camisa.

to belong to fishermen who had fled from fear. In one of
them he found a kind of dog that never barks, and in both
there were nets of palm-fibre and cordage, as well as horn
fish-hooks, bone harpoons, and other apparatus " for fishing, and several hearths. He believed that many people
lived together in one house. He gave orders that nothing
in the houses should be touched, and so it was done." The
herbage was as thick as in Andalusia during April and
May. He found much purslane and wild amaranth.[1] He
returned to the boat and went up the river for some
distance, and he says it was great pleasure to see the
bright verdure, and the birds, which he could not leave
to go back. He says that this island is the most
beautiful that eyes have seen, full of good harbours and
deep rivers, and the sea appeared as if it never rose ;
for the herbage on the beach nearly reached the waves,
which does not happen where the sea is rough. (Up
to that time they had not experienced a rough sea
among all those islands.) He says that the island is full
of very beautiful mountains, although they are not very
extensive as regards length, but high ; and all the country
is high like Sicily. It is abundantly supplied with water,
as they gathered from the Indians they had taken with
them from the island of Guanahani. These said by signs
that there are ten great rivers, and that they cannot go
round the island in twenty days. When they came near
land with the ships, two canoes came out ; and, when they
saw the sailors get into a boat and row about to find the
depth of the river where they could anchor, the canoes
fled. The Indians say that in this island there are gold
mines and pearls, and the Admiral saw a likely place for
them and mussel-shells, which are signs of them. He
understood that large ships of the Gran Can came here,
and that from here to the mainland was a voyage of ten

---

[1] Verdolagas y bledas.

days. The Admiral called this river and harbour *San Salvador*.[1]

Monday, 29th of October.

The Admiral weighed anchor from this port and sailed to the westward, to go to the city, where, as it seemed, the Indians said that there was a king. They doubled a point six leagues to the N.W.,[2] and then another point,[3] then east ten leagues. After another league he saw a river with no very large entrance, to which he gave the name of *Rio de la Luna*.[4] He went on until the hour of Vespers. He saw another river much larger than the others,[5] as the Indians told him by signs, and near he saw goodly villages of houses. He called the river *Rio de Mares*.[6] He sent two boats on shore to a village to communicate, and one of the Indians he had brought with him, for now they understood a little, and show themselves content with Christians. All the men, women, and children fled, abandoning their houses with all they contained. The Admiral gave orders that nothing should be touched. The houses were better than those he had seen before, and he believed that the houses would improve as he approached the mainland. They were made like booths, very large, and looking like tents in a camp without regular streets, but one here and another there. Within they were clean and well swept, with the furniture well made. All are of palm branches beautifully constructed. They found many images

---

[1] Puerto Naranjo. Nipe, according to Navarrete.

[2] Punta de Mulas.—N.

[3] Punta de Cabañas.—N.

[4] Puerto de Banes.—N.

[5] Puerto de las Nuevitas del Principe.—N.

[6] Afterwards *Puerto de Baracoa*, called by the Adelantado of Cuba, Diego Velasquez, *Asumpcion*. (Herrera, *Dec. I*, Lib. II, cap. xiv.)

in the shape of women, and many heads like masks,[1] very
well carved.   It was not known whether these were used
as ornaments, or to be worshipped.   They had dogs which
never bark, and wild birds tamed in their houses.   There
was a wonderful supply of nets and other fishing imple-
ments, but nothing was touched.   He believed that all the
people on the coast were fishermen, who took the fish
inland, for this island is very large, and so beautiful, that
he is never tired of praising it.   He says that he found
trees and fruits of very marvellous taste ; and adds that
they must have cows or other cattle, for he saw skulls
which were like those of cows.   The songs of the birds
and the chirping of crickets throughout the night lulled
everyone to rest, while the air was soft and healthy, and
the nights neither hot nor cold.   On the voyage through
the other islands there was great heat, but here it is
tempered like the month of May.   He attributed the heat
of the other islands to their flatness, and to the wind
coming from the east, which is hot.   The water of the
rivers was salt at the mouth, and they did not know
whence the natives got their drinking-water, though they
have sweet water in their houses.   Ships are able to turn
in this river, both entering and coming out, and there are
very good leading-marks.   He says that all this sea
appears to be constantly smooth, like the river at Seville,
and the water suitable for the growth of pearls.   He found
large shells unlike those of Spain.   Remarking on the
position of the river and port, to which he gave the name
of San Salvador,[2] he describes its mountains as lofty and
beautiful, like the *Peña de las Enamoradas*,[3] and one of

---

[1] The word is *Caratona.*   Navarrete suggests *Caratula, Careta,* or
Mascarilla.—N.
[2] The description applies exactly to *Puerto Naranjo.*   Casas
suggests *Puerto de Baracoa,* while Navarrete is confident that it is
Nipe.   [3] Near Granada.

them has another little hill on its summit, like a graceful mosque. The other river and port, in which he now was,[1] has two round mountains to the S.W., and a fine low cape running out to the W.S.W.

Tuesday, 30th of October.

He left the Rio de Mares and steered N.W., seeing a cape covered with palm trees, to which he gave the name of *Cabo de Palmas*,[2] after having made good 15 leagues. The Indians on board the caravel *Pinta* said that beyond that cape there was a river,[3] and that from the river to *Cuba* it was four days' journey. The captain of the *Pinta* reported that he understood from that, that this *Cuba* was a city, and that the land was a great continent trending far to the north. The king of that country, he gathered, was at war with the Gran Can, whom they called *Cami*, and his land or city *Fava*, with many other names. The Admiral resolved to proceed to that river, and to send a present, with the letter of the Sovereigns, to the king of that land. For this service there was a sailor who had been to Guinea, and some of the Indians of Guanahani wished to go with him, and afterwards to return to their homes. The Admiral calculated that he was forty-two[4] degrees to the north of the equinoctial line (but the handwriting is here illegible). He says that he must attempt to reach the Gran Can, who he thought was here or at the city of Cathay,[5] which belongs to him, and is very grand, as he was informed before leaving Spain. All this land, he adds, is low and beautiful, and the sea deep.

---

[1] Nuevitas del Principe.—N.

[2] "Alto de Juan Dañue."—N.

[3] Rio Maximo.—N.

[4] Wrongly transcribed. It must have been 21 in the original MS.

[5] In his letter, Toscanelli said that the usual residence of the Grand Khan was Cathay (see p. 6).

Wednesday, 31st of October.

All Tuesday night he was beating to windward, and he saw a river, but could not enter it because the entrance was narrow. The Indians fancied that the ships could enter wherever their canoes could go. Navigating onwards, he came to a cape running out very far, and surrounded by sunken rocks[1] and he saw a bay where small vessels might take shelter. He could not proceed because the wind had come round to the north, and all the coast runs N.W. and S.E. Another cape further on ran out still more.[2] For these reasons, and because the sky showed signs of a gale, he had to return to the *Rio de Mares*.

Thursday, November the 1st.

At sunrise the Admiral sent the boats on shore to the houses that were there, and they found that all the people had fled. After some time a man made his appearance. The Admiral ordered that he should be left to himself, and the sailors returned to the boats. After dinner, one of the Indians on board was sent on shore. He called out from a distance that there was nothing to fear, because the strangers were good people and would do no harm to anyone, nor were they people of the Gran Can, but they had given away their things in many islands where they had been. The Indian then swam on shore, and two of the natives took him by the arms and brought him to a house, where they heard what he had to say. When they were certain that no harm would be done to them they were reassured, and presently more than sixteen canoes came to the ships with cotton-thread and other trifles. The Admiral ordered that nothing should be taken from them, that they might understand that he sought for nothing

---

[1] Boca de Carabelas grandes.—N.   [2] Punta del Maternillo.—N.

but gold, which they call *nucay*. Thus they went to and
fro between the ships and the shore all day, and they
came to the Christians on shore with confidence. The
Admiral saw no gold whatever among them, but he says
that he saw one of them with a piece of worked silver
fastened to his nose. They said, by signs, that within
three days many merchants from inland would come to
buy the things brought by the Christians, and would give
information respecting the king of that land. So far as
could be understood from their signs, he resided at a
distance of four days' journey. They had sent many
messengers in all directions, with news of the arrival of
the Admiral. "These people", says the Admiral, "are of
the same appearance and have the same customs as those
of the other islands, without any religion so far as I know,
for up to this day I have never seen the Indians on board
say any prayer ; though they repeat the *Salve* and *Ave
Maria* with their hands raised to heaven, and they make
the sign of the cross. The language is also the same, and
they are all friends ; but I believe that all these islands are
at war with the Gran Can, whom they called *Cavila*, and his
province *Bafan*. They all go naked like the others." This
is what the Admiral says. "The river", he adds, "is very
deep, and the ships can enter the mouth, going close to the
shore. The sweet water does not come within a league
of the mouth. It is certain," says the Admiral, "that this
is the mainland, and that I am in front of *Zayto*[1] and
Guinsay,[2] a hundred leagues, a little more or less, distant

---

[1] In Toscanelli's letter it is stated that in the port of Zaiton alone
there were a hundred ships laden with pepper at one time, without
counting those laden with other spices. Zaiton was a seaport of the
province of Fokien in China, now called Chwangchan-fu, between
Fuchau and Amoy. The statement about the pepper trade was
taken by Toscanelli from Marco Polo (c. 82) (see p. 6).

[2] Quinsay of Toscanelli is the Kinsay of Marco Polo (c. 76, 77), who

the one from the other.   It is very clear that no one before has been so far as this by sea.   Yesterday, with wind from the N.W., I found it cold."

Friday, 2nd of November.

The Admiral decided upon sending two Spaniards, one named Rodrigo de Jerez, who lived in Ayamonte, and the other Luis de Torres, who had served in the household of the Adelantado of Murcia, and had been a Jew, knowing Hebrew, Chaldee, and even some Arabic.   With these men he sent two Indians, one from among those he had brought from Guanahani, and another. a native of the houses by the river-side.   He gave them strings of beads with which to buy food if they should be in need, and ordered them to return in six days.   He gave them specimens of spices, to see if any were to be found.   Their instructions were to ask for the king of that land, and they were told what to say on the part of the Sovereigns of Castille, how they had sent the Admiral with letters and a present, to inquire after his health and establish friendship, favouring him in what he might desire from them. They were to collect information respecting certain provinces, ports, and rivers of which the Admiral had notice, and to ascertain their distances from where he was.

This night the Admiral took an altitude with a quadrant, and found that the distance from the equinoctial line was 42 degrees.[1]   He says that, by his reckoning, he finds that he has gone over 1,142 leagues from the island of Hierro.[2]   He still believes that he has reached the mainland.

---

fully describes it ; now called Hangchau, south of Shanghai.   Marco Polo says it was in the province of Mangi, near Catay, and that the word means " city of heaven" (see p. 8).

[1] An erroneous transcription.   It should be 22.

[2] The true distance was 1,105 leagues.—N.

Saturday, 3rd of November.

In the morning the Admiral got into the boat, and, as the river is like a great lake at the mouth, forming a very excellent port, very deep, and clear of rocks, with a good beach for careening ships, and plenty of fuel, he explored it until he came to fresh water at a distance of two leagues from the mouth. He ascended a small mountain to obtain a view of the surrounding country, but could see nothing, owing to the dense foliage of the trees, which were very fresh and odoriferous, so that he felt no doubt that there were aromatic herbs among them. He said that all he saw was so beautiful that his eyes could never tire of gazing upon such loveliness, nor his ears of listening to the songs of birds. That day many canoes came to the ships, to barter with cotton threads and with the nets in which they sleep, called *hamacas*.

Sunday, 4th of November.

At sunrise the Admiral again went away in the boat, and landed to hunt the birds he had seen the day before. After a time, Martin Alonso Pinzon came to him with two pieces of cinnamon, and said that a Portuguese, who was one of his crew, had seen an Indian carrying two very large bundles of it ; but he had not bartered for it, because of the penalty imposed by the Admiral on anyone who bartered. He further said that this Indian carried some brown things like nutmegs. The master of the *Pinta* said that he had found the cinnamon trees. The Admiral went to the place, and found that they were not cinnamon trees. The Admiral showed the Indians some specimens of cinnamon and pepper he had brought from Castille, and they knew it, and said, by signs, that there was plenty in the vicinity, pointing to the S.E. He also showed them gold and pearls, on which certain old men said that there

F 2

was an infinite quantity in a place called *Bohio*,[1] and that the people wore it on their necks, ears, arms, and legs, as well as pearls. He further understood them to say that there were great ships and much merchandise, all to the S.E. He also understood that, far away, there were men with one eye, and others with dogs' noses who were cannibals, and that when they captured an enemy they beheaded him and drank his blood.

The Admiral then determined to return to the ship and wait for the return of the two men he had sent, intending to depart and seek for those lands, if his envoys brought some good news touching what he desired. The Admiral further says: "These people are very gentle and timid; they go naked, as I have said, without arms and without law. The country is very fertile. The people have plenty of roots called *zanahorias* (yams), with a smell like chesnuts; and they have beans of kinds very different from ours. They also have much cotton, which they do not sow, as it is wild in the mountains, and I believe they collect it throughout the year, because I saw pods empty, others full, and flowers all on one tree. There are a thousand other kinds of fruits which it is impossible for me to write about, and all must be profitable." All this the Admiral says.

Monday, 5th of November.

This morning the Admiral ordered the ship to be careened, afterwards the other vessels, but not all at the same time. Two were always to be at the anchorage, as a precaution; although he says that these people were very safe, and that without fear all the vessels might have been careened at the same time. Things being in this state,

---

[1] *Bohio* was their name for a house. The Admiral cannot have understood what they were saying. (*Las Casas.*)

the master of the *Niña*[1] came to claim a reward from the Admiral because he had found mastick, but he did not bring the specimen, as he had dropped it. The Admiral promised him a reward, and sent Rodrigo Sanchez and master Diego[2] to the trees. They collected some, which was kept to present to the Sovereigns, as well as the tree. The Admiral says that he knew it was mastick, though it ought to be gathered at the proper season. There is enough in that district for a yield of 1,000 *quintals* every year. The Admiral also found here a great deal of the plant called aloe. He further says that the *Puerto de Mares* is the best in the world, with the finest climate and the most gentle people. As it has a high, rocky cape, a fortress might be built, so that, in the event of the place becoming rich and important, the merchants would be safe from any other nations. He adds: " The Lord, in whose hands are all victories, will ordain all things for his service. An Indian said by signs that the mastick was good for pains in the stomach."

Tuesday, 6th of November.

"Yesterday, at night", says the Admiral, " the two men came back who had been sent to explore the interior. They said that after walking 12 leagues they came to a village of 50 houses, were there were a thousand inhabitants, for many live in one house. These houses are like very large booths. They said that they were received with great solemnity, according to custom, and all, both men and women, came out to see them. They were lodged in the best houses, and the people touched them, kissing their

---

[1] This was Juan Niño, Master, who, with his brother, Pero Alonso Niño, the pilot, were the owners of the caravel *Niña*.

[2] Rodrigo Sanchez of Segovia was the royal overseer in the Admiral's ship, and Master Diego was the boatswain.

hands and feet, marvelling and believing that they came
from heaven, and so they gave them to understand. They
gave them to eat of what they had. When they arrived,
the chief people conducted them by the arms to the principal house, gave them two chairs on which to sit, and all
the natives sat round them on the ground. The Indian
who came with them described the manner of living of the
Christians, and said that they were good people. Presently
the men went out, and the women came sitting round them
in the same way, kissing their hands and feet, and looking
to see if they were of flesh and bones like themselves.
They begged the Spaniards to remain with them at least
five days." The Spaniards showed the natives specimens
of cinnamon, pepper, and other spices which the Admiral
had given them, and they said, by signs, that there was
plenty at a short distance from thence to S.E., but that there
they did not know whether there was any.[1] Finding that
they had no information respecting cities, the Spaniards
returned ; and if they had desired to take those who wished
to accompany them, more than 500 men and women would
have come, because they thought the Spaniards were
returning to heaven. There came, however, a principal
man of the village and his son, with a servant. The
Admiral conversed with them, and showed them much
honour. They made signs respecting many lands and
islands in those parts. The Admiral thought of bringing
them to the Sovereigns. He says that he knew not what
fancy took them ; either from fear, or owing to the dark
night, they wanted to land. The ship was at the time
high and dry, but, not wishing to make them angry, he let
them go on their saying that they would return at dawn,

---

[1] This passage is obscure, no doubt owing to careless transcription.
Las Casas has : "and asked them if they had any there. They
answered no, but made signs that there was plenty near, towards the
S.E." (i, p. 332).

but they never came back. The two Christians met with
many people on the road going home, men and women
with a half-burnt weed in their hands, being the herbs they
are accustomed to smoke.[1] They did not find villages on
the road of more than five houses, all receiving them with
the same reverence. They saw many kinds of trees, herbs,
and sweet-smelling flowers ; and birds of many different
kinds, unlike those of Spain, except the partridges, geese,
of which there are many, and singing nightingales. They
saw no quadrupeds except the dogs that do not bark. The
land is very fertile, and is cultivated with yams and several
kinds of beans different from ours, as well as corn. There
were great quantities of cotton gathered, spun, and worked
up. In a single house they saw more than 500 *arrobas*,
and as much as 4,000 *quintals* could be yielded every year.
The Admiral said that " it did not appear to be cultivated,
and that it bore all the year round. It is very fine, and
has a large boll. All that was possessed by these people
they gave at a very low price, and a great bundle of cotton
was exchanged for the point of a needle or other trifle.
They are a people", says the Admiral, " guileless and
unwarlike. Men and women go as naked as when their
mothers bore them. It is true that the women wear a very
small rag of cotton-cloth, and they are of very good appearance, not very dark, less so than the Canarians. I hold,
most serene Princes, that if devout religious persons were
here, knowing the language, they would all turn Christians.

---

[1] Tobacco. Las Casas says that they are dried leaves rolled up in
the shape of the squibs made by the boys at Easter. Lighted at one
end, the roll is chewed, and the smoke is inhaled at the other. It has
the effect of making them sleepy and almost intoxicated, and in using
it they do not feel tired. These rolls of dried leaves are called by
them *tabacos*. Las Casas adds that he knew Spaniards in Española
who were accustomed to smoke it, and when their habit was repre-
hended as a vice, they said they could not leave off. Las Casas did
not understand what pleasure or profit they found in it.

I trust in our Lord that your Highnesses will resolve upon this with much diligence, to bring so many great nations within the Church, and to convert them ; as you have destroyed those who would not confess the Father, the Son, and the Holy Ghost. And after your days, all of us being mortal, may your kingdoms remain in peace, and free from heresy and evil, and may you be well received before the eternal Creator, to whom I pray that you may have long life and great increase of kingdoms and lordships, with the will and disposition to increase the holy Christian religion as you have done hitherto. Amen !"

" To-day I got the ship afloat, and prepared to depart on Thursday, in the name of God, and to steer S.E. in search of gold and spices, and to discover land."

These are the words of the Admiral, who intended to depart on Thursday, but, the wind being contrary, he could not go until the 12th of November.

Monday, 12th of November.

The Admiral left the port and river of *Mares* before dawn to visit the island called *Babeque*,[1] so much talked of by the Indians on board, where, according to their signs, the people gather the gold on the beach at night with candles, and afterwards beat it into bars with hammers. To go thither it was necessary to shape a course E. b. S. After having made 8 leagues along the coast, a river was sighted, and another 4 leagues brought them to another river, which appeared to be of great volume, and larger than any they had yet seen. The Admiral did not wish to stop nor to enter any of these rivers, for two reasons : the first and principal one being that wind and weather

---

[1] The Indians called the " Tierra Firme", or coast of the mainland, *Babeque* or *Caritaba*.—N.

were favourable for going in search of the said island of Babeque; the other, that, if there was a populous and famous city near the sea, it would be visible, while, to go up the rivers, small vessels are necessary, which those of the expedition were not. Much time would thus be lost; moreover, the exploration of such rivers is a separate enterprise. All that coast was peopled near the river, to which the name of *Rio del Sol* was given.

The Admiral says that, on the previous Sunday, the 11th of November, it seemed good to take some persons from amongst those at *Rio de Mares*, to bring to the Sovereigns, that they might learn our language, so as to be able to tell us what there is in their lands. Returning, they would be the mouthpieces of the Christians, and would adopt our customs and the things of the faith. "I saw and knew" (says the Admiral) "that these people are without any religion, not idolaters, but very gentle, not knowing what is evil, nor the sins of murder and theft, being without arms, and so timid that a hundred would fly before one Spaniard, although they joke with them.[1] They, however, believe and know that there is a God in heaven, and say that we have come from heaven. At any prayer that we say, they repeat, and make the sign of the cross. Thus your Highnesses should resolve to make them Christians, for I believe that, if the work was begun, in a little time a multitude of nations would be converted to our faith, with the acquisition of great lordships, peoples, and riches for Spain. Without doubt, there is in these lands a vast quantity of gold, and the Indians I have on board do not speak without reason when they say that in these islands there are places where they dig out gold, and wear it on their necks, ears, arms, and legs, the rings being very large. There are also precious stones, pearls, and an

---

[1] "aunque burlen con ellos."

infinity of spices. In this river of Mares, whence we
departed to-night, there is undoubtedly a great quantity of
mastick, and much more could be raised, because the trees
may be planted, and will yield abundantly. The leaf and
fruit are like the mastick, but the tree and leaf are larger.
As Pliny describes it, I have seen it on the island of Chios
in the Archipelago. I ordered many of these trees to be
tapped, to see if any of them would yield resin ; but, as it
rained all the time I was in that river, I could not get any,
except a very little, which I am bringing to your Highnesses. It may not be the right season for tapping, which
is, I believe, when the trees come forth after winter and
begin to flower. But when I was there the fruit was
nearly ripe. Here also there is a great quantity of cotton,
and I believe it would have a good sale here without
sending it to Spain, but to the great cities of the Gran Can,
which will be discovered without doubt, and many others
ruled over by other lords, who will be pleased to serve
your Highnesses, and whither will be brought other commodities of Spain and of the Eastern lands ; but these are
to the west as regards us. There is also here a great
yield of aloes, though this is not a commodity that will
yield great profit. The mastick, however, is important,
for it is only obtained from the said island of Chios, and
I believe the harvest is worth 50,000 ducats, if I remember
right.[1] There is here, in the mouth of the river, the best
port I have seen up to this time, wide, deep, and clear of
rocks. It is an excellent site for a town and fort, for any
ship could come close up to the walls ; the land is high,
with a temperate climate, and very good water.

"Yesterday a canoe came alongside the ship, with six

---

[1] The ducat being 9s. 2d. In the seventeenth century the value of
the mastick exported from Chios was 30,000 ducats. See also *Letter
to Santangel*, p. 15. Chios belonged to Genoa from 1346 to 1566.

youths in it. Five came on board, and I ordered them to
be detained. They are now here. I afterwards sent to
a house on the western side of the river, and seized seven
women, old and young, and three children. I did this
because the men would behave better in Spain if they had
women of their own land, than without them. For on
many occasions the men of Guinea have been brought to
learn the language in Portugal, and afterwards, when they
returned, and it was expected that they would be useful in
their land, owing to the good company they had enjoyed
and the gifts they had received, they never appeared after
arriving. Others may not act thus. But, having women,
they have the wish to perform what they are required to
do; besides, the women would teach our people their
language, which is the same in all these islands, so that
those who make voyages in their canoes are understood
everywhere. On the other hand, there are a thousand
different languages in Guinea, and one native does not
understand another.

"The same night the husband of one of the women came
alongside in a canoe, who was father of the three children
—one boy and two girls. He asked me to let him come
with them, and besought me much. They are now all
consoled at being with one who is a relation of them all.
He is a man of about 45 years of age."[1] All these are the
words of the Admiral. He also says that he had felt

---

[1] Las Casas denounces this proceeding as a breach of the law of
nations, which is not excused by the Admiral's good intentions; for
it is never right to do evil that good may come of it. St. Paul, in his
Epistle to the Romans, teaches: "non sunt facienda mala ut bona
eveniant" (Romans, iii, 8). "Certainly the Admiral acted on this
occasion inconsiderately, though in other things he was prudent."
But, on account of this act alone, Las Casas considers that he well
merited all the sorrows and misfortunes which he suffered during the
rest of his life. (Las Casas, i, pp. 334-38.)

some cold, and that it would not be wise to continue discoveries in a northerly direction in the winter. On this Monday, until sunset, he steered a course E. b. S., making 18 leagues, and reaching a cape, to which he gave the name of *Cabo de Cuba*.

Tuesday, 13th of November.

This night the ships were on a bowline, as the sailors say, beating to windward without making any progress. At sunset they began to see an opening in the mountains, where two very high peaks[1] were visible. It appeared that here was the division between the land of Cuba and that of Bohio, and this was affirmed by signs, by the Indians who were on board. As soon as the day had dawned, the Admiral made sail towards the land, passing a point which appeared at night to be distant two leagues. He then entered a large gulf, 5 leagues to the S.S.E., and there remained 5 more, to arrive at the point where, between two great mountains, there appeared to be an opening; but it could not be made out whether it was an inlet of the sea. As he desired to go to the island called Babeque, where, according to the information he had received, there was much gold; and as it bore east, and as no large town was in sight, the wind freshening more than ever, he resolved to put out to sea, and work to the east with a northerly wind. The ship made 8 miles an hour, and from ten in the forenoon, when that course was taken, until sunset, 56 miles, which is 14 leagues to the eastward from the *Cabo de Cuba*. The other land of Bohio was left to leeward. Commencing from the cape of the said gulf, he discovered, according to his reckoning, 80 miles, equal to 20 leagues, all that coast running E.S.E. and W.N.W.

---

[1] *Las Sierras del Cristal* and *Las Sierras de Moa.*—N.

Wednesday, 14th of November.

All last night the Admiral was beating to windward (he said that it would be unreasonable to navigate among those islands during the night, until they had been explored), for the Indians said yesterday that it would take three days to go from Rio de Mares to the island of Babeque, by which should be understood days' journeys in their canoes equal to about 7 leagues. The wind fell, and, the course being east, she could not lay her course nearer than S.E., and, owing to other mischances, he was detained until the morning. At sunrise he determined to go in search of a port, because the wind had shifted from north to N.E., and, if a port could not be found, it would be necessary to go back to the ports in the island of Cuba, whence they came. The Admiral approached the shore, having gone over 28 miles E.S.E. that night. He steered south ..... miles to the land, where he saw many islets and openings. As the wind was high and the sea rough, he did not dare to risk an attempt to enter, but ran along the coast W.N.W., looking out for a port, and saw many, but none very clear of rocks. After having proceeded for 64 miles, he found a very deep opening, a quarter of a mile wide, with a good port and river. He ran in with her head S.S.W., afterwards south to S.E. The port[1] was spacious and very deep, and he saw so many islands that he could not count them all, with very high land covered with trees of many kinds, and an infinite number of palms. He was much astonished to see so many lofty islands ; and assured the Sovereigns that the mountains and isles he had seen since yesterday seemed to him to be second to none in the world ; so high and clear of clouds and snow, with the sea at their bases so deep. He believes that these islands are

---

[1] Puerto de Taxamo, in Cuba.

those innumerable ones that are depicted on the maps of the world in the Far East.[1]   He believed that they yielded very great riches in precious stones and spices, and that they extend much further to the south, widening out in all directions.   He gave the name of *La Mar de Nuestra Señora*, and to the haven, which is near the mouth of the entrance to these islands, *Puerto del Principe*.   He did not enter it, but examined it from outside, until another time, on Saturday of the next week, as will there appear.   He speaks highly of the fertility, beauty, and height of the islands which he found in this gulf, and he tells the Sovereigns not to wonder at his praise of them, for that he has not told them the hundredth part.   Some of them seemed to reach to heaven, running up into peaks like diamonds. Others have a flat top like a table.   At their bases the sea is of a great depth, with enough water for a very large carrack.   All are covered with foliage and without rocks.

Thursday, 15th of November.

The Admiral went to examine these islands in the ships' boats, and speaks marvels of them, how he found mastick, and aloes without end.   Some of them were cultivated with the roots of which the Indians make bread ; and he found that fires had been lighted in several places.   He saw no fresh water.   There were some natives, but they fled. In all parts of the sea where the vessels were navigated he found a depth of 15 or 16 fathoms, and all *basa*, by which he means that the ground is sand, and not rocks ; a thing much desired by sailors, for the rocks cut their anchor cables.

---

[1] A group of innumerable islands was usually placed in the ocean to the east of Asia : and no doubt they were shown on the map of Toscanelli which Columbus took with him, as they certainly are on the globe of Martin Behaim, drawn in 1492.

Friday, 16th of November. •

As in all parts, whether islands or mainlands, that he visited, the Admiral always left a cross; so, on this occasion, he went in a boat to the entrance of these havens, and found two very large trees on a point of land, one longer than the other. One being placed over the other, made a cross, and he said that a carpenter could not have made it better. He ordered a very large and high cross to be made out of these timbers. He found canes on the beach, and did not know where they had grown, but thought they must have been brought down by some river, and washed up on the beach (in which opinion he had reason). He went to a creek on the south-east side of the entrance to the port. Here, under a height of rock and stone like a cape, there was depth enough for the largest carrack in the world close in shore, and there was a corner where six ships might lie without anchors as in a room. It seemed to the Admiral that a fortress might be built here at small cost, if at any time any famous trade[1] should arise in that sea of islands.

Returning to the ship, he found that the Indians who were on board had fished up very large shells found in those seas. He made the people examine them, to see if there was mother-o'-pearl, which is in the shells where pearls grow. They found a great deal, but no pearls, and their absence was attributed to its not being the season, which is May and June. The sailors found an animal which seemed to be a *taso*, or *taxo*.[2] They also fished with nets, and, among many others, caught a fish which was

---

[1] *Resgate. Rescate* (Las Casas).

[2] Las Casas does not seem to know the meaning of this word, and complains that Columbus does not say whether it was a land or marine beast.

exactly like a pig, not like a tunny, but all covered with
a very hard shell, without a soft place except the eyes.
It was ordered to be salted, to bring home for the Sovereigns
to see.

Saturday, 17th of November.

The Admiral got into the boat, and went to visit the
islands he had not yet seen to the S.W.   He saw many
more very fertile and pleasant islands, with a great depth
between them.   Some of them had springs of fresh water,
and he believed that the water of those streams came from
some sources at the summits of the mountains.   He went
on, and found a beach bordering on very sweet water,
which was very cold.   There was a beautiful meadow,
and many very tall palms.   They found a large nut of
the kind belonging to India, great rats, and enormous
crabs.   He saw many birds, and there was a strong smell
of musk, which made him think it must be there.   This
day the two eldest of the six youths brought from the *Rio
de Mares*, who were on board the caravel *Niña*, made their
escape.

Sunday, 18th of November.

The Admiral again went away with the boats, accompanied by many of the sailors, to set up the cross which he
had ordered to be made out of the two large trees at the
entrance to the *Puerto del Principe*, on a fair site cleared of
trees, whence there was an extensive and very beautiful
view.   He says that there is a greater rise and fall there
than in any other port he has seen, and that this is no
marvel, considering the numerous islands.   The tide is the
reverse of ours, because here, when the moon is S.S.W., it
is low water in the port.   He did not get under weigh,
because it was Sunday.

Monday, 19th of November.

The Admiral got under weigh before sunrise, in a calm. In the afternoon there was some wind from the east, and he shaped a N.N.E. course. At sunset the *Puerto del Principe* bore S.S.W. 7 leagues. He saw the island of Babeque bearing due east about 60 miles. He steered N.E. all that night, making 60 miles, and up to ten o'clock of Tuesday another dozen ; altogether 18 leagues N.E. b. W.

Tuesday, 20th of November.

They left Babeque, or the islands of Babeque, to the E.S.E., the wind being contrary ; and, seeing that no progress was being made, and the sea was getting rough, the Admiral determined to return to the *Puerto del Principe*, whence he had started, which was 25 leagues distant. He did not wish to go to the island he had called Isabella, which was twelve leagues off, and where he might have anchored that night, for two reasons : one was that he had seen two islands to the south which he wished to explore ; the other, because the Indians he brought with him, whom he had taken at the island of Guanahani, which he named San Salvador, eight leagues from Isabella, might get away, and he said that he wanted them to take to Spain. They thought that, when the Admiral had found gold, he would let them return to their homes. He came near the *Puerto del Principe*, but could not reach it, because it was night, and because the current drifted them to the N.W. He turned her head to N.E. with a light wind. At three o'clock in the morning the wind changed, and a course was shaped E.N.E., the wind being S.S.W., and changing at dawn to south and S.E. At sunset *Puerto del Principe* bore nearly S.W. by W. 48 miles, which are 12 leagues.

G

Wednesday, 21st of November.

At sunrise the Admiral steered east, with a southerly wind, but made little progress, owing to a contrary sea. At vespers he had gone 24 miles. Afterwards the wind changed to east, and he steered S. b. E., at sunset having gone 12 miles. Here he found himself forty-two degrees[1] north of the equinoctial line, as in the port of *Mares*, but he says that he kept the result from the quadrant in suspense until he reached the shore, that it might be adjusted (as it would seem that he thought this distance was too great, and he had reason, it not being possible, as these islands are only in . . . . .[2] degrees[3]).

This day Martin Alonso Pinzon parted company with the caravel *Pinta*, in disobedience to and against the wish of the Admiral, and out of avarice, thinking that an Indian who had been put on board his caravel could show him where there was much gold. So he parted company, not owing to bad weather, but because he chose. Here the Admiral says : " He had done and said many other things to me."

Thursday, 22nd of November.

On Wednesday night the Admiral steered S.S.E., with the wind east, but it was nearly calm. At 3 it began to blow from N.N.E. ; and he continued to steer south to see the land he had seen in that quarter. When the sun rose he was as far off as the day before, owing to adverse currents, the land being 40 miles off. This night Martin Alonso shaped a course to the east, to go to the island

---

[1] An erroneous transcription.   It should be 21°.

[2] A gap in the manuscript.

[3] Las Casas here interpolates some further remarks about the latitude, which are of no interest, as the figures on which he bases them are a blunder of his own in transcribing.

of Babeque, where the Indians say there is much gold. He did this in sight of the Admiral, from whom he was distant 16 miles. The Admiral stood towards the land all night. He shortened sail, and showed a lantern, because Pinzon would thus have an opportunity of joining him, the night being very clear, and the wind fair to come, if he had wished to do so.

Friday, 23rd of November.

The Admiral stood towards the land all day, always steering south with little wind, but the current would never let them reach it, being as far off at sunset as in the morning. The wind was E.N.E., and they could shape a southerly course, but there was little of it. Beyond this cape there stretched out another land or cape, also trending east, which the Indians on board called *Bohio*. They said that it was very large, and that there were people in it who had one eye in their foreheads, and others who were cannibals, and of whom they were much afraid. When they saw that this course was taken, they said that they could not talk to these people because they would be eaten, and that they were very well armed. The Admiral says that he well believes that there were such people, and that if they are armed they must have some ability. He thought that they may have captured some of the Indians, and because they did not return to their homes, the others believed that they had been eaten. They thought the same of the Christians and of the Admiral when some of them first saw the strangers.

Saturday, 24th of November.

They navigated all night, and at 3 they reached the island at the very same point they had come to the week before, when they started for the island of Babeque. At

G 2

first the Admiral did not dare to approach the shore,
because it seemed that there would be a great surf in that
mountain-girded bay. Finally he reached the sea of
Nuestra Señora, where there are many islands, and entered
a port near the mouth of the opening to the islands. He
says that if he had known of this port before he need not
have occupied himself in exploring the islands, and it
would not have been necessary to go back. He, however,
considered that the time was well spent in examining the
islands. On nearing the land he sent in the boat to sound ;
finding a good sandy bottom in 6 to 20 fathoms. He
entered the haven, pointing the ship's head S.W. and then
west, the flat island bearing north. This, with another
island near it, forms a harbour which would hold all the
ships of Spain safe from all winds. This entrance on the
S.W. side is passed by steering S.S.W., the outlet being to
the west very deep and wide. Thus a vessel can pass
amidst these islands, and he who approaches from the
north, with a knowledge of them, can pass along the coast.
These islands are at the foot of a great mountain-chain
running east and west, which is longer and higher than
any others on this coast, where there are many. A reef of
rocks outside runs parallel with the said mountains, like a
bench, extending to the entrance. On the side of the flat
island, and also to the S.E., there is another small reef, but
between them there is great width and depth. Within the
port, near the S.E. side of the entrance, they saw a large
and very fine river,[1] with more volume than any they had
yet met with, and fresh water could be taken from it as far
as the sea. At the entrance there is a bar, but within it is
very deep, 19 fathoms. The banks are lined with palms
and many other trees.

---

[1] Rio de Moa.

Sunday, 25th of November.

Before sunrise the Admiral got into the boat, and went to see a cape or point of land[1] to the S.E. of the flat island, about a league and a half distant, because there appeared to be a good river there. Presently, near to S.E. side of the cape, at a distance of two cross-bow shots, he saw a large stream of beautiful water falling from the mountains[2] above, with a loud noise. He went to it, and saw some stones shining in its bed like gold.[3] He remembered that in the river Tejo, near its junction with the sea, there was gold ; so it seemed to him that this should contain gold, and he ordered some of these stones to be collected, to be brought to the Sovereigns. Just then the sailor boys called out that they had found large pines. The Admiral looked up the hill, and saw that they were so wonderfully large that he could not exaggerate their height and straightness, like stout yet fine spindles. He perceived that here there was material for great store of planks and masts for the largest ships in Spain. He saw oaks and arbutus trees, with a good river, and the means of making water-power. The climate was temperate, owing to the height of the mountains. On the beach he saw many other stones of the colour of iron, and others that some said were like silver ore, all brought down by the river. Here he obtained a new mast and yard for the mizen of the caravel *Niña.* He came to the mouth of the river, and entered a creek which was deep and wide, at the foot of that S.E. part of the cape, which would accommodate a hundred ships without any anchor or hawsers. Eyes never beheld a better

---

[1] Punta del Mangle or del Guarico.

[2] Sierras de Moa.

[3] Las Casas says these were probably stones called *margasita*, of which there are many in these streams.

harbour. The mountains are very high, whence descend
many limpid streams, and all the hills are covered with
pines, and an infinity of diverse and beautiful trees. Two
or three other rivers were not visited.

The Admiral described all this, in much detail, to the
Sovereigns, and declared that he had derived unspeakable
joy and pleasure at seeing it, more especially the pines,
because they enable as many ships as is desired to be built
here, bringing out the rigging, but finding here abundant
supplies of wood and provisions. He affirms that he has
not enumerated a hundredth part of what there is here,
and that it pleased our Lord always to show him one thing
better than another, as well on the ground and among the
trees, herbs, fruits, and flowers, as in the people, and always
something different in each place. It had been the same
as regards the havens and the waters. Finally, he says
that if it caused him who saw it so much wonder, how much
more will it affect those who hear about it ; yet no one can
believe until he sees it.

Monday, 26th of November.

At sunrise the Admiral weighed the anchors in the
haven of *Santa Catalina*, where he was behind the flat
island, and steered along the coast in the direction of *Cabo
del Pico*, which was S.E. He reached the cape late,
because the wind failed, and then saw another cape, S.E.
b. E. 60 miles, which, when 20 miles off, was named *Cabo
de Campana*, but it could not be reached that day. They
made good 32 miles during the day, which is 8 leagues.
During this time the Admiral noted nine remarkable
ports,[1] which all the sailors thought wonderfully good, and
five large rivers ; for they sailed close along the land, so as

---

[1] Among these were the Bay of Yamanique, and the ports of Jaragua,
Taco, Cayaganueque, Nava, and Maravi.—N.

to see everything. All along the coast there are very high
and beautiful mountains, not arid or rocky, but all accessible, and very lovely. The valleys, like the mountains,
were full of tall and fine trees, so that it was a glory to
look upon them, and there seemed to be many pines.
Also, beyond the said *Cabo de Pico* to the S.E. there are
two islets, each about two leagues round, and inside them
three excellent havens and two large rivers. Along the
whole coast no inhabited places were visible from the sea.
There may have been some, and there were indications of
them, for, when the men landed, they found signs of
people and numerous remains of fires. The Admiral conjectured that the land he saw to-day S.E. of the *Cabo de
Campana* was the island called by the Indians *Bohio :* it
looked as if this cape was separated from the mainland.
The Admiral says that all the people he has hitherto met
with have very great fear of those of *Caniba* or *Canima.*
They affirm that they live in the island of *Bohio*, which
must be very large, according to all accounts. The Admiral
understood that those of Caniba come to take people from
their homes, they being very cowardly, and without knowledge of arms. For this cause it appears that these Indians
do not settle on the sea-coast, owing to being near the
land of Caniba. When the natives who were on board
saw a course shaped for that land, they feared to speak,
thinking they were going to be eaten ; nor could they rid
themselves of their fear. They declared that the Canibas
had only one eye and dogs' faces. The Admiral thought
they lied, and was inclined to believe that it was people
from the dominions of the Gran Can who took them into
captivity.

Tuesday, 27th of November.

Yesterday, at sunset, they arrived near a cape named
Campana by the Admiral ; and, as the sky was clear and

the wind light, he did not wish to run in close to the land and anchor, although he had five or six singularly good havens under his lee. The Admiral was attracted on the one hand by the longing and delight he felt to gaze upon the beauty and freshness of those lands, and on the other by a desire to complete the work he had undertaken. For these reasons he remained close hauled, and stood off and on during the night. But, as the currents had set him more than 5 or 6 leagues to the S.E. beyond where he had been at nightfall, passing the land of *Campana*, he came in sight of a great opening beyond that cape, which seemed to divide one land from another, leaving an island between them. He decided to go back, with the wind S.E., steering to the point where the opening had appeared, where he found that it was only a large bay[1]; and at the end of it, on the S.E. side, there was a point of land on which was a high and square-cut hill,[2] which had looked like an island. A breeze sprang up from the north, and the Admiral continued on a S.E. course, to explore the coast and discover all that was there. Presently he saw, at the foot of the *Cabo de Campana*, a wonderfully good port,[3] and a large river, and, a quarter of a league on, another river, and a third, and a fourth to a seventh at similar distances, from the furthest one to *Cabo de Campana* being 20 miles S.E. Most of these rivers have wide and deep mouths, with excellent havens for large ships, without sandbanks or sunken rocks. Proceeding onwards from the last of these rivers, on a S.E. course, they came to the largest inhabited place they had yet seen, and a vast concourse of people came down to the beach with loud shouts, all naked, with their darts in their hands. The Admiral desired to have speech with them, so he furled sails and anchored. The

---

[1] The port of Baracoa.—N.   [2] Monte del Yunque.—N.
[3] Port of Maravi.—N.

boats of the ship and the caravel were sent on shore, with orders to do no harm whatever to the Indians, but to give them presents. The Indians made as if they would resist the landing, but, seeing that the boats of the Spaniards continued to advance without fear, they retired from the beach. Thinking that they would not be terrified if only two or three landed, three Christians were put on shore, who told them not to be afraid, in their own language, for they had been able to learn a little from the natives who were on board. But all ran away, neither great nor small remaining. The Christians went to the houses, which were of straw, and built like the others they had seen, but found no one in any of them. They returned to the ships, and made sail at noon in the direction of a fine cape[1] to the eastward, about 8 leagues distant. Having gone about half a league, the Admiral saw, on the south side of the same bay, a very remarkable harbour,[2] and to the S.E. some wonderfully beautiful country like a valley among the mountains, whence much smoke arose, indicating a large population, with signs of much cultivation. So he resolved to stop at this port, and see if he could have any speech or intercourse with the inhabitants. It was so that, if the Admiral had praised the other havens, he must praise this still more for its lands, climate, and people. He tells marvels of the beauty of the country and of the trees, there being palms and pine trees; and also of the great valley, which is not flat, but diversified by hill and dale, the most lovely scene in the world. Many streams flow from it, which fall from the mountains.

As soon as the ship was at anchor the Admiral jumped into the boat, to get soundings in the port, which is the shape of a hammer. When he was facing the entrance he found the mouth of a river on the south side of sufficient

---

[1] Punta de Maici.—N.   [2] Puerto de Baracoa.—N.

width for a galley to enter it, but so concealed that it is
not visible until close to. Entering it for the length of
the boat, there was a depth of from 5 to 8 fathoms. In
passing up it the freshness and beauty of the trees, the
clearness of the water, and the birds, made it all so delightful
that he wished never to leave them. He said to the men
who were with him that to give a true relation to the
Sovereigns of the things they had seen, a thousand tongues
would not suffice, nor his hand to write it, for that it was
like a scene of enchantment. He desired that many other
prudent and credible witnesses might see it, and he was
sure that they would be as unable to exaggerate the
scene as he was.

The Admiral also says :—" How great the benefit that
is to be derived from this country would be, I cannot say.
It is certain that where there are such lands there must
be an infinite number of things that would be profitable.
But I did not remain long in one port, because I wished
to see as much of the country as possible, in order to make
a report upon it to your Highnesses; and besides, I do
not know the language, and these people neither understand me nor any other in my company; while the Indians
I have on board often misunderstand. Moreover, I have
not been able to see much of the natives, because they
often take to flight. But now, if our Lord pleases, I will
see as much as possible, and will proceed by little and
little, learning and comprehending; and I will make some
of my followers learn the language. For I have perceived
that there is only one language up to this point. After
they understand the advantages, I shall labour to make
all these people Christians. They will become so readily,
because they have no religion nor idolatry, and your
Highnesses will send orders to build a city and fortress,
and to convert the people. I assure your Highnesses that
it does not appear to me that there can be a more fertile

country nor a better climate under the sun, with abundant supplies of water.   This is not like the rivers of Guinea, which are all pestilential.   I thank our Lord that, up to this time, there has not been a person of my company who has so much as had a headache, or been in bed from illness, except an old man who has suffered from the stone all his life, and he was well again in two days.   I speak of all three vessels.   If it will please God that your Highnesses should send learned men out here, they will see the truth of all I have said.   I have related already how good a place *Rio de Mares* would be for a town and fortress, and this is perfectly true ; but it bears no comparison with this place, nor with the *Mar de Nuestra Señora.*   For here there must be a large population, and very valuable productions, which I hope to discover before I return to Castille.   I say that if Christendom will find profit among these people, how much more will Spain, to whom the whole country should be subject.   Your Highnesses ought not to consent that any stranger should trade here, or put his foot in the country, except Catholic Christians, for this was the beginning and end of the undertaking ; namely, the increase and glory of the Christian religion, and that no one should come to these parts who was not a good Christian."

All the above are the Admiral's words.   He ascended the river for some distance, examined some branches of it, and, returning to the mouth, he found some pleasant groves of trees, like a delightful orchard.   Here he came upon a canoe, dug out of one tree, as big as a galley of twelve benches, fastened under a boat-house made of wood, and thatched with palm-leaves, so that it could be neither injured by sun nor by the water.   He says that here would be the proper site for a town and fort, by reason of the good port, good water, good land, and abundance of fuel.

Wednesday, 28th of November.

The Admiral remained during this day, in consequence of the rain and thick weather, though he might have run along the coast, the wind being S.W., but he did not weigh, because he was unacquainted with the coast beyond, and did not know what danger there might be for the vessels. The sailors of the two vessels went on shore to wash their clothes, and some of them walked inland for a short distance. They found indications of a large population, but the houses were all empty, everyone having fled. They returned by the banks of another river, larger than that which they knew of, at the port.

Thursday, 27th of November.

The rain and thick weather continuing, the Admiral did not get under weigh. Some of the Christians went to another village to the N.W., but found no one, and nothing in the houses. On the road they met an old man who could not run away, and caught him. They told him they did not wish to do him any harm, gave him a few presents, and let him go. The Admiral would have liked to have had speech with him, for he was exceedingly satisfied with the delights of that land, and wished that a settlement might be formed there, judging that it must support a large population. In one house they found a cake of wax, which was taken to the Sovereigns, the Admiral saying that where there was wax there were also a thousand other good things. The sailors also found, in one house, the head of a man in a basket, covered with another basket, and fastened to a post of the house. They found the same things in another village. The Admiral believed that they must be the heads of some founder, or principal ancestor of a lineage, for the houses are built to contain a great number of people in each; and these should be relations, and descendants of a common ancestor.

Friday, 30th of November.

They could not get under weigh to-day because the wind was east, and dead against them. The Admiral sent 8 men well armed, accompanied by two of the Indians he had on board, to examine the villages inland, and get speech with the people. They came to many houses, but found no one and nothing, all having fled. They saw four youths who were digging in their fields, but, as soon as they saw the Christians, they ran away, and could not be overtaken. They marched a long distance, and saw many villages and a most fertile land, with much cultivation and many streams of water. Near one river they saw a canoe dug out of a single tree, 95 *palmos* long, and capable of carrying 150 persons.

Saturday, 1st of December.

They did not depart, because there was still a foul wind, with much rain. The Admiral set up a cross at the entrance of this port, which he called *Puerto Santo*,[1] on some bare rocks. The point is that which is on the S.E. side of the entrance; but he who has to enter should make more over to the N.W.; for at the foot of both, near the rock, there are 12 fathoms and a very clean bottom. At the entrance of the port, towards the S.E. point, there is a reef of rocks above water,[2] sufficiently far from the shore to be able to pass between if it is necessary; for both on the side of the rock and the shore there is a depth of

---

[1] Puerto de Baracoa.—N.

[2] This reef actually exists on the S.E. side of the entrance to this port, which is described with great accuracy by Columbus.—N.

12 to 15 fathoms : and, on entering, a ship's head should
be turned S.W.

Sunday, 2nd of December.

The wind was still contrary, and they could not depart.
Every night the wind blows on the land, but no vessel
need be alarmed at all the gales in the world, for they cannot blow home by reason of a reef of rocks at the opening
to the haven.[1] A sailor-boy found, at the mouth of the
river, some stones which looked as if they contained gold ;
so they were taken to be shown to the Sovereigns. The
Admiral says that there are great rivers at the distance of
a lombard shot.

Monday, 3rd of December.

By reason of the continuance of an easterly wind the
Admiral did not leave this port. He arranged to visit a
very beautiful headland a quarter of a league to the S.E.
of the anchorage. He went with the boats and some
armed men. At the foot of the cape there was the mouth
of a fair river, and on entering it they found the width to
be a hundred paces, with a depth of one fathom. Inside
they found 12, 5, 4, and 2 fathoms, so that it would hold
all the ships there are in Spain. Leaving the river, they
came to a cove in which were five very large canoes, so
well constructed that it was a pleasure to look at them.
They were under spreading trees, and a path led from
them to a very well-built boat-house, so thatched that
neither sun nor rain could do any harm. Within it there
was another canoe made out of a single tree like the others,
like a galley with 17 benches. It was a pleasant sight to
look upon such goodly work. The Admiral ascended a

---

[1] Here Las Casas puts "&c.", evidently omitting some valuable
sailing directions.

mountain, and afterwards found the country level, and cultivated with many things of that land, including such calabashes, as it was a glory to look upon them. In the middle there was a large village, and they came upon the people suddenly ; but, as soon as they were seen, men and women took to flight. The Indian from on board, who was with the Admiral, cried out to them that they need not be afraid, as the strangers were good people. The Admiral made him give them bells, copper ornaments, and glass beads, green and yellow, with which they were well content. He saw that they had no gold nor any other precious thing, and that it would suffice to leave them in peace. The whole district was well peopled, the rest having fled from fear. The Admiral assures the Sovereigns that ten thousand of these men would run from ten, so cowardly and timid are they. No arms are carried by them, except wands, on the point of which a short piece of wood is fixed, hardened by fire, and these they are very ready to exchange. Returning to where he had left the boats, he sent back some men up the hill, because he fancied he had seen a large apiary. Before those he had sent could return, they were joined by many Indians, and they went to the boats, where the Admiral was waiting with all his people. One of the natives advanced into the river near the stern of the boat, and made a long speech, which the Admiral did not understand. At intervals the other Indians raised their hands to heaven, and shouted. The Admiral thought he was assuring him that he was pleased at his arrival ; but he saw the Indian who came from the ship change the colour of his face, and turn as yellow as wax, trembling much, and letting the Admiral know by signs that he should leave the river, as they were going to kill him. He pointed to a cross-bow which one of the Spaniards had, and showed it to the Indians, and the Admiral let it be understood that they would all be slain, because that cross-bow carried far and killed people. He also took a sword and drew it out of the sheath, showing it to them, and saying the same, which, when they had heard, they all took to flight; while the Indian from the ship still trembled from cowardice, though he was a tall, strong man. The Admiral did not want to leave the river, but pulled towards the place where the natives had assembled in great numbers, all painted, and as naked as when their mothers bore them. Some had tufts of feathers on their heads, and all had their bundles of darts.

The Admiral says: "I came to them, and gave them some mouthfuls of bread, asking for the darts, for which I gave in exchange copper ornaments, bells, and glass beads. This made them peaceable, so that they came to the boats again, and gave us what they had. The sailors had killed a turtle, and the shell was in the boat in pieces. The sailor-boys gave them some in exchange for a bundle of darts. These are like the other people we have seen, and with the same belief that we came from heaven. They are ready to give whatever thing they have in exchange for any trifle without saying it is little; and I believe they would do the same with gold and spices if they had any. I saw a fine house, not very large, and with two doors, as all the rest have. On entering, I saw a marvellous work, there being rooms made in a peculiar way, that I scarcely know how to describe it. Shells and other things were fastened to the ceiling. I thought it was a temple, and I called them and asked, by signs, whether prayers were offered up there. They said that they were not, and one of them climbed up and offered me all the things that were there, of which I took some."

Tuesday, 4th of December.

The Admiral made sail with little wind, and left that port, which he called *Puerto Santo*. After going two leagues, he saw the great river[1] of which he spoke yesterday. Passing along the land, and beating to windward on S.E. and W.N.W. courses, they reached *Cabo Lindo*,[2] which is E.S.E. 5 leagues from *Cabo del Monte*. A league and a half from *Cabo del Monte* there is an important but rather narrow river, which seemed to have a good entrance, and to be deep. Three-quarters of a league further on, the Admiral saw another very large river, and he thought it must have its source at a great distance. It had a hundred paces at its mouth, and no bar, with a depth of 8 fathoms. The Admiral sent the boat in, to take soundings, and they found the water fresh until it enters the sea.

This river had great volume, and must have a large population on its banks. Beyond *Cabo Lindo* there is a great bay, which would be open for navigation to E.N.E. and S.E. and S.S.W.

Wednesday, 5th of December.

All this night they were beating to windward off *Cape Lindo*, to reach the land to the east, and at sunrise the Admiral sighted another cape,[3] two and a half leagues to the east. Having passed it, he saw that the land trended S. and S.W., and presently saw a fine high cape in that direction, 7 leagues distant.[4] He would have wished to go

---

[1] Rio Boma.—N.   [2] Punta del Fraile.—N.

[3] Punta de los Azules.—N.

[4] The eastern end of Cuba, called *Punta del Maici*.—N. Las Casas says that Punta del Maici was not the extreme point. It was the point named by the Admiral "Cabo de Cuba". He must be correct, for he had the chart drawn by the Admiral himself, in his possession (i, p. 340). The Admiral named the extreme east point of Cuba "Alpha et Omega"; and Las Casas says that in his time it had the native name of "Punta de Bayatiquiri". (*Las Casas*, i, p. 360; ii, p. 51.)

H

there, but his object was to reach the island of Babeque,
which, according to the Indians, bore N.E.; so he gave up
the intention. He could not go to Babeque either, because
the wind was N.E.[1] Looking to the S.E., he saw land,
which was a very large island, according to the information of the Indians, well peopled, and called by them
Bohio.[2] The Admiral says that the inhabitants of Cuba, or
Juana,[3] and of all the other islands, are much afraid of the
inhabitants of Bohio, because they say that they eat people.
The Indians relate other things, by signs, which are very
wonderful; but the Admiral did not believe them. He
only inferred that those of Bohio must have more clever-
ness and cunning to be able to capture the others, who,
however, are very poor-spirited. The wind veered from
N.E. to North, so the Admiral determined to leave Cuba,
or Juana, which, up to this time, he had supposed to be
the mainland, on account of its size, having coasted along
it for 120 leagues.[4] He shaped a course S.E. b. E., the
land he had sighted bearing S.E.; taking this precaution
because the wind always veered from N. to N.E. again,
and thence to east and S.E. The wind increased, and he
made all sail, the current helping them; so that they
were making 8 miles an hour from the morning until one
in the afternoon (which is barely 6 hours, for they say that
the nights were nearly 15 hours). Afterwards they went
10 miles an hour, making good 88 miles by sunset,
equal to 22 leagues, all to the S.E. As night was coming

---

[1] Babeque is a name that does not occur again. Probably its use
by the Admiral arose from some word that had been misunderstood.

[2] Hayti, or Española. The name Bohio is a mistake (*Las Casas*, i, 359).

[3] The Admiral gave the name of Juana to Cuba, in honour of
Prince Juan, only son of Ferdinand and Isabella.

[4] "I found it so large that I thought it must be the mainland—the
province of Cathay" (*Letter to Santangel*, v. 2). Further on he says:
"I learnt from Indians whom I seized, that their land was certainly
an island" (*ibid.*, p. 3). But he remained in doubt.

on, the Admiral ordered the caravel *Niña,* being a good
sailer, to proceed ahead, so as to sight a harbour at daylight. Arriving at the entrance of a port which was like
the Bay of Cadiz, while it was still dark, a boat was sent in
to take soundings, which showed a light from a lantern.
Before the Admiral could beat up to where .the caravel
was, hoping that the boat would show a leading-mark for
entering the port, the candle in the lantern went out.
The caravel, not seeing the light, showed a light to the
Admiral, and, running down to him, related what had
happened. The boat's crew then showed another light,
and the caravel made for it; but the Admiral could not
do so, and was standing off and on all night.

Thursday, 6th of December.

When daylight arrived the Admiral found himself four
leagues from the port, to which he gave the name of *Puerto
Maria,*[1] and to a fine cape bearing S.S.W. he gave the
name of *Cabo del Estrella.*[2] It seemed to be the furthest
point of the island towards the south, distant 28 miles.
Another point of land, like an island, appeared about 40
miles to the east. To another fine point, 54 miles to the
east, he gave the name of *Cabo del Elefante,*[3] and he called
another, 28 miles to the S.E., *Cabo de Cinquin.* There was
a great opening or bay, which might be the mouth of a
river,[4] distant 20 miles. It seemed that between *Cabo del
Elefante* and that of *Cinquin* there was a great opening,[5]
and some of the sailors said that it formed an island, to
which the name of *Isla de la Tortuga* was given. The
island appeared to be very high land, not closed in with
mountains, but with beautiful valleys, well cultivated, the

---

[1] The port of St. Nicholas Mole, in Hayti.
[2] Cape of St. Nicholas.
[3] Punta Palmista.   [4] Puerto Escudo.
[5] The channel between Tortuga Island and the main.

crops appearing like the wheat on the plain of Cordova in
May. That night they saw many fires, and much smoke,
as if from workshops, in the day time; it appeared to be a
signal made by people who were at war. All the coast of
this land trends to the east.

At the hour of vespers the Admiral reached this port, to
which he gave the name of *Puerto de San Nicolas*, in honour
of St. Nicholas, whose day it was[1]; and on entering it he
was astonished at its beauty and excellence. Although he
had given great praise to the ports of Cuba, he had no
doubt that this one not only equalled, but excelled them,
and none of them are like it. At the entrance it is a
league and a half wide, and a vessel's head should be
turned S.S.E., though, owing to the great width, she may
be steered on any bearing that is convenient; proceeding
on this course for two leagues. On the south side of the
entrance the coast forms a cape, and thence the course is
almost the same as far as a point where there is a fine
beach, and a plain covered with fruit-bearing trees of
many kinds; so that the Admiral thought there must be
nutmegs and other spices among them, but he did not
know them, and they were not ripe. There is a river
falling into the harbour, near the middle of the beach.
The depth of this port is surprising, for, until reaching the
land, for a distance of .....[2] the lead did not reach the
bottom at 40 fathoms; and up to this length there are
15 fathoms with a very clean bottom. Throughout the
port there is a depth of 15 fathoms, with a clean bottom,
at a short distance from the shore; and all along
the coast there are soundings with clean bottom, and
not a single sunken rock. Inside, at the length of a

---

[1] When he saw it at a distance he had given it the name of *Puerto
Maria*, but, having entered it on St. Nicholas's Day, he changed the
name, thinking the new one more appropriate.

[2] A gap in the manuscript.—N.

boat's oar from the land, there are 5 fathoms.   Beyond
the limit of the port to the S.S.E. a thousand carracks
could beat up.   One branch of the port to the N.E. runs
into the land for a long half league, and always the same
width, as if it had been measured with a cord. Being in this
creek, which is 25 paces wide, the principal entrance to
the harbour is not in sight, so that it appears land-locked.[1]
The depth of this creek is 11 fathoms throughout, all with
clean bottom ; and close to the land, where one might
put the gangboards on the grass, there are eight fathoms.

The whole port is open to the air, and clear of trees.
All the island appeared to be more rocky than any that
had been discovered.   The trees are smaller, and many of
them of the same kinds as are found in Spain, such as the
ilex, the arbutus, and others, and it is the same with the
herbs.   It is a very high country, all open and clear, with
a very fine air, and no such cold has been met with elsewhere, though it cannot be called cold except by comparison.   Towards the front of the haven there is a
beautiful valley, watered by a river ; and in that district
there must be many inhabitants, judging from the number
of large canoes, like galleys, with 15 benches.   All the
natives fled as soon as they saw the ships.   The Indians
who were on board had such a longing to return to their
homes that the Admiral considered whether he should not
take them back when he should depart from here.   They
were already suspicious, because he did not shape a course
towards their country ; whence he neither believed what
they said, nor could he understand them, nor they him,
properly.   The Indians on board had the greatest fear in
the world of the people of this island.   In order to get
speech of the people it would be necessary to remain some
days in harbour ; but the Admiral did not do so, because
he had to continue his discoveries, and because he could

---

[1] This is the "Carenero", within the port of St. Nicholas.—N.

not tell how long he might be detained.   He trusted in
our Lord that the Indians he brought with him would
understand the language of the people of this island ; and
afterwards he would communicate with them, trusting
that it might please God's Majesty that he might find
trade in gold before he returned.

Friday, 7th of December.

At daybreak the Admiral got under weigh, made sail,
and left the port of St. Nicholas.   He went on with the
wind in the west for two leagues, until he reached the
point which forms the *Carenero*, when the angle in the
coast bore S.E., and the *Cabo de la Estrella* was 24 miles
to the S.W.   Thence he steered along the coast eastward
to *Cabo Cinquin* about 48 miles, 20 of them being on an
E.N.E. coast.   All the coast is very high, with a deep sea.
Close in shore there are 20 to 30 fathoms, and at the
distance of a lombard-shot there is no bottom ; all which
the Admiral discovered that day, as he sailed along the
coast with the wind S.W., much to his satisfaction.   The
cape, which runs out in the port of St. Nicholas the length
of a shot from a lombard, could be made an island by
cutting across it, while to sail round it is a circuit of 3 or
4 miles.   All that land is very high, not clothed with very
high trees, but with ilex, arbutus, and others proper to the
land of Castille.   Before reaching *Cape Cinquin* by two
leagues, the Admiral discovered an opening in the mountains, through which he could see a very large valley,
covered with crops like barley, and he therefore judged
that it must sustain a large population.   Behind there was
a high range of mountains.   On reaching *Cabo Cinquin*,
the *Cabo de la Tortuga* bore N.E. 32 miles.[1]   Off *Cabo*

---

[1] It should be north 11 miles.—N.

Cinquin, at the distance of a lombard-shot, there is a high rock, which is a good landmark. The Admiral being there, he took the bearing of *Cabo del Elefante*, which was E.S.E. about 70 miles,[1] the intervening land being very high. At a distance of 6 leagues there was a conspicuous cape,[2] and he saw many large valleys and plains, and high mountains inland, all reminding him of Spain. After 8 leagues he came to a very deep but narrow river, though a carrack might easily enter it, and the mouth without bar or rocks. After 16 miles there was a wide and deep harbour,[3] with no bottom at the entrance, nor, at 3 paces from the shore, less than 15 fathoms ; and it runs inland a quarter of a league. It being yet very early, only one o'clock in the afternoon, and the wind being aft and blowing fresh, yet, as the sky threatened much rain, and it was very thick, which is dangerous even on a known coast, how much more in an unknown country, the Admiral resolved to enter the port, which he called *Puerto de la Concepcion.* He landed near a small river at the point of the haven, flowing from valleys and plains, the beauty of which was a marvel to behold. He took fishing-nets with him ; and, before he landed, a skate, like those of Spain, jumped into the boat, this being the first time they had seen fish resembling the fish of Castille. The sailors caught and killed others. Walking a short distance inland, the Admiral found much land under cultivation, and heard the singing of nightingales and other birds of Castille. Five men were seen, but they would not stop, running away. The Admiral found myrtles and other Spanish plants, while land and mountains were like those of Castille.

---

[1] This is another error of the transcriber. It should be 11 miles.
[2] Puerto Escudo.—N.   [3] Bahia Mosquito.—N.

Saturday, 8th of December.

In this port there was heavy rain, with a fresh breeze
from the north. The harbour is protected from all winds
except the north ; but even this can do no harm whatever,
because there is a great surf outside, which prevents such
a sea within the river as would make a ship work on her
cables. After midnight the wind veered to N.E., and then
to East, from which winds this port is well sheltered by
the island of Tortuga, distant 36 miles.[1]

Sunday, 9th of December.

To-day it rained, and the weather was wintry, like
October in Castille.   No habitations had been seen except
a very beautiful house in the *Puerto de S. Nicolas*, which
was better built than any that had been in other parts.
" The island is very large," says the Admiral : " it would
not be much if it has a circumference of 200 leagues.   All
the parts he had seen were well cultivated.   He believed
that the villages must be at a distance from the sea,
whither they went when the ships arrived ; for they all
took to flight, taking everything with them, and they
made smoke-signals, like a people at war." This port has
a width of a thousand paces at its entrance, equal to
a quarter of a league.   There is neither bank nor reef
within, and there are scarcely soundings close in shore.
Its length, running inland, is 3,000 paces, all clean, and
with a sandy bottom ; so that any ship may anchor in it
without fear, and enter it without precaution.   At the upper
end there are the mouths of two rivers, with the most
beautiful campaign country, almost like the lands of Spain :

---

[1] A blunder of the transcriber.   It should be 11 miles.

these even have the advantage ; for which reasons the Admiral gave the name of the said island *Isla Española*.[1]

Monday, 10th of December.

It blew hard from the N.E., which made them drag their anchors half a cable's length. This surprised the Admiral, who had seen that the anchors had taken good hold of the ground. As he saw that the wind was foul for the direction in which he wanted to steer, he sent six men on shore, well armed, to go two or three leagues inland, and endeavour to open communications with the natives. They came and returned without having seen either people or houses. But they found some hovels, wide roads, and some places where many fires had been made. They saw excellent lands, and many mastick trees, some specimens of which they took ; but this is not the time for collecting it, as it does not coagulate.

Tuesday, 11th of December.

The Admiral did not depart, because the wind was still east and S.E. In front of this port, as has been said, is the island of La Tortuga. It appears to be a large island, with the coast almost like that of Española, and the distance between them is about ten leagues.[2] It is well to know that from the *Cabo de Cinquin*, opposite Tortuga, the coast trends to the south. The Admiral had a great desire to see that channel between these two islands, and to examine the island of Española, which is the most beautiful thing in the world. According to what the Indians said who were on board, he would have to go to the island of *Babeque*. They declared that it was very large, with great mountains, rivers, and valleys ; and that

---

[1] See *Letter to Santangel*, p. 3.

[2] One of the commonest blunders of the careless scribe who made the copy of the Journal of Columbus was to write leagues instead of miles. The distance is 11 miles.

the island of *Bohio* was larger than Juana, which they call Cuba, and that it is not surrounded by water. They seem to imply that there is mainland behind Española, and they call it *Caritaba*, and say it is of vast extent. They have reason in saying that the inhabitants are a clever race, for all the people of these islands are in great fear of those of Caniba. So the Admiral repeats, what he has said before, that Caniba is nothing else but the Gran Can, who ought now to be very near. He sends ships to capture the islanders ; and as they do not return, their countrymen believe that they have been eaten. Each day we understand better what the Indians say, and they us, so that very often we are intelligible to each other. The Admiral sent people on shore, who found a great deal of mastick, but did not gather it. He says that the rains make it, and that in Chios they collect it in March. In these lands, being warmer, they might take it in January. They caught many fish like those of Castille—dace,[1] salmon, hake,[2] dory,[3] gilt heads,[4] skates,[5] *corbinas*,[6] shrimps,[7] and they saw sardines. They found many aloes.

Wednesday, 12th of December.

The Admiral did not leave the port to-day, for the same reason : a contrary wind. He set up a great cross on the west side of the entrance, on a very picturesque height, "in sign", he says, "that your Highnesses hold this land for your own, but chiefly as a sign of our Lord Jesus Christ." This being done, three sailors strolled into the woods to see the trees and bushes. Suddenly they came upon a crowd of people, all naked like the rest. They called

---

[1] *Albures*, a river fish : roach or dace.
[2] *Pijota*, a word in the Galician dialect for a cod or hake.
[3] *Gallo*.   [4] *Pampano*.   [5] *Liza*.
[6] I have failed to find the English equivalent for the name of this fish.   [7] *Camarones*.

to them, and went towards them, but they ran away. At last they caught a woman; for I had ordered that some should be caught, that they might be treated well, and made to lose their fear. This would be a useful event, for it could scarcely be otherwise, considering the beauty of the country. So they took the woman, who was very young and beautiful, to the ship, where she talked to the Indians on board; for they all speak the same language. The Admiral caused her to be dressed, and gave her glass beads, hawks' bells, and brass ornaments; then he sent her back to the shore very courteously, according to his custom. He sent three of the crew with her, and three of the Indians he had on board, that they might open communications with her people. The sailors in the boat, who took her on shore, told the Admiral that she did not want to leave the ship, but would rather remain with the other women he had seized at the port of Mares, in the island of Juana or Cuba. The Indians who went to put the woman on shore said that the natives came in a canoe, which is their caravel, in which they navigate from one place to another; but when they came to the entrance of the harbour, and saw the ships, they turned back, left the canoe, and took the road to the village. The woman pointed out the position of the village. She had a piece of gold in her nose, which showed that there was gold in that island.

Thursday, 13th of December.

The three men who had been sent by the Admiral with the woman returned at 3 o'clock in the morning, not having gone with her to the village, because the distance appeared to be long, or because they were afraid. They said that next day many people would come to the ships, as they would have been reassured by the news brought them by the woman. The Admiral, with the desire of ascertaining whether there were any profitable commodities

in that land, being so beautiful and fertile, and of having
some speech with the people, and being desirous of serving the Sovereigns, determined to send again to the village,
trusting in the news brought by the woman that the
Christians were good people.   For this service he selected
nine men well armed, and suited for such an enterprise,
with whom an Indian went from those who were on
board.   They reached the village,[1] which is 4½ leagues to
the S.E., and found that it was situated in a very large
and open valley.   As soon as the inhabitants saw the
Christians coming they all fled inland, leaving all their
goods behind them.   The village consisted of a thousand
houses, with over three thousand inhabitants.   The Indian
whom the Christians had brought with them ran after the
fugitives, saying that they should have no fear, for the
Christians did not come from Cariba, but were from
heaven, and that they gave many beautiful things to all
the people they met.   They were so impressed with what
he said, that upwards of two thousand came close up to
the Christians, putting their hands on their heads, which
was a sign of great reverence and friendship; and they
were all trembling until they were reassured.   The Christians related that, as soon as the natives had cast off their
fear, they all went to the houses, and each one brought
what he had to eat, consisting of yams,[2] which are roots
like large radishes, which they sow and cultivate in all
their lands, and is their staple food.   They make bread of
it, and roast it.   The yam has the smell of a chestnut, and
anyone would think he was eating chestnuts.   They gave
their guests bread and fish, and all they had.   As the
Indians who came in the ship had understood that the

---

[1] This village is now known by the name of *Gros Morne*.   It is
situated on the banks of the *Rio de los Tres Reyes*, which empties
itself into the sea half-a-mile west of *Puerto de Paz*.—N.

[2] " Pan de niames."

Admiral wanted to have some parrots, one of those who accompanied the Spaniards mentioned this, and the natives brought out parrots, and gave them as many as they wanted, without asking anything for them. The natives asked the Spaniards not to go that night, and that they would give them many other things that they had in the mountains. While all these people were with the Spaniards, a great multitude was seen to come, with the husband of the woman whom the Admiral had honoured and sent away. They wore hair over their shoulders, and came to give thanks to the Christians for the honour the Admiral had done them, and for the gifts. The Christians reported to the Admiral that this was a handsomer and finer people than any that had hitherto been met with. But the Admiral says that he does not see how they can be a finer people than the others, giving to understand that all those he had found in the other islands were very well conditioned. As regards beauty, the Christians said there was no comparison, both men and women, and that their skins are whiter than the others. They saw two girls whose skins were as white as any that could be seen in Spain. They also said, with regard to the beauty of the country they saw, that the best land in Castille could not be compared with it. The Admiral also, comparing the lands they had seen before with these, said that there was no comparison between them, nor did the plain of Cordova come near them, the difference being as great as between night and day. They said that all these lands were cultivated, and that a very wide and large river passed through the centre of the valley, and could irrigate all the fields. All the trees were green and full of fruit, and the plants tall and covered with flowers. The roads were broad and good. The climate was like April in Castille; the nightingale and other birds sang as they do in Spain during that month, and it was the most pleasant place in the world. Some birds sing sweetly at night. The,

crickets and frogs are heard a good deal. The fish are
like those of Spain. They saw much aloe and mastick,
and cotton-fields. Gold was not found, and it is not wonderful that it should not have been found in so short a time.

Here the Admiral calculated the number of hours in the
day and night, and from sunrise to sunset. He found that
twenty half-hour glasses passed,[1] though he says that here
there may be a mistake, either because they were not
turned with equal quickness, or because some sand may
not have passed. He also observed with a quadrant, and
found that he was 34 degrees from the equinoctial line.[2]

Friday, 14th of December.

The Admiral left the *Puerto de la Concepcion* with
the land-breeze, but soon afterwards it fell calm (and this
is experienced every day by those who are on this coast).
Later an east wind sprang up, so he steered N.N.E., and
arrived at the island of Tortuga. He sighted a point
which he named *Punta Pierna*, E.N.E. of the end of the
island 12 miles ; and from thence another point was seen
and named *Punta Lanzada*, in the same N.E. direction 16
miles. Thus from the end of Tortuga to *Punta Aguda*
the distance is 44 miles, which is 11 leagues E.N.E. Along
this route there are several long stretches of beach. The
island of Tortuga is very high, but not mountainous, and
is very beautiful and populous, like Española, and the land
is cultivated, so that it looked like the plain of Cordova.
Seeing that the wind was foul, and that he could not steer
for the island of *Baneque*,[3] he determined to return to the
Puerto de la Concepcion whence he had come ; but he could
not fetch a river which is two leagues to the east of that
port.

---

[1] Another blunder in transcribing.
[2] Another transcriber's blunder. It should be 20°.
[3] Elsewhere called Babeque.

Saturday, 15th of December.

Once more the Admiral left the *Puerto de la Concepcion*, but, on leaving the port, he was again met by a contrary east wind. He stood over to Tortuga, and then steered with the object of exploring the river he had been unable to reach yesterday ; nor was he able to fetch the river this time, but he anchored half a league to leeward of it, where there was clean and good anchoring ground. As soon as the vessels were secured, he went with the boats to the river, entering an arm of the sea, which proved not to be the river. Returning, he found the mouth, there being only one, and the current very strong. He went in with the boats to find the villagers that had been seen the day before. He ordered a tow-rope to be got out and manned by the sailors, who hauled the boats up for a distance of two lombard-shots. They could not get further owing to the strength of the current. He saw some houses, and the large valley where the villages were, and he said that a more beautiful valley he had never seen, this river flowing through the centre of it. He also saw people at the entrance, but they all took to flight. He further says that these people must be much hunted, for they live in such a state of fear. When the ships arrived at any port, they presently made smoke signals throughout the country ; and this is done more in this island of Española and in Tortuga, which is also a large island, than in the others that were visited before. He called this valley *Valle del Paraiso*, and the river *Guadalquivir;* because he says that it is the size of the Guadalquivir at Cordova. The banks consist of shingle, suitable for walking.

Sunday, 16th of December.

At midnight the Admiral made sail with the land-breeze to get clear of that gulf. Passing along the coast of

Española on a bowline, for the wind had veered to the east, he met a canoe in the middle of the gulf, with a single Indian in it. The Admiral was surprised how he could have kept afloat with such a gale blowing. Both the Indian and his canoe were taken on board, and he was given glass beads, bells, and brass trinkets, and taken in the ship, until she was off a village 17 miles from the former anchorage, where the Admiral came to again. The village appeared to have been lately built, for all the houses were new. The Indian then went on shore in his canoe, bringing the news that the Admiral and his companions were good people; although the intelligence had already been conveyed to the village from the place where the natives had their interview with the six Spaniards. Presently more than five hundred natives with their king came to the shore opposite the ships, which were anchored very close to the land. Presently one by one, then many by many, came to the ship without bringing anything with them, except that some had a few grains of very fine gold in their ears and noses, which they readily gave away. The Admiral ordered them all to be well treated; and he says: "for they are the best people in the world, and the gentlest; and above all I entertain the hope in our Lord that your Highnesses will make them all Christians, and that they will be all your subjects, for as yours I hold them." He also saw that they all treated the king with respect, who was on the sea-shore. The Admiral sent him a present, which he received in great state. He was a youth of about 21 years of age, and he had with him an aged tutor, and other councillors who advised and answered him, but he uttered very few words. One of the Indians who had come in the Admiral's ship spoke to him, telling him how the Christians had come from heaven, and how they came in search of gold, and wished to find the island of *Baneque.* He said that it was well, and that there was

much gold in the said island. He explained to the alguazil
of the Admiral[1] that the way they were going was the right
way, and that in two days they would be there ; adding,
that if they wanted anything from the shore he would give
it them with great pleasure. This king, and all the others,
go naked as their mothers bore them, as do the women
without any covering, and these were the most beautiful
men and women that had yet been met with. They are
fairly white, and if they were clothed and protected from
the sun and air, they would be almost as fair as people in
Spain. This land is cool, and the best that words can
describe. It is very high, yet the top of the highest
mountain could be ploughed with bullocks ; and all is
diversified with plains and valleys. In all Castille there
is no land that can be compared with this for beauty and
fertility. All this island, as well as the island of Tortuga,
is cultivated like the plain of Cordova. They raise on
these lands crops of yams, which are small branches, at the
foot of which grow roots[2] like carrots, which serve as
bread. They powder and knead them, and make them
into bread ; then they plant the same branch in another
part, which again sends out four or five of the same roots,
which are very nutritious, with the taste of chesnuts.
Here they have the largest the Admiral had seen in any
part of the world, for he says that they have the same
plant in Guinea. At this place they were as thick as a
man's leg. All the people were stout and lusty, not thin,
like the natives that had been seen before, and of a very
pleasant manner, without religious belief. The trees were
so luxuriant that the leaves left off being green, and were

---

[1] Diego de Arana of Cordova, a near relation of Beatriz Henriquez,
the mother of the Admiral's son Fernando.

[2] *Dioscorea alata.* The stem has a woody tissue, with a large
farinaceous tuber attached, which sometimes weighs 30 lbs.

I

dark coloured with verdure. It was a wonderful thing to see those valleys, and rivers of sweet water, and the cultivated fields, and land fit for cattle, though they have none, for orchards, and for anything in the world that a man could seek for.

In the afternoon the king came on board the ship, where the Admiral received him in due form, and caused him to be told that the ships belonged to the Sovereigns of Castille, who were the greatest Princes in the world. But neither the Indians who were on board, who acted as interpreters, nor the king, believed a word of it. They maintained that the Spaniards came from heaven, and that the Sovereigns of Castille must be in heaven, and not in this world. They placed Spanish food before the king to eat, and he ate a mouthful, and gave the rest to his councillors and tutor, and to the rest who came with him.

"Your Highnesses may believe that these lands are so good and fertile, especially these of the island of Española, that there is no one who would know how to describe them, and no one who could believe if he had not seen them. And your Highnesses may believe that this island, and all the others, are as much yours as Castille. Here there is only wanting a settlement and the order to the people to do what is required. For I, with the force I have under me, which is not large, could march over all these islands without opposition. I have seen only three sailors land, without wishing to do harm, and a multitude of Indians fled before them. They have no arms, and are without warlike instincts; they all go naked, and are so timid that a thousand would not stand before three of our men. So that they are good to be ordered about, to work and sow, and do all that may be necessary, and to build towns, and they should be taught to go about clothed and to adopt our customs."

Monday, 17th of December.

It blew very hard during the night from E.N.E., but there was not much sea, as this part of the coast is enclosed and sheltered by the island of Tortuga. The sailors were sent away to fish with nets. They had much intercourse with the natives, who brought them certain arrows of the *Caribas* or *Canibales*. They are made of reeds, pointed with sharp bits of wood hardened by fire, and are very long. They pointed out two men who wanted certain pieces of flesh on their bodies, giving to understand that the *Canibales* had eaten them by mouthfuls. The Admiral did not believe it. Some Christians were again sent to the village, and, in exchange for glass beads, obtained some pieces of gold beaten out into fine leaf. They saw one man, whom the Admiral supposed to be Governor of that province, called by them *Cacique*, with a piece of gold leaf as large as a hand, and it appears that he wanted to barter with it. He went into his house, and the other remained in the open space outside. He cut the leaf into small pieces, and each time he came out he brought a piece and exchanged it. When he had no more left, he said by signs that he had sent for more, and that he would bring it another day. The Admiral says that all these things, and the manner of doing them, with their gentleness and the information they gave, showed these people to be more lively and intelligent than any that had hitherto been met with. In the afternoon a canoe arrived from the island of Tortuga with a crew of forty men; and when they arrived on the beach, all the people of the village sat down in sign of peace, and nearly all the crew came on shore. The Cacique rose by himself, and, with words that appeared to be of a menacing character, made them go back to the canoe and

I 2

shove off. He took up stones from the beach and threw
them into the water, all having obediently gone back into
the canoe. He also took a stone and put it in the hands
of my Alguazil,[1] that he might throw it. He had been
sent on shore with the Secretary[2] to see if the canoe had
brought anything of value. The Alguazil did not wish to
throw the stone. That Cacique showed that he was well
disposed to the Admiral. Presently the canoe departed,
and afterwards they said to the Admiral that there was
more gold in Tortuga than in Española, because it is
nearer to Baneque. The Admiral did not think that there
were gold mines either in Española or Tortuga, but that
the gold was brought from *Baneque* in small quantities,
there being nothing to give in return. That land is so
rich that there is no necessity to work much to sustain
life, nor to clothe themselves, as they go naked. He
believed that they were very near the source, and that
our Lord would point out where the gold has its origin.
He had information that from here to *Baneque*[3] was four
days' journey, about 34 leagues, which might be traversed
with a fair wind in a single day.

Tuesday, 18th of December.

The Admiral remained at the same anchorage, because
there was no wind, and also because the Cacique had said
that he had sent for gold. The Admiral did not expect
much from what might be brought, but he wanted to
understand better whence it came. Presently he ordered
the ship and caravel to be adorned with arms and dressed
with flags, in honour of the feast of Santa Maria de la

---

[1] Diego de Arana.
[2] Rodrigo de Escobedo.
[3] Las Casas suggests that this name *Baneque* may possibly mean
Jamaica or the mainland.

O——,[1] or commemoration of the Annunciation, which was on that day, and many rounds were fired from the lombards. The king of that island of Española had got up very early and left his house, which is about five leagues away, reaching the village at three in the morning. There were several men from the ship in the village, who had been sent by the Admiral to see if any gold had arrived. They said that the king came with two hundred men; that he was carried in a litter by four men; and that he was a youth, as has already been said. To-day, when the Admiral was dining under the poop, the king came on board with all his people.

The Admiral says to the Sovereigns: "Without doubt, his state, and the reverence with which he is treated by all his people, would appear good to your Highnesses, though they all go naked. When he came on board, he found that I was dining at a table under the poop, and, at a quick walk, he came to sit down by me, and did not wish that I should give place by coming to receive him or rising from the table, but that I should go on with my dinner. I thought that he would like to eat of our viands, and ordered them to be brought for him to eat. When he came under the poop, he made signs with his hand that all the rest should remain outside, and so they did, with the greatest possible promptitude and reverence. They all sat on the deck, except the men of mature age, whom I believe to be his councillors and tutor, who came and sat at his feet. Of the viands which I put before him, he took of each as much as would serve to taste it,[2] sending the rest to his people, who all partook of the dishes. The same thing in drinking: he just touched with his lips,

---

[1] The Feast of the Annunciation. (*Las Casas.*)

[2] "Hacer la salva", the quantity taken by the taster before it was eaten by guests.

giving the rest to his followers. They were all of fine
presence and very few words. What they did say, so far
as I could make out, was very clear and intelligent. The
two at his feet watched his mouth, speaking to him and
for him, and with much reverence. After dinner, an
attendant brought a girdle, made like those of Castille,
but of different material, which he took and gave to me,
with pieces of worked gold, very thin. I believe they get
very little here, but they say that they are very near the
place where it is found, and where there is plenty. I saw
that he was pleased with some drapery I had over my
bed, so I gave it him, with some very good amber beads
I wore on my neck, some coloured shoes, and a bottle of
orange-flower water. He was marvellously well content,
and both he and his tutor and councillors were very sorry
that they could not understand me, nor I them. However, I knew that they said that, if I wanted anything, the
whole island was at my disposal. I sent for some beads
of mine, with which, as a charm, I had a gold *excelente*,[1]
on which your Highnesses were stamped. I showed it to
him, and said, as I had done yesterday, that your Highnesses ruled the best part of the world, and that there
were no Princes so great. I also showed him the royal
standards, and the others with a cross, of which he thought
much. He said to his councillors what great lords your
Highnesses must be to have sent me from so far, even
from heaven to this country, without fear. Many other
things passed between them which I did not understand,
except that it was easy to see that they held everything to
be very wonderful."

When it got late, and the king wanted to go, the
Admiral sent him on shore in his boat very honourably,

---

[1] A coin worth two *castellanos*. The *castellano* was worth 490
maravedis.

and saluted him with many guns. Having landed, he got into his litter, and departed with his 200 men, his son being carried behind on the shoulders of an Indian, a man highly respected. All the sailors and people from the ships were given to eat, and treated with much honour wherever they liked to stop. One sailor said that he had stopped in the road and seen all the things given by the Admiral. A man carried each one before the king, and these men appeared to be among those who were most respected. His son came a good distance behind the king, with a similar number of attendants, and the same with a brother of the king, except that the brother went on foot, supported under the arms by two honoured attendants. This brother came to the ship after the king, and the Admiral presented him with some of the things used for barter. It was then that the Admiral learnt that a king was called *Cacique* in their language. This day little gold was got by barter, but the Admiral heard from an old man that there were many neighbouring islands, at a distance of a hundred leagues or more, as he understood, in which much gold is found; and there is even one island that was all gold. In the others there was so much that it was said they gather it with sieves, and they fuse it and make bars, and work it in a thousand ways. They explained the work by signs. This old man pointed out to the Admiral the direction and position, and he determined to go there, saying that if the old man had not been a principal councillor of the king he would detain him, and make him go, too; or if he knew the language he would ask him, and he believed, as the old man was friendly with him and the other Christians, that he would go of his own accord. But as these people were now subjects of the King of Castille, and it would not be right to injure them, he decided upon leaving him. The Admiral set up a very large cross in the centre of the square of that village, the Indians giving much help ; they made prayers and worshipped it, and, from the feeling they show, the Admiral trusted in our Lord that all the people of those islands would become Christians.

Wednesday, 19th of December.

This night the Admiral got under weigh to leave the gulf formed between the islands of Tortuga and Española, but at dawn of day a breeze sprang up from the east, against which he was unable to get clear of the strait between the two islands during the whole day.   At night he was unable to reach a port which was in sight.[1]   He made out four points of land, and a great bay with a river, and beyond he saw a large bay,[2] where there was a village, with a valley behind it among high mountains covered with trees, which appeared to be pines.   Over the Two Brothers[3] there is a very high mountain-range running N.E. and S.W., and E.S.E. from the *Cabo de Torres* is a small island to which the Admiral gave the name of *Santo Tomas,* because to-morrow was his vigil.   The whole circuit of this island alternates with capes and excellent harbours, so far as could be judged from the sea.   Before coming to the island on the west side, there is a cape which runs far into the sea, in part high, the rest low ; and for this reason the Admiral named it *Cabo alto y bajo.*[4]   From the road[5] of Torres to E.S.E. 60 miles, there is a mountain higher than any that reaches the sea,[6] and from a distance it looks like an island, owing to a depression on the land side.   It was named *Monte Caribata,* because that province

---

[1] El Puerto de la Granja.—N.
[2] The bay of Puerto Margot.—N.
[3] Las Casas says there was no such name used in his time.
[4] Point and Island of Margot.—N.
[5] *Camino* for Cabo (?).   [6] Mountain over Guarico.

was called *Caribata*. It is very beautiful, and covered with green trees, without snow or clouds. The weather was then, as regards the air and temperature, like March in Castille, and as regards vegetation, like May. The nights lasted 14 hours.

Thursday, 20th of December.

At sunrise they entered a port between the island of *Santo Tomas* and the *Cabo de Caribata*,[1] and anchored. This port is very beautiful, and would hold all the ships in Christendom. The entrance appears impossible from the sea to those who have never entered, owing to some reefs of rocks which run from the mountainous cape almost to the island. They are not placed in a row, but one here, another there, some towards the sea, others near the land. It is therefore necessary to keep a good look-out for the entrances, which are wide and with a depth of 7 fathoms, so that they can be used without fear. Inside the reefs there is a depth of 12 fathoms. A ship can lie with a cable made fast, against any wind that blows. At the entrance of this port there is a channel on the west side of a sandy islet with 7 fathoms, and many trees on its shore. But there are many sunken rocks in that direction, and a look-out should be kept up until the port is reached. Afterwards there is no need to fear the greatest storm in the world. From this port a very beautiful cultivated valley is in sight, descending from the S.E., surrounded by such lofty mountains that they appear to reach the sky, and covered with green trees. Without doubt there are mountains here which are higher than the island of Tenerife in the Canaries, which is held to be the highest yet known. On this side of the island of *Santo Tomas*, at

---

[1] Bahia de Acúl.

a distance of a league, there is another islet, and beyond it another, forming wonderful harbours; though a good look-out must be kept for sunken rocks. The Admiral also saw villages, and smoke made by them.

Friday, 21st of December.

To-day the Admiral went with the ship's boats to examine this port, which he found to be such that it could not be equalled by any he had yet seen; but, having praised the others so much, he knew not how to express himself, fearing that he will be looked upon as one who goes beyond the truth. He therefore contents himself with saying that he had old sailors with him who say the same. All the praises he has bestowed on the other ports are true, and that this is better than any of them is equally true. He further says: " I have traversed the sea for 23 years,[1] without leaving it for any time worth counting, and I saw all in the east and the west, going on the route of the north, which is England, and I have been to Guinea, but in all those parts there will not be found perfection of harbours . . . .[2] always found . . . .[3] better than another, that I, with good care, saw written ; and I again affirm it was well written, that this one is better than all others, and will hold all the ships of the world, secured with the oldest cables. From the entrance to the end is a distance of five leagues.[4] The Admiral saw some very well cultivated lands, although they are all so,

---

[1] This is one of the passages which fixes the date of the great discoverer's birth. He went to sea at 14, and had been at sea 23 years when he first came to Spain in 1483, which makes his age 46. He was, therefore, born in the year 1447.

[2] A gap of a line and a half in the manuscript.

[3] Another gap in the manuscript.

[4] The distance is six miles. This is another instance of the transcriber substituting leagues for miles.

and he sent two of the boat's crew to the top of a hill to
see if any village was near, for none could be seen from the
sea.   At about ten o'clock that night, certain Indians
came in a canoe to see the Admiral and the Christians, and
they were given presents, with which they were much
pleased.   The two men returned, and reported that they
had seen a very large village at a short distance from the
sea.[1]   The Admiral ordered the boat to row towards the
place where the village was until they came near the land,
when he saw two Indians, who came to the shore apparently
in a state of fear.   So he ordered the boats to stop, and
the Indians that were with the Admiral were told to assure
the two natives that no harm whatever was intended to
them.   Then they came nearer the sea, and the Admiral
nearer the land.   As soon as the natives had got rid of
their fear, so many came that they covered the ground,
with women and children, giving a thousand thanks.
They ran hither and thither to bring us bread made of
yams, which they call *ajes*, which is very white and good,
and water in calabashes, and in earthen jars made like
those of Spain, and everything else they had and that they
thought the Admiral could want, and all so willingly and
cheerfully that it was wonderful.   " It cannot be said that,
because what they gave was worth little, therefore they
gave liberally, because those who had pieces of gold gave
as freely as those who had a calabash of water ; and it is
easy to know when a thing is given with a hearty desire
to give."   These are the Admiral's words.   " These people
have no spears nor any other arms, nor have any of the
inhabitants of the whole island, which I believe to be very
large.   They go naked as when their mothers bore them,
both men and women.   In Cuba and the other islands the
women wear a small clout of cotton in front, as well as the

---

[1] Acúl.

men, as soon as they have passed the age of twelve years, but here neither old nor young do so. Also, the men in the other islands jealously hide their women from the Christians, but here they do not." The women have very beautiful bodies, and they were the first to come and give thanks to heaven, and to bring what they had, especially things to eat, such as bread of *ajes* (yams), nuts, and four or five kinds of fruits, some of which the Admiral ordered to be preserved, to be taken to the Sovereigns. He says that the women did not do less in other ports before they were hidden ; and he always gave orders that none of his people should annoy them ; that nothing should be taken against their wills, and that everything that was taken should be paid for. Finally, he says that no one could believe that there could be such good-hearted people, so free to give, anxious to let the Christians have all they wanted, and, when visitors arrived, running to bring every- thing to them.

Afterwards the Admiral sent six Christians to the village to see what it was like, and the natives showed them all the honour they could devise, and gave them all they had ; for no doubt was any longer entertained that the Admiral and all his people had come from heaven ; and the same was believed by the Indians who were brought from the other islands, although they had now been told what they ought to think. When the six Christians had gone, some canoes came with people to ask the Admiral to come to their village when he left the place where he was. *Canoa* is a boat in which they navigate, some large and others small. Seeing that this village of the Chief was on the road, and that many people were waiting there for him, the Admiral went there ; but, before he could depart, an enormous crowd came to the shore, men, women, and children, crying out to him not to go, but to stay with them. The messengers from the other Chief, who had come to invite him, were waiting with their

canoes, that he might not go away, but come to see their
Chief, and so he did.   On arriving where the Chief was
waiting for him with many things to eat, he ordered that all
the people should sit down, and that the food should be
taken to the boats, where the Admiral was, on the sea-shore.
When he saw that the Admiral had received what he sent,
all or most of the Indians ran to the village, which was
near, to bring more food, parrots, and other things they
had, with such frankness of heart that it was marvellous.
The Admiral gave them glass beads, brass trinkets, and
bells : not because they asked for anything in return, but
because it seemed right, and, above all, because he now
looked upon them as future Christians, and subjects of the
Sovereigns, as much as the people of Castille.   He further
says that they want nothing except to know the language
and be under governance; for all they may be told to do will
be done without any contradiction.   The Admiral left this
place to go to the ships, and the people, men, women, and
children, cried out to him not to go, but remain with them.
After the boats departed, several canoes full of people
followed after them to the ship, who were received with
much honour, and given to eat.   There had also come before
another Chief from the west, and many people even came
swimming, the ship being over a good half-league from the
shore.   I sent certain persons to the Chief, who had gone
back, to ask him about these islands.   He received them
very well, and took them to his village, to give them
some large pieces of gold.   They arrived at a large river,
which the Indians crossed by swimming.   The Christians
were unable, so they turned back.   In all this district there
are very high mountains which seem to reach the sky, so
that the mountain in the island of Tenerife appears as
nothing in height and beauty, and they are all green with
trees.   Between them there are very delicious valleys, and
at the end of this port, to the south, there is a valley so

large that the end of it is not visible, though no mountains intervene, so that it seems to be 15 or 20 leagues long. A river flows through it, and it is all inhabited and cultivated, and as green as Castille in May or June; but the night contains 14 hours, the land being so far north. This port is very good for all the winds that can blow, being enclosed and deep, and the shores peopled by a good and gentle race without arms or evil designs. Any ship may lie within it without fear that other ships will enter at night to attack her, because, although the entrance is over two leagues wide, it is protected by reefs of rocks which are barely awash; and there is only a very narrow channel through the reef, which looks as if it had been artificially made, leaving an open door by which ships may enter. In the entrance there are 7 fathoms of depth up to the shore of a small flat island, which has a beach fringed with trees. The entrance is on the west side, and a ship can come without fear until she is close to the rock. On the N.W. side there are three islands, and a great river a league from the cape on one side of the port. It is the best harbour in the world, and the Admiral gave it the name of *Puerto de la mar de Santo Tomas*, because to-day it was that Saint's day. The Admiral called it a sea, owing to its size.

Saturday, 22nd of December.

At dawn the Admiral made sail to shape a course in search of the islands which the Indians had told him contained much gold, some of them having more gold than earth. But the weather was not favourable, so he anchored again, and sent away the boat to fish with a net. The Lord of that land,[1] who had a place near there, sent a large canoe full of people, including one of his principal

---

[1] This was Guacangari, Lord of Marien, afterwards the tried and steadfast friend of the Admiral.

attendants, to invite the Admiral to come with the ships to his land, where he would give him all he wanted. The Chief sent, by this servant, a girdle which, instead of a bag, had attached to it a mask with two large ears made of beaten gold, the tongue, and the nose. These people are very open-hearted, and whatever they are asked for they give most willingly; while, when they themselves ask for anything, they do so as if receiving a great favour. So says the Admiral. They brought the canoe alongside the boat, and gave the girdle to a boy; then they came on board with their mission. It took a good part of the day before they could be understood. Not even the Indians who were on board understood them well, because they have some differences of words for the names of things. At last their invitation was understood by signs. The Admiral determined to start to-morrow, although he did not usually sail on a Sunday, owing to a devout feeling, and not on account of any superstition whatever. But in the hope that these people would become Christians through the willingness they show, and that they will be subjects of the Sovereigns of Castille, and because he now holds them to be so, and that they may serve with love, he wished and endeavoured to please them. Before leaving, to-day, the Admiral sent six men to a large village three leagues to the westward, because the Chief had come the day before and said that he had some pieces of gold. When the Christians arrived, the Secretary of the Admiral, who was one of them, took the Chief by the hand. The Admiral had sent him, to prevent the others from imposing upon the Indians. As the Indians are so simple, and the Spaniards so avaricious and grasping, it does not suffice that the Indians should give them all they want in exchange for a bead or a bit of glass, but the Spaniards would take everything without any return at all. The Admiral always prohibits this, although, with the exception of gold, the things given by the Indians

are of little value.   But the Admiral, seeing the simplicity
of the Indians, and that they will give a piece of gold in
exchange for six beads, gave the order that nothing should
be received from them unless something had been given in
exchange.   Thus the Chief took the Secretary by the
hand and led him to his house, followed by the whole
village, which was very large.   He made his guests eat,
and the Indians brought them many cotton fabrics, and
spun-cotton in skeins.   In the afternoon the Chief gave
them three very fat geese and some small pieces of gold.
A great number of people went back with them, carrying
all the things they had got by barter, and they also carried
the Spaniards themselves across streams and muddy places.
The Admiral ordered some things to be given to the Chief,
and both he and his people were very well satisfied, truly
believing that the Christians had come from heaven, so that
they considered themselves fortunate in beholding them.
On this day more than 120 canoes came to the ships, all
full of people, and all bringing something, especially their
bread and fish, and fresh water in earthen jars.   They also
brought seeds of good kinds, and there was a grain which
they put into a porringer of water and drank it.   The
Indians who were on board said that this was very wholesome.

Sunday, 23rd of December.

The Admiral could not go with the ships to that land
whither he had been invited by the Chief, because there
was no wind.   But he sent, with the three messengers who
were waiting for the boats, some people, including the
Secretary.   While they were gone, he sent two of the
Indians he had on board with him to the villages which
were near the anchorage.   They returned to the ship with
a chief, who brought the news that there was a great
quantity of gold in that island of Española, and that

people from other parts came to buy it. They said that
here the Admiral would find as much as he wanted.
Others came, who confirmed the statement that there was
much gold in the island, and explained the way it was
collected. The Admiral understood all this with much
difficulty ; nevertheless, he concluded that there was a very
great quantity in those parts, and that, if he could find the
place whence it was got, there would be abundance ; and, if
not, there would be nothing. He believed there must be
a great deal, because, during the three days that he had
been in that port, he had got several pieces of gold, and
he could not believe that it was brought from another
land. "Our Lord, who holds all things in his hands, look
upon me, and grant what shall be for his service." These
are the Admiral's words. He says that, according to his
reckoning, a thousand people had visited the ship, all of
them bringing something. Before they come alongside,
at a distance of a crossbow-shot, they stand up in the
canoe with what they bring in their hands, crying out,
"Take it ! take it !" He also reckoned that 500 came to
the ship swimming, because they had no canoes, the ship
being near a league from the shore. Among the visitors,
five chiefs had come, sons of chiefs, with all their families
of wives and children, to see the Christians. The Admiral
ordered something to be given to all, because such gifts
were all well employed. "May our Lord favour me by
his clemency, that I may find this gold, I mean the mine
of gold, which I hold to be here, many saying that they
know it." These are his words. The boats arrived at
night, and said that there was a grand road as far as
they went, and they found many canoes, with people
who went to see the Admiral and the Christians, at the
mountain of *Caribatan*. They held it for certain that,
if the Christmas festival was kept in that port,[1] all the

---

[1] Port of Guarico.—N.

K

people of the island would come, which they calculated to be larger than England. All the people went
with them to the village,[1] which they said was the
largest, and the best laid out with streets, of any they
had seen. The Admiral says it is part of the *Punta Santa*,[2]
almost three leagues S.E. The canoes go very fast with
paddles ; so they went ahead to apprise the *Cacique*, as
they call the chief. They also have another greater name
—*Nitayno ;* but it was not clear whether they used it for
lord, or governor, or judge. At last the Cacique came to
them, and joined them in the square, which was clean-
swept, as was all the village. The population numbered
over 2,000 men. This king did great honour to the people
from the ship, and every inhabitant brought them something to eat and drink. Afterwards the king gave each
of them cotton cloths such as women wear, with parrots
for the Admiral, and some pieces of gold. The people
also gave cloths and other things from their houses to the
sailors ; and as for the trifles they got in return, they
seemed to look upon them as relics. When they wanted
to return in the afternoon, he asked them to stay until the
next day, and all the people did the same. When they
saw that the Spaniards were determined to go, they accompanied them most of the way, carrying the gifts of the
Cacique on their backs as far as the boats, which had been
left at the mouth of the river.

Monday, 24th of December.

Before sunrise the Admiral got under weigh with the
land-breeze. Among the numerous Indians who had
come to the ship yesterday, and had made signs that there

---

[1] Guarico.

[2] Columbus has not mentioned this point before. It is now called
San Honorato.—N.

was gold in the island, naming the places whence it was collected, the Admiral noticed one who seemed more fully informed, or who spoke with more willingness, so he asked him to come with the Christians and show them the position of the gold mines.   This Indian has a companion or relation with him, and among other places they mentioned where gold was found, they named *Cipango*, which they called *Civao*. Here they said that there was a great quantity of gold, and that the Cacique carried banners of beaten gold.   But they added that it was very far off to the eastward.

Here the Admiral addresses the following words to the Sovereigns: " Your Highnesses may believe that there is no better nor gentler people in the world. Your Highnesses ought to rejoice that they will soon become Christians, and that they will be taught the good customs of your kingdom.   A better race there cannot be, and both the people and the lands are in such quantity that I know not how to write it. I have spoken in the superlative degree of the country and people of Juana, which they call Cuba, but there is as much difference between them and this island and people as between day and night.   I believe that no one who should see them could say less than I have said, and I repeat that the things and the great villages of this island of Española, which they call *Bohio*, are wonderful.   All here have a loving manner and gentle speech, unlike the others, who seem to be menacing when they speak.   Both men and women are of good stature, and not black.   It is true that they all paint, some with black, others with other colours, but most with red. I know that they are tanned by the sun, but this does not affect them much.   Their houses and villages are pretty, each with a chief, who acts as their judge, and who is obeyed by them.   All these lords use few words, and have excellent manners.   Most of their orders are given by a sign with the hand, which is understood with surprising quickness." All these are the words of the Admiral.

He who would enter the sea of *Santo Tomé*[1] ought to stand for a good league across the mouth to a flat island in the middle, which was named *La Amiga*,[2] pointing her head towards it. When the ship is within a stone's-throw of it the course should be altered to make for the eastern shore, leaving the west side, and this shore, and not the other, should be kept on board, because a great reef runs out from the west, and even beyond that there are three sunken rocks. This reef comes within a lombard-shot of the *Amiga* island. Between them there are seven fathoms at least, with a gravelly bottom. Within, a harbour will be found large enough for all the ships in the world, which would be there without need of cables. There is another reef, with sunken rocks, on the east side of the island of *Amiga*, which are extensive and run out to sea, reaching within two leagues of the cape. But it appeared that between them there was an entrance, within two lombard-shots of *Amiga*, on the west side of *Monte Caribatan*, where there was a good and very large port.[3]

Tuesday, 25th of December.   Christmas.

Navigating yesterday, with little wind, from *Santo Tomé* to *Punta Santa*, and being a league from it, at about eleven o'clock at night the Admiral went down to get some sleep, for he had not had any rest for two days and a night. As it was calm, the sailor who steered the ship thought he would go to sleep, leaving the tiller in charge of a boy. The Admiral had forbidden this throughout the voyage, whether it was blowing or whether it was calm. The boys were never to be entrusted with the helm. The Admiral

---

[1] Entrance of the Bay of Açul.—N.   [2] Isla de Ratos.—N.
[3] Puerto Frances.—N.

had no anxiety respecting sand-banks and rocks, because, when he sent the boats to that king on Sunday, they had passed to the east of *Punta Santa* at least three leagues and a half, and the sailors had seen all the coast, and the rocks there are from *Punta Santa*, for a distance of three leagues to the E.S.E. They saw the course that should be taken, which had not been the case before, during this voyage. It pleased our Lord that, at twelve o'clock at night, when the Admiral had retired to rest, and when all had fallen asleep, seeing that it was a dead calm and the sea like glass, the tiller being in the hands of a boy, the current carried the ship on one of the sand-banks. If it had not been night the bank could have been seen, and the surf on it could be heard for a good league. But the ship ran upon it so gently that it could scarcely be felt. The boy, who felt the helm and heard the rush of the sea, cried out. The Admiral at once came up, and so quickly that no one had felt that the ship was aground. Presently the master of the ship,[1] whose watch it was, came on deck. The Admiral ordered him and others to launch the boat, which was on the poop, and lay out an anchor astern. The master, with several others, got into the boat, and the Admiral thought that they did so with the object of obeying his orders. But they did so in order to take refuge with the caravel, which was half a league to leeward. The caravel would not allow them to come on board, acting judiciously, and they therefore returned to the ship ; but the caravel's boat arrived first. When the Admiral saw that his own people fled in this way, the water rising and the ship being across the sea, seeing no other course, he ordered the masts to be cut away and the ship to be

---

[1] The master, who was also the owner, of the Admiral's ship was Juan de la Cosa of Santoña, afterwards well known as a draughtsman and pilot

lightened as much as possible, to see if she would come off.
But, as the water continued to rise, nothing more could be
done. Her side fell over across the sea, but it was nearly
calm. Then the timbers[1] opened, and the ship was lost.
The Admiral went to the caravel to arrange about the
reception of the ship's crew, and as a light breeze was
blowing from the land, and continued during the greater
part of the night, while it was unknown how far the bank
extended, he hove her to until daylight. He then went
back to the ship, inside the reef; first having sent a boat
on shore with Diego de Arana of Cordova, Alguazil of the
Fleet, and Pedro Gutierrez, Gentleman of the King's Bed-
chamber, to inform the king, who had invited the ships to
come on the previous Saturday. His town was about a
league and a half from the sand-bank. They reported
that he wept when he heard the news, and he sent all his
people with large canoes to unload the ship. This was
done, and they landed all there was between decks in a
very short time. Such was the great promptitude and
diligence shown by that king. He himself, with brothers
and relations, were actively assisting as well in the ship as
in the care of the property when it was landed, that all
might be properly guarded. Now and then he sent one of
his relations weeping to the Admiral, to console him,
saying that he must not feel sorrow or annoyance, for he
would supply all that was needed. The Admiral assured
the Sovereigns that there could not have been such good
watch kept in any part of Castille, for that there was not
even a needle missing. He ordered that all the property
should be placed by some houses which the king placed at
his disposal, until they were emptied, when everything
would be stowed and guarded in them. Armed men were

---

[1] *Conventos*, a word meaning the spaces filled with timber, between
the ribs. See Herrera, *Dec. I*, Lib. I, cap. 18.—N.

placed round the stores to watch all night. "The king and all his people wept. They are a loving people, without covetousness, and fit for anything ; and I assure your Highnesses that there is no better land nor people. They love their neighbours as themselves, and their speech is the sweetest and gentlest in the world, and always with a smile. Men and women go as naked as when their mothers bore them. Your Highnesses should believe that they have very good customs among themselves. The king is a man of remarkable presence, and with a certain self-contained manner that is a pleasure to see. They have good memories, wish to see everything, and ask the use of what they see." All this is written by the Admiral.[1]

Wednesday, 26th of December.

To-day, at sunrise, the king of that land came to the caravel *Niña*, where the Admiral was, and said to him, almost weeping, that he need not be sorry, for that he would give him all he had; that he had placed two large houses at the disposal of the Christians who were on shore, and that he would give more if they were required, and as many canoes as could load from the ship and discharge on shore, with as many people as were wanted. This had all been done yesterday, without so much as a needle being missed. "So honest are they," says the Admiral, "without any covetousness for the goods of others, and so above all was that virtuous king." While the Admiral was talking to him, another canoe arrived from a different place, bringing some pieces of gold, which the people in the canoe wanted to exchange for a hawk's bell; for there was nothing they

---

[1] Fernando Columbus, in the *Historie* (cap. xxxii), copies this account of the shipwreck by his father, the Admiral. His version differs somewhat in the expressions, but is the same in substance as the text from the copy of Las Casas.—N.

desired more than these bells. They had scarcely come
alongside when they called and held up the gold, saying
Chuq chuq for the bells, for they are quite mad about them.
After the king had seen this, and when the canoes which
came from other places had departed, he called the
Admiral and asked him to give orders that one of the bells
was to be kept for another day, when he would bring four
pieces of gold the size of a man's hand. The Admiral
rejoiced to hear this, and afterwards a sailor, who came
from the shore, told him that it was wonderful what pieces
of gold the men on shore were getting in exchange for next
to nothing. For a needle they got a piece of gold worth
two *castellanos*, and that this was nothing to what it would
be within a month. The king rejoiced much when he saw
that the Admiral was pleased. He understood that his
friend wanted much gold, and he said, by signs, that he knew
where there was, in the vicinity, a very large quantity; so
that he must be in good heart, for he should have as much
as he wanted. He gave some account of it, especially
saying that in *Cipango*, which they call *Cibao*, it is so abundant that it is of no value, and that they will bring it,
although there is also much more in the island of *Española*,
which they call *Bohio*, and in the province of *Caritaba*.
The king dined on board the caravel with the Admiral
and afterwards went on shore, where he received the
Admiral with much honour. He gave him a collation
consisting of three or four kinds of yams, with shellfish
and game, and other viands they have, besides the
bread they call *cazavi*. He then took the Admiral to
see some groves of trees near the houses, and they were
accompanied by at least a thousand people, all naked. The
Lord had on a shirt and a pair of gloves, given to him by
the Admiral, and he was more delighted with the gloves
than with anything else. In his manner of eating, both
as regards the high-bred air and the peculiar cleanliness,

he clearly showed his nobility.   After he had eaten, he
remained some time at table, and they brought him certain
herbs, with which he rubbed his hands.   The Admiral
thought that this was done to make them soft, and they
also gave him water for his hands.   After the meal he took
the Admiral to the beach.   The Admiral then sent for a
Turkish bow and a quiver of arrows, and took a shot at a
man of his company, who had been warned.   The chief,
who knew nothing about arms, as they neither have them
nor use them, thought this a wonderful thing.   He, however, began to talk of those of *Caniba*, whom they call
Caribes.   They come to capture the natives, and have bows
and arrows without iron, of which there is no memory in
any of these lands, nor of steel, nor any other metal except
gold and copper.   Of copper the Admiral had only seen
very little.   The Admiral said, by signs, that the Sovereigns
of Castille would order the Caribs to be destroyed, and
that all should be taken with their heads tied together.
He ordered a lombard and a hand-gun to be fired off, and
seeing the effect caused by its force and what the shots pene-
trated, the king was astonished.   When his people heard
the explosion they all fell on the ground.   They brought
the Admiral a large mask, which had pieces of gold for the
eyes and ears and in other parts, and this they gave, with
other trinkets of gold that the same king had put on the
head and round the neck of the Admiral, and of other
Christians, to whom they also gave many pieces.   The
Admiral received much pleasure and consolation from
these things, which tempered the anxiety and sorrow he
felt at the loss of the ship.   He knew our Lord had
caused the ship to stop here, that a settlement might
be formed.   " From this", he says, "originated so many
things that, in truth, the disaster was really a piece of
good fortune.   For it is certain that, if I had not lost the
ship, I should have gone on without anchoring in this

place, which is within a great bay, having two or three
reefs of rock. I should not have left people in the country
during this voyage, nor even, if I had desired to leave them,
should I have been able to obtain so much information, nor
such supplies and provisions for a fortress. And true it is that
many people had asked me to give them leave to remain.
Now I have given orders for a tower and a fort, both well
built, and a large cellar, not because I believe that such de-
fences will be necessary. I believe that with the force I have
with me I could subjugate the whole island, which I believe
to be larger than Portugal, and the population double. But
they are naked and without arms, and hopelessly timid.
Still, it is advisable to build this tower, being so far from
your Highnesses. The people may thus know the skill of
the subjects of your Highnesses, and what they can do ;
and will obey them with love and fear. So they make
preparations to build the fortress, with provision of bread
and wine for more than a year, with seeds for sowing, the
ship's boat, a caulker and carpenter, a gunner and cooper.
Many among these men have a great desire to serve your
Highnesses and to please me, by finding out where the
mine is whence the gold is brought. Thus everything is
got in readiness to begin the work. Above all, it was so
calm that there was scarcely wind nor wave when the ship
ran aground." This is what the Admiral says ; and he
adds more to show that it was great good luck, and the
settled design of God, that the ship should be lost in order
that people might be left behind. If it had not been for
the treachery of the master and his boat's crew, who were
all or mostly his countrymen,[1] in neglecting to lay out the
anchor so as to haul the ship off in obedience to the

---

[1] Juan de la Cosa, the master, was a native of Santoña, on the north
coast of Spain. There were two other Santoña men on board, and
several from the north coast.

Admiral's orders, she would have been saved.   In that
case, the same knowledge of the land as has been gained
in these days would not have been secured, for the
Admiral always proceeded with the object of discovering,
and never intended to stop more than a day at any
one place, unless he was detained by the wind.   Still, the
ship was very heavy and unsuited for discovery.   It was
the people of Palos who obliged him to take such a ship,
by not complying " with what they had promised to the
King and Queen, namely, to supply suitable vessels for
this expedition.   This they did not do.   Of all that there
was on board the ship, not a needle, nor a board, nor
a nail was lost, for she remained as whole as when she
sailed, except that it was necessary to cut away and level
down in order to get out the jars and merchandise, which
were landed and carefully guarded."   He trusted in God
that, when he returned from Spain, according to his intention, he would find a ton of gold collected by barter by
those he was to leave behind, and that they would have
found the mine, and spices in such quantities that the
Sovereigns would, in three years, be able to undertake
and fit out an expedition to go and conquer the Holy
Sepulchre.   " Thus", he says, " I protest to your Highnesses that all the profits of this my enterprise may be
spent in the conquest of Jerusalem.   Your Highnesses
may laugh, and say that it is pleasing to you, and that,
without this, you entertain that desire."   These are the
Admiral's words.

Thursday, 27th of December.

The king of that land came alongside the caravel at
sunrise, and said that he had sent for gold, and that he
would collect all he could before the Admiral departed ;
but he begged him not to go.   The king and one of his

brothers, with another very intimate relation, dined with the Admiral, and the two latter said they wished to go to Castille with him. At this time the news came that the caravel *Pinta* was in a river at the end of this island. Presently the Cacique sent a canoe there, and the Admiral sent a sailor in it. For it was wonderful how devoted the Cacique was to the Admiral. The necessity was now evident of hurrying on preparations for the return to Castille.

Friday, 28th of December.

The Admiral went on shore to give orders and hurry on the work of building the fort, and to settle what men should remain behind. The king, it would seem, had watched him getting into the boat, and quickly went into his house, dissimulating, sending one of his brothers to receive the Admiral, and conduct him to one of the houses that had been set aside for the Spaniards, which was the largest and best in the town. In it there was a couch made of palm matting, where they sat down. Afterwards the brother sent an attendant to say that the Admiral was there, as if the king did not know that he had come. The Admiral, however, believed that this was a feint in order to do him more honour. The attendant gave the message, and the Cacique came in great haste, and put a large soft piece of gold he had in his hand round the Admiral's neck. They remained together until the evening, arranging what had to be done.

Saturday, 29th of December.

A very youthful nephew of the king came to the caravel at sunrise, who showed a good understanding and disposition. As the Admiral was always working to find out the origin of the gold, he asked everyone, for he could now understand somewhat by signs. This youth told him

that, at a distance of four days' journey, there was an
island to the eastward called *Guarionex*, and others called
Macorix, *Mayonic*, *Fuma*, *Cibao*, and *Coroay*,[1] in which
there was plenty of gold. The Admiral wrote these names
down, and now understood what had been said by a
brother of the king, who was annoyed with him, as the
Admiral understood. At other times the Admiral had
suspected that the king had worked against his knowing
where the gold had its origin and was collected, that he
might not go away to barter in another part of the island.
For there are such a number of places in this same island
that it is wonderful. After nightfall the king sent a large
mask of gold, and asked for a washhand basin and jug.
The Admiral thought he wanted them for patterns to copy
from, and therefore sent them.

Sunday, 30th of December.

The Admiral went on shore to dinner, and came at a
time when five kings had arrived, all with their crowns,
who were subject to this king, named *Guacanagari*. They
represented a very good state of affairs, and the Admiral
says to the Sovereigns that it would have given them
pleasure to see the manner of their arrival. On landing,
the Admiral was received by the king, who led him by the
arms to the same house where he was yesterday, where
there were chairs, and a couch on which the Admiral sat.
Presently the king took the crown off his head and put it
on the Admiral's head, and the Admiral took from his
neck a collar of beautiful beads of several different colours,
which looked very well in all its parts, and put it on the
king. He also took off a cloak of fine material, in which
he had dressed himself that day, and dressed the king in

---

[1] These were not islands, but provinces of Española, Guarionex
was the chief of the "Vega Real".

it, and sent for some coloured boots, which he put on his feet, and he put a large silver ring on his finger, because he had heard that he had admired greatly a silver ornament worn by one of the sailors. The king was highly delighted and well satisfied, and two of those kings who were with him came with him to where the Admiral was, and each gave him a large piece of gold. At this time an Indian came and reported that it was two days since he left the caravel *Pinta* in a port to the eastward. The Admiral returned to the caravel, and Vicente Anes,[1] the captain, said that he had seen the rhubarb plant, and that they had it on the island *Amiga*, which is at the entrance of the sea of *Santo Tomé*, six leagues off, and that he had recognised the branches and roots. They say that rhubarb forms small branches above ground, and fruit like green mulberries, almost dry, and the stalk, near the root, is as yellow and delicate as the best colour for painting, and underground the root grows like a large pear.[2]

Monday, 31st of December.

To-day the Admiral was occupied in seeing that water and fuel were taken on board for the voyage to Spain, to give early notice to the Sovereigns, that they might despatch ships to complete the discoveries. For now the business appeared to be so great and important that the Admiral was astonished. He did not wish to go until he had examined all the land to the eastward, and explored the coast, so as to know the route to Castille, with a view to sending sheep and cattle. But as he had been left with only a single vessel, it did not appear prudent to encounter the dangers that are inevitable in making discoveries. He

---

[1] For Yañez. Vicente Yañez Pinzon.
[2] See *Letter to Santangel*, p. 15.

complained that all this inconvenience had been caused by
the caravel *Pinta* having parted company.

Tuesday, 1st of January 1493.

At midnight the Admiral sent a boat to the island
Amiga to bring the rhubarb. It returned at vespers with
a bundle of it. They did not bring more because they had
no spade to dig it up with ; it was taken to be shown to
the Sovereigns. The king of that land said that he had sent
many canoes for gold. The canoe returned that had been
sent for tidings of the *Pinta*, without having found her.
The sailor who went in the canoe said that twenty leagues
from there he had seen a king who wore two large plates
of gold on his head, but when the Indians in the canoe
spoke to him he took them off. He also saw much gold
on other people. The Admiral considered that the King
Guacanagari ought to have prohibited his people from
selling gold to the Christians, in order that it might all pass
through his hands. But the king knew the places, as
before stated, where there was such a quantity that it was
not valued. The spicery also is extensive, and is worth
more than pepper or *manegueta*.[1] He left instructions to
those who wished to remain that they were to collect as
much as they could.

Wednesday, 2nd of January.

In the morning the Admiral went on shore to take leave of
the King Guacanagari, and to depart from him in the name
of the Lord. He gave him one of his shirts. In order to
show him the force of the lombards, and what effect they
had, he ordered one to be loaded and fired into the side of
the ship that was on shore, for this was apposite to the conversation respecting the Caribs, with whom Guacanagari
was at war. The king saw whence the lombard-shot

---

[1] See note at page 154.

came, and how it passed through the side of the ship
and went far away over the sea. The Admiral also
ordered a skirmish of the crews of the ships, fully armed,
saying to the Cacique that he need have no fear of the
Caribs even if they should come. All this was done that
the king might look upon the men who were left behind as
friends, and that he might also have a proper fear of them.
The king took the Admiral to dinner at the house where he
was established, and the others who came with him. The
· Admiral strongly recommended to his friendship Diego de
Arana, Pedro Gutierrez, and Rodrigo Escovedo, whom he
left jointly as his lieutenants over the people who remained
behind, that all might be well regulated and governed for
the service of their Highnesses. The Cacique showed much
love for the Admiral, and great sorrow at his departure,
especially when he saw him go on board. A relation of
that king said to the Admiral that he had ordered a statue
of pure gold to be made, as big as the Admiral, and that
it would be brought within ten days. The Admiral
embarked with the intention of sailing presently, but there
was no wind.

He left on that island of Española, which the Indians
called *Bohio*, 39 men[1] with the fortress,[2] and he says that

---

[1] The actual number was 44, according to the official list, namely:

1. Diego de Arana of Cordova (*Alguazil Mayor*).	7. Castillo of Seville (*Assayer*).
	8. Antonio of Jaen.
2. Rodrigo de Escobedo (*Secretary*).	9. Alvaro Perez Osorio.
	10. Cristoval de Alamo of Niebla.
3. Pedro Gutierrez (*Gentleman of the King's Bedchamber*).	11. Diego Garcia of Xeres.
	12. Diego de Tordoya of Cabeza de Vaca.
4. Bachiller Bernardo de Tapia (*Volunteer*).	13. Diego de Capilla of Almeden.
5. Alonzo Velez of Seville.	14. Diego of Mambles.
6. Alonzo Perez Osorio.	15. Diego de Mendoza.

---

[2] To which he gave the name of "Villa de la Navidad", because
the ship was lost on Christmas Day.

they were great friends of Guacanagari. The lieutenants placed over them were Diego de Arana of Cordova, Pedro Gutierrez, Gentleman of the King's Bedchamber, and Rodrigo de Escovedo, a native of Seogvia, nephew of Fray Rodrigo Perez, with all the powers he himself received from the Sovereigns. He left behind all the merchandise which had been provided for bartering, which was much, that they might trade for gold. He also left bread for a year's supply, wine, and much artillery. He also left the ship's boat, that they, most of them being sailors, might go, when the time seemed convenient, to discover the gold mine, in order that the Admiral, on his return, might find much gold. They were also to find a good site for a town, for this was not altogether a desirable port ; especially as the gold the natives brought came from the east ; also, the farther to the east the nearer to Spain. He also left seeds for sowing, and his officers, the Alguazil and Secretary, as well as a ship's carpenter, a caulker, a good gunner well

16. Diego de Montalvan of Jaen.	30. Juan del Barco of Avila.
17. Domingo de Bermeo.	31. Pedro Carbacho of Caceres.
18. Francisco de Godoy of Seville.	32. Pedro of Talavera.
19. Francisco de Vergara of Seville.	33. Sebastian of Majorca.
20. Francisco of Aranda.	34. Tallarte (Alard ?) of Lajes
21. Francisco Henao of Avila.	(an Englishman).
22. Francisco Jimenes of Seville.	35. Diego de Torpa.
23. Gabriel Baraona of Belmonte.	36. Francisco Fernandez.
24. Gonzalo Fernandez of Sego-	37. Hernando de Porcuna.
via.	38. Juan de Urminga.
25. Gonzalo Fernandez of Leon.	39. Juan de Morcillo.
26. Guillelmo (Irish, native of	40. Juan de Villar.
Galway).	41. Juan de Mendoza.
27. Jorge Gonzales of Trigueros.	42. Martin de Logrosan.
28. Juan de Cueva.	43. Pedro de Foronda.
29. Juan Patiño of La Sarena.	44. Tristan de San Jorge.

The names are given in a document printed by Navarrete ; which is a notice to the next of kin to apply for wages due, dated Burgos, December 20th, 1507. Oviedo and Herrera say that a surgeon named Maestre Juan was also left behind

L

acquainted with artillery, a cooper, a physician, and a. tailor, all being seamen as well.[1]

Thursday, 3rd of January.

The Admiral did not go to-day, because three of the Indians whom he had brought from the islands, and who had staid behind, arrived, and said that the others with their women would be there at sunrise.[2] The sea also was rather rough, so that they could not land from the boat. He determined to depart to-morrow, with the grace of God. The Admiral said that if he had the caravel *Pinta* with him he could make sure of shipping a ton of gold, because he could then follow the coasts of these islands, which he would not do alone, for fear some accident might impede his return to Castille, and prevent him from reporting all he had discovered to the Sovereigns. If it was certain that the caravel *Pinta* would arrive safely in Spain with Martin Alonso Pinzon, he would not hesitate to act as he desired ; but as he had no certain tidings of him, and as he might return and tell lies to the Sovereigns, that he might not receive the punishment he deserved for having done so much harm in having parted company without permission, and impeded the good service that might have been done ; the Admiral could only trust in our Lord that he would grant favourable weather, and remedy all things.

Friday, 4th of January.

At sunrise the Admiral weighed the anchor, with little wind, and turned her head N.W. to get clear of the reef, by another channel wider than the one by which he

---

[1] Herrera gives the farewell speech of the Admiral to those who were left behind at Navidad. (*Dec. I*, Lib. I, cap. xx.)

[2] Las Casas says that the Admiral brought ten or twelve Indians to Castille with him. (*Ibid.*, I, p. 419.)

entered, which, with others, is very good for coming in front of the *Villa de la Navidad*, in all which the least depth is from 3 to 9 fathoms. These two channels run N.W. and S.E., and the reefs are long, extending from the *Cabo Santo* to the *Cabo de Sierpe* for more than six leagues, and then a good three leagues out to sea. At a league outside *Cabo Santo* there are not more than 8 fathoms of depth, and inside that cape, on the east side, there are many sunken rocks, and channels to enter between them. All this coast trends N.W. and S.E., and it is all beach, with the land very level for about a quarter of a league inland. After that distance there are very high mountains, and the whole is peopled with a very good race, as they showed themselves to the Christians. Thus the Admiral navigated to the east, shaping a course for a very high mountain, which looked like an island, but is not one, being joined to the mainland by a very low neck. The mountain has the shape of a very beautiful tent.[1] He gave it the name of *Monte Cristi*. It is due east of *Cabo Santo*, at a distance of 18 leagues.[2] That day, owing to the light wind, they could not reach within six leagues of Monte Cristi. He discovered four very low and sandy islets,[3] with a reef extending N.W. and S.E. Inside, there is a large gulf,[4] which extends from this mountain to the S.E. at least twenty leagues,[5] which must all be shallow, with many sand-banks, and inside numerous rivers which are not navigable. At the same time the sailor who was sent in the canoe to get tidings of the *Pinta* reported that '

---

[1] *Alfaneque;* which Las Casas explains as *Tienda de Campo.* Hazard (*Santo Domingo*, 1873, p. 352) says it is called the *Morro*, and *La Grange* (the barn), "name given by Columbus". *Alfaneque* means a booth or tent, not a barn.

[2] It is N. 80° E. 70 leagues.—N.

[3] Los siete Hermanos.—N.   [4] Bahia de Manzanillo.—N.

[5] Should be S.W. three leagues.

he saw a river[1] into which ships might enter.   The Admiral
anchored at a distance of six leagues[2] from *Monte Cristi*, in
19 fathoms, and so kept clear of many rocks and reefs.
Here he remained for the night.   The Admiral gives
notice to those who would go to the *Villa de la Navidad*
that, to make *Monte Cristi*, he should stand off the land
two leagues, etc.   (But as the coast is now known it is not
given here.)   The Admiral concluded that Cipango was
in that island, and that it contained much gold, spices,
mastick, and rhubarb.

Saturday, 5th of January.

At sunrise the Admiral made sail with the land-breeze,
and saw that to the S.S.E.[3] of *Monte Cristi*, between it
and an island, there seemed to be a good port to anchor
in that night.   He shaped an E.S.E. course, afterwards
S.S.E., for six leagues round the high land, and found
a depth of 17 fathoms, with a very clean bottom, going on
for three leagues with the same soundings.   Afterwards it
shallowed to 12 fathoms up to the *morro* of the mountain,
and off the *morro*, at one league, the depth of 9 fathoms
was found, the bottom clean, and all fine sand.   The
Admiral followed the same course until he came between
the mountain and the island,[4] where he found 3½ fathoms
at low water, a very good port, and here he anchored.[5]
He went in the boat to the islet, where he found remains of
fire and footmarks, showing that fishermen had been there.

---

[1] Rio Tapion, in the Bahia de Manzanillo.—N.
[2] A mistake for three leagues.
[3] Should be W.S.W.
[4] Isla Cabra.
[5] Anchorage of Monte Cristi.   It is now a depôt for receiving
mahogany and other woods from the neighbouring country, to be
shipped in small schooners to Puerto Plata.   At one time it was a
much more important place.   (*Hazard*, p. 353.)

Here they saw many stones painted in colours, or a quarry of such stones, very beautifully worked by nature, suited for the building of a church or other public work, like those he found on the island of San Salvador. On this islet he also found many plants of mastick. He says that this *Monte Cristi* is very fine and high, but accessible, and of a very beautiful shape, all the land round it being low, a very fine plain, from which the height rises, looking at a distance like an island disunited from other land.[1] Beyond the mountain, to the east, he saw a cape at a distance of 24 miles, which he named *Cabo del Becerro*,[2] whence to the mountain for two leagues there are reefs of rocks, though it appeared as if there were navigable channels between them. It would, however, be advisable to approach in daylight, and to send a boat ahead to sound. From the mountain eastward to *Cabo del Becerro*, for four leagues, there is a beach, and the land is low, but the rest is very high, with beautiful mountains and some cultivation. Inland, a chain of mountains runs N.E. and S.W., the most beautiful he had seen, appearing like the hills of Cordova. Some other very lofty mountains appear in the distance towards the south and S.E., and very extensive green valleys with large rivers : all this in such quantity that he did not believe he had exaggerated a thousandth part. Afterwards he saw, to the eastward of the mountain, a land which appeared like that of *Monte Cristi* in size and beauty. Further to the east and N.E. there is land which is not so high, extending for some hundred miles or near it.

Sunday, 6th of January.

That port is sheltered from all winds, except north and N.W., and these winds seldom blow in this region. Even

---

[1] Las Casas says that this is an accurate description.
[2] Punta Rucia.

when the wind is from those quarters, shelter may be found near the islet in 3 or 4 fathoms. At sunset the Admiral made sail to proceed along the coast, the course being east, except that it is necessary to look out for several reefs of stone and sand, within which there are good anchorages, with channels leading to them. After noon it blew fresh from the east. The Admiral ordered a sailor to go to the mast-head to look out for reefs, and he saw the caravel *Pinta* coming, with the wind aft, and she joined the Admiral. As there was no place to anchor, owing to the rocky bottom, the Admiral returned for ten leagues to *Monte Cristi*, with the *Pinta* in company. Martin Alonso Pinzon came on board the caravel *Niña*, where the Admiral was, and excused himself by saying that he had parted company against his will, giving reasons for it. But the Admiral says that they were all false; and that on the night when Pinzon parted company he was influenced by pride and covetousness. He could not understand whence had come the insolence and disloyalty with which Pinzon had treated him during the voyage. The Admiral had taken no notice, because he did not wish to give place to the evil works of Satan, who desired to impede the voyage. It appeared that one of the Indians, who had been put on board the caravel by the Admiral with others, had said that there was much gold in an island called *Baneque*, and, as Pinzon's vessel was light and swift, he determined to go there, parting company with the Admiral, who wished to remain and explore the coasts of Juana and Española, with an easterly course. When Martin Alonso arrived at the island of *Baneque* he found no gold. He then went to the coast of Española, on information from the Indians that there was a great quantity of gold and many mines in that island of Española, which the Indians call *Bohio*. He thus arrived near the *Villa de Navidad*, about 15 leagues from it,

having then been absent more than twenty days, so that
the news brought by the Indians was correct, on account
of which the King Guacanagari sent a canoe, and the
Admiral put a sailor on board; but the *Pinta* must have
gone before the canoe arrived. The Admiral says that
the *Pinta* obtained much gold by barter, receiving large
pieces the size of two fingers in exchange for a needle.
Martin Alonso took half, dividing the other half among
the crew. The Admiral then says: "Thus I am con-
vinced that our Lord miraculously caused that vessel to
remain here, this being the best place in the whole island
to form a settlement, and the nearest to the gold mines."
He also says that he knew "of another great island,[1] to
the south of the island of Juana, in which there is more
gold than in this island, so that they collect it in bits the
size of beans, while in Española they find the pieces the
size of grains of corn.[2] They call that island *Yamaye*.
The Admiral also heard of an island further east, in which
there were only women, having been told this by many
people. He was also informed that *Yamaye* and the
island of Española were ten days' journey in a canoe from
the mainland, which would be about 70 or 80 leagues, and
that there the people wore clothes.

Monday, 7th of January.

This day the Admiral took the opportunity of caulking
the caravel, and the sailors were sent to cut wood. They
found mastick and aloes in abundance.

----

[1] Jamaica.

[2] Las Casas says that the pieces were even as large as a loaf of
bread of Alcalá, or as a quarter loaf of Valladolid, and that he had
seen them of that size. He adds that many are found weighing a
pound to eight pounds in Española

Tuesday, 8th of January.

As the wind was blowing fresh from the east and S.E., the Admiral did not get under weigh this morning. He ordered the caravel to be filled up with wood and water and with all other necessaries for the voyage. He wished to explore all the coast of Española in this direction. But those he appointed to the caravels as captains were brothers, namely, Martin Alonso Pinzon and Vicente Anes. They also had followers who were filled with pride and avarice, considering that all now belonged to them, and unmindful of the honour the Admiral had done them. They had not and did not obey his orders, but did and said many unworthy things against him ; while Martin Alonso had deserted him from the 21st of November until the 6th of January without cause or reason, but from disaffection. All these things had been endured in silence by the Admiral in order to secure a good end to the voyage. He determined to return as quickly as possible, to get rid of such an evil company, with whom he thought it necessary to dissimulate, although they were a mutinous set, and though he also had with him many good men ; for it was not a fitting time for dealing out punishment.

The Admiral got into the boat and went up the river[1] which is near, towards the S.S.W. of *Monte Cristi*, a good league. This is where the sailors went to get fresh water for the ships. He found that the sand at the mouth of the river, which is very large and deep, was full of very fine gold, and in astonishing quantity. The Admiral thought that it was pulverized in the drift down the river, but in a

---

[1] This is the large river *Yaqui*, which contains much gold in its sand. It was afterwards called the "Santiago". Las Casas thinks that Columbus may have found gold on this occasion, but that much of what he saw was *margasita*. (*Las Casas*, i, p. 428.)

short time he found many grains as large as horse-beans, while there was a great deal of the fine powder.

As the fresh water mixed with the salt when it entered the sea, he ordered the boat to go up for the distance of a stone's-throw. They filled the casks from the boat, and when they went back to the caravel they found small bits of gold sticking to the hoops of the casks and of the barrel. The Admiral gave the name of *Rio del Oro* to the river.[1] Inside the bar it is very deep, though the mouth is shallow and very wide. The distance to the *Villa de la Navidad* is 17 leagues,[2] and there are several large rivers on the intervening coast, especially three which probably contain much more gold than this one, because they are larger. This river is nearly the size of the Guadalquivir at Cordova, and from it to the gold mines the distance is not more than 20 leagues.[3] The Admiral further says that he did not care to take the sand containing gold, because their Highnesses would have it all as their property at their town of Navidad ; and because his first object was now to bring the news and to get rid of the evil company that was with him, whom he had always said were a mutinous set.

Wednesday, 9th of January.

The Admiral made sail at midnight, with the wind S.E., and shaped an E.N.E. course, arriving at a point named *Punta Roja*,[4] which is 60 miles[5] east of *Monte Cristi*, and anchored under its lee three hours before nightfall.

---

[1] Afterwards called the *Rio de Santiago*.
[2] This should be 8 leagues.
[3] Las Casas says the distance to the mines is not 4 leagues.
[4] Punta Isabelica.
[5] The distance is 10½ leagues, or 42 of the Italian miles used by Columbus.

He did not venture to go out at night, because there are many reefs, until they are known. Afterwards, if, as will probably be the case, channels are found between them, the anchorage, which is good and well sheltered, will be profitable. The country between *Monte Cristi* and this point where the Admiral anchored is very high land, with beautiful plains, the range running east and west, all green and cultivated, with numerous streams of water, so that it is wonderful to see such beauty. In all this country there are many turtles, and the sailors took several when they came on shore to lay their eggs at *Monte Cristi*, as large as a great wooden buckler.

On the previous day, when the Admiral went to the *Rio del Oro*, he saw three mermaids,[1] which rose well out of the sea ; but they are not so beautiful as they are painted, though to some extent they have the form of a human face. The Admiral says that he had seen some, at other times, in Guinea, on the coast of the Manequeta.[2]

---

[1] The mermaids of Columbus are the *manatis*, or sea-cows of the Caribean Sea and great South American rivers. They are now scarcely ever seen out at sea. Their resemblance to human beings, when rising in the water, must have been very striking. They have small rounded heads, and cervical vertebræ which form a neck, enabling the animal to turn its head about. The fore-limbs also, instead of being pectoral fins, have the character of the arm and hand of the higher mammalia. These peculiarities, and their very human way of suckling their young, holding it by the forearm, which is movable at the elbow-joint, suggested the idea of mermaids. The congener of the *manati*, which had been seen by Columbus on the coast of Guinea, is the *dugong*.

[2] Las Casas has " en la costa de Guinea, donde se coja la *mane-queta*" (i, 430). *Amomum Melequeta*, an herbaceous, reed-like plant, three to five feet high, is found along the coast of Africa, from Sierra Leone to the Congo. Its seeds were called " Grains of Paradise", or *maniguetta*, and the coast alluded to by Columbus, between Liberia and Cape Palmas, was hence called the Grain Coast. The grains were used as a condiment, like pepper, and in making the spiced wine called *hippocras*. At present, about 1,705 cwts. are exported,

The Admiral says that this night, in the name of our Lord, he would set out on his homeward voyage without any further delay whatever, for he had found what he sought, and he did not wish to have further cause of offence with Martin Alonso until their Highnesses should know the news of the voyage and what had been done. Afterwards he says, " I will not suffer the deeds of evil-disposed persons, with little worth, who, without respect for him to whom they owe their positions, presume to set up their own wills with little ceremony."

Thursday, 10th of January.

He departed from the place where he had anchored, and at sunset he reached a river, to which he gave the name of *Rio de Gracia*, three leagues to the S.E. He came to at the mouth,[1] where there is good anchorage on the east side. There is a bar with no more than two fathoms of water, and very narrow across the entrance. It is a good and well-sheltered port, except that there it is often misty, owing to which the caraval *Pinta*, under Martin Alonso, received a good deal of damage. He had been here bartering for 16 days, and got much gold, which was what Martin Alonso wanted. As soon as he heard from the Indians that the Admiral was on the coast of the same island of Española, and that he could not avoid him, Pinzon came to him. He wanted all the people of the ship to swear that he had not been there more than six days. But his treachery was so public that it could not be concealed. He had made a law that half of all the gold that was collected was his. When he left this port he

---

chiefly from Cape Coast Castle and Accra ; used in cattle medicines and to give pungency to cordials. See *Hanbury's Pharmacographia*, p. 590.

[1] Rio Chuzona chica.—N.

took four men and two girls by force. But the Admiral
ordered that they should be clothed and put on shore to
return to their homes. "This", the Admiral says, "is a
service of your Highnesses. For all the men and women
are subjects of your Highnesses, as well in this island as in
the others. Here, where your Highnesses already have a
settlement, the people ought to be treated with honour and
favour, seeing that this island has so much gold and such
good spice-yielding lands."

Friday, 11th of January.

At midnight the Admiral left the *Rio de Gracia* with
the land-breeze, and steered eastward until he came to a
cape named *Belprado*, at a distance of four leagues. To
the S.E. is the mountain to which he gave the name of
Monte de Plata,[1] eight leagues distant. Thence from the
cape *Belprado* to E.S.E. is the point named *Angel*, eighteen
leagues distant; and from this point to the *Monte de
Plata* there is a gulf, with the most beautiful lands in the
world, all high and fine lands which extend far inland.
Beyond there is a range of high mountains running east and
west, very grand and beautiful. At the foot of this mountain
there is a very good port,[2] with 14 fathoms in the entrance.
The mountain is very high and beautiful, and all the country
is well peopled. The Admiral believed there must be fine
rivers and much gold. At a distance of 4 leagues E.S.E.

---

[1] So called because the summit is always covered with white or
silver clouds. A monastery of Dominicans was afterwards built on
Monte de Plata, in which Las Casas began to write his history of the
Indies in the year 1527. (*Las Casas*, iv, p. 254.)

[2] Puerto de Plata, where a flourishing seaport town was afterwards
established; founded by Ovanda in 1502. It had fallen to decay in
1606. In 1822 it was again a flourishing place, but was destroyed by
the Spaniards in 1865.

of *Cabo del Angel* there is a cape named *Punta del Hierro,*[1]
and on the same course, 4 more leagues, a point is reached
named *Punta Seca.*[2] Thence, 6 leagues further on, is *Cabo
Redondo,*[3] and further on *Cabo Frances,* where a large bay[4]
is formed, but there did not appear to be anchorage in it.
A league further on is *Cabo del Buen Tiempo,* and thence,
a good league S.S.E., is *Cabo Tajado.*[5] Thence, to the
south, another cape was sighted at a distance of about
15 leagues. To-day great progress was made, as wind and
tide were favourable. The Admiral did not venture to
anchor for fear of the rocks, so he was hove-to all night.

Saturday, 12th of January.

Towards dawn the Admiral filled and shaped a course
to the east with a fresh wind, running 20 miles before daylight, and in two hours afterwards 24 miles. Thence he saw
land to the south,[6] and steered towards it, distant 48 miles.
During the night he must have run 28 miles N.N.E., to
keep the vessels out of danger. When he saw the land, he
named one cape that he saw *Cabo de Padre y Hijo,* because
at the east point there are two rocks, one larger than the
other.[7] Afterwards, at two leagues to the eastward, he saw
a very fine bay between two grand mountains. He saw
that it was a very large port with a very good approach ; but,
as it was very early in the morning, and as the greater part
of the time it was blowing from the east, and then they
had a N.N.W. breeze, he did not wish to delay any more.

---

[1] Punta Macuris. The distance is 3, not 4 leagues.—N.

[2] Punta Sesua. The distance is only one league.—N.

[3] Cabo de la Roca. It should be 5, not 6 leagues.—N.

[4] Bahia Escocesa.

[5] Las Casas says that none of these names were retained, even in
his time.

[6] This was the Peninsula of Samana.   [7] Isla Yazual.—N.

He continued his course to the east as far as a very high and beautiful cape, all of scarped rock, to which he gave the name of *Cabo del Enamorado*,[1] which was 32 miles to the east of the port named *Puerto Sacro*.[2] On rounding the cape, another finer and loftier point came in sight,[3] like Cape St. Vincent in Portugal, 12 miles east of *Cabo del Enamorado*. As soon as he was abreast of the *Cabo del Enamorado*, the Admiral saw that there was a great bay[4] between this and the next point, three leagues across, and in the middle of it a small island.[5] The depth is great at the entrance close to the land. He anchored here in twelve fathoms, and sent the boat on shore for water, and to see if intercourse could be opened with the natives, but they all fled. He also anchored to ascertain whether this was all one land with the island of Española, and to make sure that this was a gulf, and not a channel, forming another island. He remained astonished at the great size of Española.

Sunday, 13th of January.

The Admiral did not leave the port, because there was no land-breeze with which to go out. He wished to shift to another better port, because this was rather exposed. He also wanted to wait, in that haven, the conjunction of the sun and moon, which would take place on the 17th of this month, and their opposition with Jupiter and conjunction with Mercury, the sun being in opposition to Jupiter,[6]

---

[1] Cabro Cabron, or Lover's Cape; the extreme N.E. point of the sland, rising nearly 2,000 feet above the sea.

[2] Puerto Yaqueron.

[3] Cabo Samana; called Cabo de San Theramo afterwards by Columbus.

[4] The Bay of Samana.   [5] Cayo de Levantados.

[6] Las Casas thinks that the text is here corrupt, owing to the mistakes of the transcriber from the book of the navigation of the

which is the cause of high winds. He sent the boat on
shore to a beautiful beach to obtain yams for food. They
found some men with bows and arrows, with whom they
stopped to speak, buying two bows and many arrows from
them. They asked one of them to come on board the
caravel and see the Admiral; who says that he was very
wanting in reverence, more so than any native he had yet
seen. His face was all stained with charcoal, but in all
parts there is the custom of painting the body different
colours. He wore his hair very long, brought together and
fastened behind, and put into a small net of parrots'
feathers.[1] He was naked, like all the others. The Admiral
supposed that he belonged to the Caribs,[2] who eat men,
and that the gulf he had seen yesterday formed this part
of the land into an island by itself. The Admiral asked
about the Caribs, and he pointed to the east, near at hand,
which means that he saw the Admiral yesterday before he
entered the bay. The Indian said there was much gold to
the east, pointing to the poop of the caravel, which was a
good size, meaning that there were pieces as large. He
called gold *tuob*, and did not understand *caona*,[3] as they
call it in the first part of the island that was visited, nor
nozay, the name in San Salvador and the other islands.
Copper is called *tuob* in Española. He also spoke of

Admiral (i, p. 433). Doubtless, stormy weather was predicted under
the above conditions in the Old World, in some almanack on board,
and Columbus prudently considered whether he would wait a few
days to see if similar causes produced like effects in the New World.
He, however, did not wait until the 17th.

[1] Las Casas says that the *Ciguayos* wore their hair in this
way.

[2] According to Las Casas, these were not Caribs, for no Caribs
were ever settled in Española.

[3] *Caona* is the name for gold in the greater part of Española, but
there were two or three dialects.

the island of *Goanin*,[1] where there was much *tuob*. The
Admiral says that he had received notices of these islands
from many persons; that in the other islands the natives
were in great fear of the *Caribs*, called by some of them
Caniba, but in Española *Carib*. He thought they must be
an audacious race, for they go to all these islands and eat
the people they can capture. He understood a few words,
and the Indians who were on board comprehended more,
there being a difference in the languages owing to the
great distance between the various islands. The Admiral
ordered that the Indian should be fed, and given pieces of
green and red cloth, and glass beads, which they like very
much, and then sent on shore. He was told to bring gold
if he had any, and it was believed that he had, from some
small things he brought with him. When the boat reached
the shore there were fifty-five men behind the trees, naked,
and with very long hair,[2] as the women wear it in Castille.
Behind the head they wore plumes of feathers of parrots
and other birds, and each man carried a bow. The Indian
landed, and signed to the others to put down their bows
and arrows, and a piece of a staff, which is like . . . . ,[3]
very heavy, carried instead of a sword.[4] As soon as they
came to the boat the crew landed, and began to buy the
bows and arrows and other arms, in accordance with an
order of the Admiral. Having sold two bows, they did

---

[1] Las Casas says that *Goanin* was not the name of an island, but
the word for base gold (*oro bajo?*).

[2] These were the *Ciguayos*, according to Las Casas, who inhabited
the mountains and coasts of the north of Española from nearly as far
as *Puerto de Plata* to *Higuey*.

[3] A gap in the original manuscript.

[4] This is the *macana*, made of palm-wood, and very hard. Las
Casas says that these wooden swords are very hard and heavy. They
are not sharp, but two fingers thick on all sides, and with one blow
they will cleave through a helmeted head to the brain (i p. 435).

not want to give more, but began to attack the Spaniards, and to take hold of them. They were running back to pick up their bows and arrows where they had laid them aside, and took cords in their hands to bind the boat's crew. Seeing them rushing down, and being prepared— for the Admiral always warned them to be on their guard —the Spaniards attacked the Indians, and gave one a stab with a knife in the buttocks, wounding another in the breast with an arrow. Seeing that they could gain little, although the Christians were only seven and they numbered over fifty, they fled, so that none were left, throwing bows and arrows away. The Christians would have killed many, if the pilot, who was in command, had not prevented them. The Spaniards presently returned to the caravel with the boat. The Admiral regretted the affair for one reason, and was pleased for another. They would have fear of the Christians, and they were no doubt an ill-conditioned people, probably Caribs, who eat men. But the Admiral felt alarm lest they should do some harm to the 39 men left in the fortress and town of *Navidad*, in the event of their coming here in their boat. Even if they are not Caribs, they are a neighbouring people, with similar habits, and fearless, unlike the other inhabitants of the island, who are timid, and without arms. The Admiral says all this, and adds that he would have liked to have captured some of them. He says that they lighted many smoke signals, as is the custom in this island of Española.

Monday, 14th of January.

This evening the Admiral wished to find the houses of the Indians and to capture some of them, believing them to be Caribs. For, owing to the strong east and north-east winds and the heavy sea, he had remained during the day. Many Indians were seen on shore. The Admiral, there-

M

fore, ordered the boat to be sent on shore, with the crew
well armed. Presently the Indians came to the stern of
the boat, including the man who had been on board the
day before, and had received presents from the Admiral.
With him there came a king, who had given to the said
Indian some beads in token of safety and peace for the
boat's crew. This king, with three of his followers, went
on board the boat and came to the caravel. The Admiral
ordered them to be given biscuit and treacle to eat, and
gave the chief a red cap, some beads, and a piece of red
cloth. The others were also given pieces of cloth. The
chief said that next day he would bring a mask made of
gold, affirming that there was much here, and in *Carib*[1]
and *Matinino*.[2] They afterwards went on shore well
satisfied.

The Admiral here says that the caravels were making
much water, which entered by the keel ; and he complains
of the caulkers at Palos, who caulked the vessels very
badly, and ran away when they saw that the Admiral had
detected the badness of their work, and intended to oblige
them to repair the defect. But, notwithstanding that the
caravels were making much water, he trusted in the favour
and mercy of our Lord, for his high Majesty well knew
how much controversy there was before the expedition
could be despatched from Castille, that no one was in the
Admiral's favour save Him alone who knew his heart, and
after God came your Highnesses, while all others were
against him without any reason. He further says : "And
this has been the cause that the royal crown of your
Highnesses has not a hundred *cuentos* of revenue more
than after I entered your service, which is seven years ago
in this very month, the 20th of January.[3] The increase

---

[1] Puerto Rico.   [2] Probably Martinique or Guadaloupe.
[3] By this calculation the Admiral entered the service of the Catholic
Sovereigns on January 20th, 1486.

will take place from now onwards. For the almighty God will remedy all things." These are his words.

Tuesday, 15th of January.

The Admiral now wished to depart, for there was nothing to be gained by further delay, after these occurrences and the tumult with the Indians. To-day he had heard that all the gold was in the district of the town of *Navidad*, belonging to their Highnesses; and that in the island of *Carib*[1] there was much copper, as well as in *Matinino*. The intercourse at *Carib* would, however, be difficult, because the natives are said to eat human flesh. Their island would be in sight from thence, and the Admiral determined to go there, as it was on the route, and thence to *Matinino*, which was said to be entirely peopled by women, without men. He would thus see both islands, and might take some of the natives. The Admiral sent the boat on shore, but the king of that district had not come, for his village was distant. He, however, sent his crown of gold, as he had promised; and many other natives came with cotton, and bread made from yams, all with their bows and arrows. After the bartering was finished, four youths came to the caravel. They appeared to the Admiral to give such a clear account of the islands to the eastward, on the same route as the Admiral would have to take, that he determined to take them to Castille with him. He says that they had no iron nor other metals; at least none was seen, but it was impossible to know much of the land in so short a time, owing to the difficulty with the language, which the Admiral could not understand except by guessing, nor could they know what was said to them, in such a few days. The bows of these people are as large as those of France or England. The arrows are similar to

---

[1] Puerto Rico.

M 2

the darts of the natives who have been met with previously, which are made of young canes, which grow very straight, and a *vara* and a half or two *varas* in length. They point them with a piece of sharp wood, a *palmo* and a half long, and at the end some of them fix a fish's tooth, but most of them anoint it with an herb. They do not shoot as in other parts, but in a certain way which cannot do much harm. Here they have a great deal of fine and long cotton, and plenty of mastick. The bows appeared to be of yew, and there is gold and copper. There is also plenty of *aji,*[1] which is their pepper, which is more valuable than pepper, and all the people eat nothing else, it being very wholesome. Fifty caravels might be annually loaded with it from Española. The Admiral says that he found a great deal of weed in this bay, the same as was met with at sea when he came on this discovery. He therefore supposed that there were islands to the eastward, in the direction of the position where he began to meet with it; for he considers it certain that this weed has its origin in shallow water near the land, and, if this is the case, these Indies must be very near the Canary Islands. For this reason he thought the distance must be less than 400 leagues.

Wednesday, 16th of January.

They got under weigh three hours before daylight, and left the gulf, which was named *Golfo de las Flechas,*[2] with the land-breeze. Afterwards there was a west wind, which was fair to go to the island of *Carib* on an E.N.E. course. This was where the people live of whom all the natives of the other islands are so frightened, because they roam over the sea in canoes without number, and eat the men

---

[1] Capsicum. In Quichua it is called *uchu*.

[2] Gulf of the Arrows. This was the Bay of *Samana*, into which the river *Yuna* flows.

they can capture. The Admiral steered the course indicated by one of the four Indians he took yesterday in the
Puerto de las Flechas. After having sailed about 64 miles,
the Indians made signs that the island was to the S.E.[1]
The Admiral ordered the sails to be trimmed for that
course, but, after having proceeded on it for two leagues,
the wind freshened from a quarter which was very favourable for the voyage to Spain. The Admiral had noticed
that the crew were downhearted when he deviated from
the direct route home, reflecting that both caravels were
leaking badly, and that there was no help but in God.
He therefore gave up the course leading to the islands,
and shaped a direct course for Spain E.N.E. He sailed
on this course, making 48 miles, which is 12 leagues, by
sunset. The Indians said that by that route they would
fall in with the island of *Matinino,* peopled entirely by
women without men, and the Admiral wanted very much
to take five or six of them to the Sovereigns. But he
doubted whether the Indians understood the route well,
and he could not afford to delay, by reason of the leaky
condition of the caravels. He, however, believed the story,
and that, at certain seasons, men came to them from the
island of Carib, distant ten or twelve leagues. If males
were born, they were sent to the island of the men; and if
females, they remained with their mothers. The Admiral
says that these two islands cannot have been more than
15 or 20 leagues to the S.E. from where he altered course,
the Indians not understanding how to point out the direction. After losing sight of the cape, which was named
San Theramo,[2] which was left 16 leagues to the west, they
went for 12 leagues E.N.E. The weather was very fine.

---

[1] Puerto Rico. It would have been distant about 30 leagues.

[2] Now called *Cabo del Engaño*, the extreme eastern point of
Española. It had the same name when Las Casas wrote.

Thursday, 17th of January.

The wind went down at sunset yesterday, the caravels having sailed 14 glasses, each a little less than half-an-hour, at 4 miles an hour, making 28 miles. Afterwards the wind freshened, and they ran all that watch, which was 10 glasses. Then another six until sunrise at 8 miles an hour, thus making altogether 84 miles, equal to 21 leagues, to the E.N.E., and until sunset 44 miles, or 11 leagues, to the east. Here a booby came to the caravel, and afterwards another. The Admiral saw a great deal of gulf-weed.

Friday, 18th of January.   .

During the night they steered E.S.E., with little wind, for 40 miles, equal to 10 leagues, and then 30 miles, or 7½ leagues, until sunrise. All day they proceeded with little wind to E.N.E. and N.E. by E., more or less, her head being sometimes north and at others N.N.E., and, counting one with the other, they made 60 miles, or 15 leagues. There was little weed, but yesterday and to-day the sea appeared to be full of tunnies. The Admiral believed that they were on their way to the tunny-fisheries of the Duke, at Conil and Cádiz.[1] He also thought they were near some islands, because a frigate-bird flew round the caravel, and afterwards went away to the S.S.E. He said that to the S.E. of the island of Española were the islands of *Carib*, *Matinino*, and many others.

---

[1] The Duke here alluded to was the redoubtable warrior, Don Rodrigo Ponce de Leon, conqueror of Zahara and Alhama, and one of the chief leaders in the war with Granada. Henry IV created him Marquis of Cadiz in 1470, and he was also made Duke of Cadiz. He died in the end of August 1492, soon after the departure of Columbus. The Crown then resumed the dukedom of Cadiz, and his grandson and successor was created Duke of Arcos instead. The *almadravas*, or tunny fisheries of Rota, near Cadiz, were inherited by the Duke, as well as those of Conil, a little fishing town 6 leagues east of Cadiz.

Saturday, 19th of January.

During the night they made good 56 miles N.N.E., and 64 N.E. by N. After sunrise they steered N.E. with the wind fresh from S.W., and afterwards W.S.W. 84 miles, equal to 21 leagues. The sea was again full of small tunnies. There were boobies, frigate-birds, and terns.

Sunday, 20th of January.

It was calm during the night, with occasional slants of wind, and they only made 20 miles to the N.E. After sunrise they went 11 miles S.E., and then 36 miles N.N.E., equal to 9 leagues. They saw an immense quantity of small tunnies, the air very soft and pleasant, like Seville in April or May, and the sea, for which God be given many thanks, always very smooth. Frigate-birds, sandpipers, and other birds were seen.

Monday, 21st of January.

Yesterday, before sunset, they steered N.E. b. E., with the wind east, at the rate of 8 miles an hour until midnight, equal to 56 miles. Afterwards they steered N.N.E. 8 miles an hour, so that they made 104 miles, or 26 leagues, during the night N.E. by N. After sunrise they steered N.N.E. with the same wind, which at times veered to N.E., and they made good 88 miles in the eleven hours of daylight, or 21 leagues: except one that was lost by delay caused by closing with the *Pinta* to communicate. The air was colder, and it seemed to get colder as they went further north, and also that the nights grew longer owing to the narrowing of the sphere. Many boatswain-birds and terns were seen, as well as other birds, but not so many fish, perhaps owing to the water being colder. Much weed was seen.

Tuesday, 22nd of January.

Yesterday, after sunset, they steered N.N.E. with an east wind. They made 8 miles an hour during five glasses, and three before the watch began, making eight glasses, equal to 72 miles, or 18 leagues. Afterwards they went N.E. by N. for six glasses, which would be another 18 miles. Then, during four glasses of the second watch N.E. at six miles an hour, or three leagues. From that time to sunset, for eleven glasses, E.N.E. at 6 leagues an hour,[1] equal to seven leagues. Then E.N.E. until 11 o'clock, 32 miles. Then the wind fell, and they made no more during that day. The Indians swam about. They saw boatswain-birds and much weed.

Wednesday, 23rd of January.

To-night the wind was very changeable, but, making the allowances applied by good sailors, they made 84 miles, or 21 leagues, N.E. by N. Many times the caravel *Niña* had to wait for the *Pinta*, because she sailed badly when on a bowline, the mizen being of little use owing to the weakness of the mast. If her captain, Martin Alonso Pinzon, had taken the precaution to provide her with a good mast in the Indies, where there are so many and such excellent spars, instead of deserting his commander from motives of avarice, he would have done better. They saw many boatswain-birds and much weed. The heavens have been clouded over during these last days, but there has been no rain. The sea has been as smooth as a river, for which many thanks be given to God. After sunrise they went

---

[1] An error of the transcriber for miles. Other figures have been wrongly copied. Each glass being half-an-hour, going six miles an hour, they would have made 33 miles in five hours and a half.—N.

free, and made 30 miles, or 7¼ leagues N.E. During the
rest of the day E.N.E. another 30 miles.

Thursday, 24th of January.

They made 44 miles, or 11 leagues, during the night,
allowing for many changes in the wind, which was
generally N.E. After sunrise until sunset E.N.E. 14
leagues.

Friday, 25th of January.

They steered during part of the night E.N.E. for 13
glasses, making 9¼ leagues. Then N.N.E. 6 miles. The
wind fell, and during the day they only made 28 miles
E.N.E., or 7 leagues. The sailors killed a tunny and a
very large shark, which was very welcome, as they now
had nothing but bread and wine, and some yams from the
Indies.

Saturday, 26th of January.

This night they made 56 miles, or 14 leagues, E.S.E.
After sunrise they steered E.S.E., and sometimes S.E.,
making 40 miles up to 11 o'clock. Afterwards they went
on another tack, and then on a bowline, 24 miles, or
6 leagues, to the north, until night.

Sunday, 27th of January.

Yesterday, after sunset, they steered N.E. and N.E.
by N. at the rate of five miles an hour, which in thirteen
hours would be 65 miles, or 16¼ leagues. After sunrise
they steered N.E. 24 miles, or 6 leagues, until noon, and
from that time until sunset 3 leagues E.N.E.

Monday, 28th of January.

All night they steered E.N.E. 36 miles, or 9 leagues.
After sunrise until sunset E.N.E. 20 miles, or 5 leagues.

The weather was temperate and pleasant.   They saw boatswain-birds, sandpipers, and much weed.

Tuesday, 29th of January.

They steered E.N.E. 39 miles, or 9½ leagues, and during the whole day 8 leagues.   The air was very pleasant, líke April in Castille, the sea smooth, and fish they call *dorados* came on board.

Wednesday, 30th of January.

All this night they made 6 leagues E.N.E., and in the day S.E. by S. 13½ leagues.   Boatswain-birds, much weed, and many tunnies.

Thursday, 31st of January.

This night they steered N.E. by N. 30 miles, and afterwards N.E. 35 miles, or 16 leagues.   From sunrise to night E.N.E. 13½ leagues.   They saw boatswain-birds and terns.

Friday, 1st of February.

They made 16½ leagues E.N.E. during the night, and went on the same course during the day 29¼ leagues. The sea very smooth, thanks be to God.

Saturday, 2nd of February.

They made 40 miles, or 10 leagues, E.N.E. this night. In the daytime, with the same wind aft, they went 7 miles an hour, so that in eleven hours they had gone 77 miles, or 9¼ leagues.   The sea was very smooth, thanks be to God, and the air very soft.   They saw the sea so covered with weed that, if they had not known about it before, they would have been fearful of sunken rocks.   They saw terns.

Sunday, 3rd of February.

This night, the wind being aft and the sea very smooth, thanks be to God, they made 29 leagues. The North Star appeared very high, as it does off Cape St. Vincent. The Admiral was unable to take the altitude, either with the astrolabe or with the quadrant, because the rolling caused by the waves prevented it. That day he steered his course E.N.E., going 10 miles an hour, so that in eleven hours he made 27 leagues.

Monday, 4th of February.

During the night the course was N.E. by E., going twelve miles an hour part of the time, and the rest ten miles. Thus they made 130 miles, or 32 leagues and a half. The sky was very threatening and rainy, and it was rather cold, by which they knew that they had not yet reached the Azores. After sunrise the course was altered to east. During the whole day they made 77 miles, or 19¼ leagues.

Tuesday, 5th of February.

This night they steered east, and made 55 miles, or 13½ leagues. In the day they were going ten miles an hour, and in eleven hours made 110 miles, or 27½ leagues. They saw sandpipers, and some small sticks, a sign that they were near land.

Wednesday, 6th of February.

They steered east during the night, going at the rate of eleven miles an hour, so that in the thirteen hours of the night they made 143 miles, or 35¼ leagues. They saw many birds. In the day they went 14 miles an hour, and made 154 miles, or 38½ leagues; so that, including night and day, they made 74 leagues, more or less. Vicente

Anes[1] said that they had left the island of Flores to the north and Madeira to the east. Roldan said that the island of Fayal, or San Gregorio, was to the N.N.E. and Puerto Santo to east. There was much weed.

Thursday, 7th of February.

This night they steered east, going ten miles an hour, so that in thirteen hours they made 130 miles, or 32½ leagues. In the daytime the rate was eight miles an hour, in eleven hours 88 miles, or 22 leagues. This morning the Admiral found himself 65 leagues south of the island of Flores, and the pilot Pedro Alonso, being further north, according to his reckoning, passed between Terceira and Santa Maria to the east, passing to windward of the island of Madeira, twelve leagues further north. The sailors saw a new kind of weed, of which there is plenty in the islands of the Azores.

Friday, 8th of February.

They went three miles an hour to the eastward for some time during the night, and afterwards E.S.E., going twelve miles an hour. From sunrise to noon they made 27 miles, and the same distance from noon till sunset, equal to 13 leagues S.S.E.

Saturday, 9th of February.

For part of this night they went 3 leagues S.S.E., and afterwards S. by E., then N.E. 5 leagues until ten o'clock in the forenoon, then 9 leagues east until dark.

Sunday, 10th of February.

From sunset they steered east all night, making 130 miles, or 32½ leagues. During the day they went at

---

[1] It should be Yañez.

the rate of nine miles an hour, making 99 miles, or 24½ leagues, in eleven hours.

In the caravel of the Admiral, Vicente Yañez and the two pilots, Sancho Ruiz and Pedro Alonso Niño, and Roldan,[1] made charts and plotted the route. They all made the position a good deal beyond the islands of the Azores to the east, and, navigating to the north, none of them touched Santa Maria, which is the last of all the Azores. They made the position five leagues beyond it, and were in the vicinity of the islands of Madeira and Puerto Santo. But the Admiral was very different from them in his reckoning, finding the position very much in rear of theirs. This night he found the island of Flores to the north, and to the east he made the direction to be towards Nafe in Africa, passing to leeward of the island of Madeira to the north . . . . . leagues.[2] So that the pilots were nearer to Castille than the Admiral by 150 leagues. The Admiral says that, with the grace of God, when they reach the land they will find out whose reckoning was most correct. He also says that he went 263 leagues from the island of Hierro to the place where he first saw the gulf-weed.

Monday, 11th of February.

This night they went twelve miles an hour on their course, and during the day they ran 16½ leagues. They saw many birds, from which they judged that land was near.

---

[1] Las Casas says that the pilot Roldan afterwards lived for many years in the city of San Domingo, owning several houses in the principal streets.

[2] A gap in the original manuscript.

Tuesday, 12th of February.

They went six miles an hour on an east course during the night, altogether 73 miles, or 18¼ leagues. At this time they began to encounter bad weather with a heavy sea; and, if the caravel had not been very well managed, she must have been lost. During the day they made 11 or 12 leagues with much difficulty and danger.

Wednesday, 13th of February.

From sunset until daylight there was great trouble with the wind, and the high and tempestuous sea. There was lightning three times to the N.N.E.—a sign of a great storm coming either from that quarter or its opposite. They were lying-to most of the night, afterwards showing a little sail, and made 52 miles, which is 13 leagues. In the day the wind moderated a little, but it soon increased again. The sea was terrific, the waves crossing each other, and straining the vessels. They made 55 miles more, equal to 13½ leagues.

Thursday, 14th of February.

This night the wind increased, and the waves were terrible, rising against each other, and so shaking and straining the vessel that she could make no headway, and was in danger of being stove in. They carried the main-sail very closely reefed, so as just to give her steerage-way, and proceeded thus for three hours, making 20 miles. Meanwhile, the wind and sea increased, and, seeing the great danger, the Admiral began to run before it, there being nothing else to be done. The caravel *Pinta* began to run before the wind at the same time, and Martin Alonso ran her out of sight,[1] although the Admiral kept

---

[1] Martin Alonso Pinzon succeeded in bringing the caravel *Pinta*

showing lanterns all night, and the other answered. It would seem that she could do no more, owing to the force of the tempest, and she was taken far from the route of the Admiral. He steered that night E.N.E., and made 54 miles, equal to 13 leagues. At sunrise the wind blew still harder, and the cross sea was terrific. They continued to show the closely-reefed mainsail, to enable her to rise from between the waves, or she would otherwise have been swamped. An E.N.E. course was steered, and afterwards N.E. by E. for six hours, making 7½ leagues. The Admiral ordered that a pilgrimage should be made to Our Lady of Guadaloupe, carrying a candle of 6 lbs. of weight in wax, and that all the crew should take an oath that the pilgrimage should be made by the man on whom the lot fell. As many beans were got as there were persons on board, and on one a cross was cut with a knife. They were then put into a cap and shaken up. The first who put in his hand was the Admiral, and he drew out the bean with a cross, so the lot fell on him ; and he was bound to go on the pilgrimage and fulfil the vow. Another lot was drawn, to go on pilgrimage to Our Lady of Loreto, which is in the march of Ancona, in the Papal territory, a house where Our Lady works many and great miracles. The lot fell on a sailor of the port of Santa Maria, named Pedro de Villa, and the Admiral promised to pay his travelling expenses. Another pilgrimage was agreed upon, to watch for one night in Santa Clara[1] at Moguer, and have a Mass said, for which they again used the beans, including the one with a cross. The lot again fell on the Admiral. After

---

into port at Bayona in Galicia. He went thence to Palos, arriving in the evening of the same day as the *Niña* with the Admiral. Pinzon died very soon afterwards. Oviedo says : "Fuesse a Palos a su casa, é murió desde a pocas dias, porque yba muy doliente" (II, cap. vi).

[1] Las Casas says that this was a church much frequented by sailors (i, p. 446).

this the Admiral and all the crew made a vow that, on
arriving at the first land, they would all go in procession,
in their shirts, to say their prayers in a church dedicated
to Our Lady.

Besides these general vows made in common, each
sailor made a special vow; for no one expected to escape,
holding themselves for lost, owing to the fearful weather
from which they were suffering. The want of ballast
increased the danger of the ship, which had become light,
owing to the consumption of the provisions and water.
On account of the favourable weather enjoyed among the
islands, the Admiral had omitted to make provision for
this need, thinking that ballast might be taken on board
at the island inhabited by women, which he had intended
to visit. The only thing to do was to fill the barrels that
had contained wine or fresh water with water from the sea,
and this supplied a remedy.

Here the Admiral writes of the causes which made him
fear that he would perish, and of others that gave him
hope that God would work his salvation, in order that
such news as he was bringing to the Sovereigns might not
be lost. It seemed to him that the strong desire he felt
to bring such great news, and to show that all he had said
and offered to discover had turned out true, suggested the
fear that he would not be able to do so, and that each
stinging insect would be able to thwart and impede the
work. He attributes this fear to his little faith, and to his
want of confidence in Divine Providence. He was com-
forted, on the other hand, by the mercies of God in having
vouchsafed him such a victory, in the discoveries he had
made, and in that God had complied with all his desires
in Castille, after much adversity and many misfortunes.
As he had before put all his trust in God, who had
heard him and granted all he sought, he ought now to
believe that God would permit the completion of what

had been begun, and ordain that he should be saved. Especially as he had freed him on the voyage out, when he had still greater reason to fear, from the trouble caused by the sailors and people of his company, who all with one voice declared their intention to return, and protested that they would rise against him. But the eternal God gave him force and valour to withstand them all, and in many other marvellous ways had God shown his will in this voyage besides those known to their Highnesses. Thus he ought not to fear the present tempest, though his weakness and anxiety prevent him from giving tranquillity to his mind. He says further that it gave him great sorrow to think of the two sons he had left at their studies in Cordova, who would be left orphans, without father or mother, in a strange land; while the Sovereigns would not know of the services he had performed in this voyage, nor would they receive the prosperous news which would move them to help the orphans. To remedy this, and that their Highnesses might know how our Lord had granted a victory in all that could be desired respecting the Indies, and that they might understand that there were no storms in those parts, which may be known by the herbs and trees which grow even within the sea[1]; also that the Sovereigns might still have information, even if he perished in the storm, he took a parchment and wrote on it as good an account as he could of all he had discovered, entreating anyone who might pick it up to deliver it to the Sovereigns. He rolled this parchment up in waxed cloth, fastened it very securely, ordered a large wooden barrel to

---

[1] The Admiral thought that there could be no great storms in the countries he had discovered, because trees (mangroves) actually grew with their roots in the sea. The herbage on the beach nearly reached the waves, which does not happen when the sea is rough. See *ante*, p. 60.

N

be brought, and put it inside, so that no one else knew
what it was. They thought that it was some act of
devotion, and so he ordered the barrel to be thrown
into the sea.[1] Afterwards, in the showers and squalls,
the wind veered to the west, and they went before it, only
with the foresail, in a very confused sea, for five hours.
They made 2½ leagues N.E. They had taken in the reefed
mainsail, for fear some wave of the sea should carry all
away.

Friday, 15th of February.

Last night, after sunset, the sky began to clear towards
the west, showing that the wind was inclined to come from
that quarter. The Admiral added the bonnet[2] to the
mainsail. The sea was still very high, although it had
gone down slightly. They steered E.N.E., and went four
miles an hour, which made 13 leagues during the eleven
hours of the night. After sunrise they sighted land. It
appeared from the bows to bear E.N.E. Some said it was
the island of Madeira, others that it was the rock of Cintra,
in Portugal, near Lisbon. Presently the wind headed to
E.N.E., and a heavy sea came from the west, the caravel
being 5 leagues from the land. The Admiral found by his
reckoning that he was close to the Azores, and believed

---

[1] It is stated, in the *Vita dell Ammiraglio*, by his son Fernando
Columbus, that the Admiral wrote a duplicate of this letter, and placed
it in a second barrel, which was kept on board until the ship should
sink (*Historie*, cap. xxxvi). Lamartine (*Christophe Colomb.*, N. XLVII)
has a curious but unauthenticated story, that several casks with documents were thrown overboard, and that one was picked up three
centuries afterwards. Lafuente (*Historia General de España*, vol. ix,
p. 463) even gives the name of the vessel that picked up one of the
documents of Columbus, and the date, 27 Aug. 1852. But the story
is unworthy of credit.

[2] The bonnet was a small sail, usually cut to a third the size of
the mizen, or a fourth of the mainsail. It was secured through eyelet-
holes to the leech of the mainsail, in the manner of a studding sail.

that this was one of them. The pilots and sailors thought it was the land of Castille.[1]

Saturday, 16th of February.

All that night the Admiral was standing off and on to keep clear of the land, which they now knew to be an island, sometimes standing N.E., at others N.N.E., until sunrise, when they tacked to the south to reach the island, which was now concealed by a great mist. Another island was in sight from the poop, at a distance of eight leagues. Afterwards, from sunrise until dark, they were tacking to reach the land against a strong wind and head-sea. At the time of repeating the *Salve*, which is just before dark, some of the men saw a light to leeward, and it seemed that it must be on the island they first saw yesterday. All night they were beating to windward, and going as near as they could, so as to see some way to the island at sunrise. That night the Admiral got a little rest, for he had not slept nor been able to sleep since Wednesday, and his legs were very sore from long exposure to the

---

[1] On this day the Admiral dated the letter to Santangel, the Escribano de Racion ; which was translated by Mr. Major for the Hakluyt Society (*Select Letters of Columbus*, 1870). A copy of this letter was made, a few days afterwards, to be sent to Gabriel Sanchez, the Treasurer of Aragon. These letters are very brief *compendia* of the Journal. The *Santangel Letter* was first printed at Barcelona in April 1493 (unique copy in possession of Mr. Quaritch, folio, two leaves). The next edition, also printed in April 1493, at Seville, is represented by a unique copy in the Ambrosian Library at Milan (quarto, four leaves). There is a manuscript copy at Simancas, which is a transcript made about 70 years ago, but it is not known from what original. A manuscript transcript of the *Sanchez Letter*, written about 1600, was bought by Varnhagen at Valencia, and printed there by him in 1858. A Latin translation of it, by Leander de Cosco, had been printed three times, in 1493, at Rome ; and a fourth edition exists, probably printed at Naples.

wet and cold.   At sunrise[1] he steered S.S.W., and reached
the island at night, but could not make out what island it
was, owing to the thick weather.

Monday, 18th of February.

Yesterday, after sunset, the Admiral was sailing round
the island, to see where he could anchor and open communications.   He let go one anchor, which he presently
lost, and then stood off and on all night.   After sunrise
he again reached the north side of the island, where he
anchored, and sent the boat on shore.   They had speech
with the people, and found that it was the island of Santa
Maria, one of the Azores.   They pointed out the port[2] to
which the caravel should go.   They said that they had
never seen such stormy weather as there had been for the
last fifteen days, and they wondered how the caravel
could have escaped.   They gave many thanks to God, and
showed great joy at the news that the Admiral had discovered the Indies.   The Admiral says that his navigation had been very certain, and that he had laid the
discoveries down on the chart.   Many thanks were due to
our Lord, although there had been some delay.   But he
was sure that he was in the region of the Azores, and that
this was one of them.   He pretended to have gone over
more ground, to mislead the pilots and mariners who
pricked off the charts, in order that he might remain
master of that route to the Indies, as, in fact, he did.   For
none of the others kept an accurate reckoning, so that no
one but himself could be sure of the route to the Indies.

Tuesday, 19th of February.

After sunset three natives of the island came to the

---

[1] This was on Sunday, 17th of February.
[2] The port of San Lorenzo.

beach and hailed. The Admiral sent the boat, which
returned with fowls and fresh bread. It was carnival
time, and they brought other things which were sent
by the captain of the island, named Juan de Castañeda,
saying that he knew the Admiral very well, and that
he did not come to see him because it was night, but
that at dawn he would come with more refreshments,
bringing with him three men of the boat's crew, whom
he did not send back owing to the great pleasure he
derived from hearing their account of the voyage. The
Admiral ordered much respect to be shown to the messengers, and that they should be given beds to sleep in
that night, because it was late, and the town was far off.
As on the previous Thursday, when they were in the midst
of the storm, they had made a vow to go in procession to
a church of Our Lady as soon as they came to land, the
Admiral arranged that half the crew should go to comply
with their obligation to a small chapel, like a hermitage,
near the shore; and that he would himself go afterwards
with the rest. Believing that it was a peaceful land, and
confiding in the offers of the captain of the island, and
in the peace that existed between Spain and Portugal,
he asked the three men to go to the town and arrange
for a priest to come and say Mass. The half of the crew
then went in their shirts, in compliance with their vow.
While they were at their prayers, all the people of the
town, horse and foot, with the captain at their head, came
and took them all prisoners. The Admiral, suspecting
nothing, was waiting for the boat to take him and the
rest to accomplish the vow. At 11 o'clock, seeing that
they did not come back, he feared that they had been
detained, or that the boat had been swamped, all the island
being surrounded by high rocks. He could not see what
had taken place, because the hermitage was round a point.
He got up the anchor, and made sail until he was in full

view of the hermitage, and he saw many of the horsemen
dismount and get into the boat with arms.   They came to
the caravel to seize the Admiral.   The captain stood up in
the boat, and asked for an assurance of safety from the
Admiral, who replied that he granted it ; but, what out-
rage was this, that he saw none of his people in the
boat ?   The Admiral added that they might come on
board, and that he would do all that might be proper.
The Admiral tried, with fair words, to get hold of this
captain, that he might recover his own people, not
considering that he broke faith by giving him security,
because he had offered peace and security, and had then
broken his word.   The captain, as he came with an evil
intention, would not come on board.   Seeing that he did
not come alongside, the Admiral asked that he might be
told the reason for the detention of his men, an act which
would displease the King of Portugal, because the Portuguese received much honour in the territories of the King
of Castille, and were as safe as if they were in Lisbon.
He further said that the Sovereigns had given him letters
of recommendation to all the Lords and Princes of the
world, which he would show the captain if he would come
on board ; that he was the Admiral of the Ocean Sea, and
Viceroy of the Indies, which belonged to their Highnesses,
and that he would show the commissions signed with their
signatures, and attested by their seals, which he held up
from a distance.   He added that his Sovereigns were in
friendship and amity with the King of Portugal, and had
ordered that all honour should be shown to ships that
came from Portugal.   Further, that if the captain did not
surrender his people, he would still go on to Castille, as he
had quite sufficient to navigate as far as Seville, in which
case the captain and his followers would be severely
punished for their offence.   Then the captain and those
with him replied that they did not know the King and

Queen of Castille there, nor their letters, nor were they afraid of them, and they would give the Admiral to understand that this was Portugal, almost menacing him.   On hearing this the Admiral was much moved, thinking that some cause of disagreement might have arisen between the two kingdoms during his absence, yet he could not endure that they should not be answered reasonably. Afterwards he turned to the captain, and said that he should go to the port with the caravel, and that all that had been done would be reported to the King his Lord. The Admiral made those who were in the caravel bear witness to what he said, calling to the captain and all the others, and promising that he would not leave the caravel until a hundred Portuguese had been taken to Castille, and all that island had been laid waste.   He then returned to anchor in the port where he was first, the wind being very unfavourable for doing anything else.

Wednesday, 20th of February.

The Admiral ordered the ship to be repaired, and the casks to be filled alongside for ballast.   This was a very bad port, and he feared he might have to cut the cables. This was so, and he made sail for the island of San Miguel ; but there is no good port in any of the Azores for the weather they then experienced, and there was no other remedy but to go to sea.

Thursday, 21st of February.

Yesterday the Admiral left that island of Santa Maria for that of San Miguel, to see if a port could be found to shelter his vessel from the bad weather.   There was much wind and a high sea, and he was sailing until night without being able to see either one land or the other, owing to the thick weather caused by wind and sea.   The Admiral says he was in much anxiety, because he only had three sailors who knew their business, the rest knowing nothing of seamanship. He was lying-to all that night, in great danger and trouble. Our Lord showed him mercy in that the waves came in one direction, for if there had been a cross sea they would have suffered much more. After sunrise the island of San Miguel was not in sight, so the Admiral determined to return to Santa Maria, to see if he could recover his people and boat, and the anchors and cables he had left there.

The Admiral says that he was astonished at the bad weather he encountered in the region of these islands. In the Indies he had navigated throughout the winter without the necessity for anchoring, and always had fine weather, never having seen the sea for a single hour in such a state that it could not be navigated easily. But among these islands he had suffered from such terrible storms. The same had happened in going out as far as the Canary Islands, but as soon as they were passed there was always fine weather, both in sea and air. In concluding these remarks, he observes that the sacred theologians and wise men said well when they placed the terrestrial paradise in the Far East, because it is a most temperate region. Hence these lands that he had now discovered must, he says, be in the extreme East.

Friday, 22nd of February.

Yesterday the Admiral came-to off Santa Maria, in the place or port where he had first anchored. Presently a man came down to some rocks at the edge of the beach, hailing that they were not to remain there. Soon afterwards the boat came with five sailors, two priests, and a scrivener. They asked for safety, and when it was granted by the Admiral, they came on board, and, as it was night

they slept on board, the Admiral showing them all the
civility he could.   In the morning they asked to be shown
the authority of the Sovereigns of Castille, by which the
voyage had been made.   The Admiral felt that they did
this to give some colour of right to what they had done,
and to show that they had right on their side.   As they
· were unable to secure the person of the Admiral, whom
they intended to get into their power when they came with
the boat armed, they now feared that their game might not
turn out so well, thinking, with some fear, of what the
Admiral had threatened, and which he proposed to put into
execution.   In order to get his people released, the Admiral
displayed the general letter of the Sovereigns to all Princes
and Lords, and other documents, and having given them of
what he had, the Portuguese went on shore contented, and
presently released all the crew and the boat.   The Admiral
heard from them that if he had been captured also, they
never would have been released, for the captain said that
those were the orders of the King his Lord.

Saturday, 23rd of February.

Yesterday the weather began to improve, and the
Admiral got under weigh to seek a better anchorage,
where he could take in wood and stones for ballast ; but
he did not find one until late.

. Sunday, 24th of February.

He anchored yesterday in the afternoon, to take in wood
and stones, but the sea was so rough that they could not
land from the boat, and during the first watch it came on
to blow from the west and S.W.   He ordered sail to be
made, owing to the great danger there is off these islands in
being at anchor with a southerly gale, and as the wind
was S.W. it would go round to south.   As it was a good

wind for Castille, he gave up his intention of taking in wood and stones, and shaped an easterly course until sunset, going seven miles an hour for six hours and a half, equal to 45½ miles.   After sunset he made six miles an hour, or 66 miles in eleven hours, altogether 111 miles, equal to 28 leagues.

Monday, 25th of February.

Yesterday, after sunset, the caravel went at the rate ot five miles an hour on an easterly course, and in the eleven hours of the night she made 65 miles, equal to 16¼ leagues. From sunrise to sunset they made another 16½ leagues with a smooth sea, thanks be to God.   A very large bird, like an eagle, came to the caravel.

Tuesday, 26th of February.

Yesterday night the caravel steered her course in a smooth sea, thanks be to God.   Most of the time she was going eight miles an hour, and made a hundred miles, equal to 25 leagues.   After sunrise there was little wind and some rain-showers.   They made about 8 leagues E.N.E.

Wednesday, 27th of February.

During the night and day she was off her course, owing to contrary winds and a heavy sea.   She was found to be 125 leagues from Cape St. Vincent, and 80 from the island of Madeira, 106 from Santa Maria.   It was very troublesome to have such bad weather just when they were at the very door of their home.

Thursday, 28th of February.

The same weather during the night, with the wind from south and S.E., sometimes shifting to N.E. and E.N.E., and it was the same all day.

Friday, 1st of March.

To-night the course was E.N.E., and they made twelve leagues. During the day, 23½ leagues on the same course.

Saturday, 2nd of March.

The course was E.N.E., and distance made good 28 leagues during the night, and 20 in the day.

Sunday, 3rd of March.

After sunset the course was east; but a squall came down, split all the sails, and the vessel was in great danger; but God was pleased to deliver them. They drew lots for sending a pilgrim in a shirt to Santa Maria de la Cinta at Huelva, and the lot fell on the Admiral. The whole crew also made a vow to fast on bread and water during the first Saturday after their arrival in port. They had made 60 miles before the sails were split. Afterwards they ran under bare poles, owing to the force of the gale and the heavy sea. They saw signs of the neighbourhood of land, finding themselves near Lisbon.

Monday, 4th of March.

During the night they were exposed to a terrible storm, expecting to be overwhelmed by the cross-seas, while the wind seemed to raise the caravel into the air, and there was rain and lightning in several directions. The Admiral prayed to our Lord to preserve them, and in the first watch it pleased our Lord to show land, which was reported by the sailors. As it was advisable not to reach it before it was known whether there was any port to which he could run for shelter, the Admiral set the mainsail, as there was no other course but to proceed, though in great danger. Thus God preserved them until daylight, though all the time they were in infinite fear and trouble. When

it was light, the Admiral knew the land, which was the
rock of Cintra, near the river of Lisbon, and he resolved
to run in because there was nothing else to be done. So
terrible was the storm, that in the village of Cascaes, at
the mouth of the river, the people were praying for the
little vessel all that morning. After they were inside, the
people came off, looking upon their escape as a miracle.
At the third hour they passed Rastelo, within the river of
Lisbon, where they were told that such a winter, with so
many storms, had never before been known, and that
25 ships had been lost in Flanders, while others had been
wind-bound in the river for four months. Presently the
Admiral wrote to the King of Portugal, who was then at
a distance of nine leagues, to state that the Sovereigns of
Castille had ordered him to enter the ports of his Highness, and ask for what he required for payment, and
requesting that the King would give permission for the
caravel to come to Lisbon, because some ruffians, hearing
that he had much gold on board, might attempt a robbery
in an unfrequented port, knowing that they did not come
from Guinea, but from the Indies.[1]

Tuesday, 5th of March.

To-day the great ship of the King of Portugal was also
at anchor off Rastelo, with the best provision of artillery
and arms that the Admiral had ever seen. The master of her,
named Bartolomé Diaz, of Lisbon, came in an armed boat
to the caravel, and ordered the Admiral to get into the
boat, to go and give an account of himself to the agents of
the king and to the captain of that ship. The Admiral
replied that he was the Admiral of the Sovereigns of
Castille, and that he would not give an account to any
such persons, nor would he leave the ship except by force,

---

[1] On this day the Admiral dated the postscript to his letter to the
Escribano de Racion, which was written at sea on February 15th.

as he had not the power to resist. The master replied
that he must then send the master of the caravel. The
Admiral answered that neither the master nor any other
person should go except by force, for if he allowed anyone
to go, it would be as if he went himself; and that such
was the custom of the Admirals of the Sovereigns of
Castille, rather to die than to submit, or to let any of
their people submit. The master then moderated his
tone, and told the Admiral that if that was his determina-
tion he might do as he pleased. He, however, requested
that he might be shown the letters of the Kings of Castille, if they were on board. The Admiral readily showed
them, and the master returned to the ship and reported
what had happened to the captain, named Alvaro Dama.
That officer, making great festival with trumpets and drums,
came to the caravel to visit the Admiral, and offered to
do all that he might require.

Wednesday, 6th of March.

As soon as it was known that the Admiral came from
the Indies, it was wonderful how many people came from
Lisbon to see him and the Indians, giving thanks to
our Lord, and saying that the heavenly Majesty had given
all this to the Sovereigns of Castille as a reward for their
faith and their great desire to serve God.

Thursday, 7th of March.

To-day an immense number of people came to the
caravel, including many knights, and amongst them the
agents of the king, and all gave infinite thanks to our
Lord for so wide an increase of Christianity granted
by our Lord to the Sovereigns of Castille; and they
said that they received it because their Highnesses had
worked and laboured for the increase of the religion of
Christ.

Friday, 8th of March.

To-day the Admiral received a letter from the King of Portugal,[1] brought by Don Martin de Noroña, asking him to visit him where he was, as the weather was not suitable for the departure of the caravel. He complied, to prevent suspicion, although he did not wish to go, and went to pass the night at Sacanben. The king had given orders to his officers that all that the Admiral, his crew, and the caravel were in need of should be given without payment, and that all the Admiral wanted should be complied with.

Saturday, 9th of March.

To-day the Admiral left Sacanben, to go where the king was residing, which was at Valparaiso, nine leagues from Lisbon. Owing to the rain, he did not arrive until night. The king caused him to be received very honourably by the principal officers of his household ; and the king himself received the Admiral with great favour, making him sit down, and talking very pleasantly.[2] He offered to give orders that everything should be done for the service of the Sovereigns of Castille, and said that the successful termination of the voyage had given him great pleasure. He said further that he understood that, in the capitulation between the Sovereigns and himself, that conquest belonged to him. The Admiral replied that he had not seen the capitulation, nor knew more than that the Sovereigns had ordered him not to go either to Lamina or to any other

---

[1] This was João II, son of Affonso V, who had the correspondence with Toscanelli. João II succeeded in 1481, and died in 1495, when he was succeeded by his cousin Manoel, Duke of Bejar.

[2] Las Casas, quoting from the Portuguese historian, Garcia de Resende, says that the courtiers proposed to pick a quarrel with Columbus, and to kill him ; but that the King João II would not allow it (i, p. 465).

port of Guinea, and that this had been ordered to be proclaimed in all the ports of Andalusia before he sailed. The king graciously replied that he held it for certain that there would be no necessity for any arbitrators. The Admiral was assigned as a guest to the Prior of Crato, who was the principal person present, and from whom he received many favours and civilities.

Sunday, 10th of March.

To-day, after Mass, the king repeated that if the Admiral wanted anything he should have it. He conversed much with the Admiral respecting his voyage, always ordering him to sit down, and treating him with great favour.

Monday, 11th of March.

To-day the Admiral took leave of the king, who entrusted him with some messages to the Sovereigns, and always treating him with much friendliness. He departed after dinner, Don Martin de Noroña being sent with him, and all the knights set out with him, and went with him some distance, to do him honour. Afterwards he came to a monastery of San Antonio, near a place called Villafranca, where the Queen was residing.[1] The Admiral went to do her reverence and to kiss her hand, because she had sent to say that he was not to go without seeing her. The Duke[2] and the Marquis were with her, and the Admiral was received with much honour. He departed at night, and went to sleep at Llandra.

---

[1] The Queen of João II was his cousin Leonor, daughter of Don Fernando, Duke of Viseu, his uncle. The Queen's brother had been killed by her husband the King with his own hand, as a traitor. Her other brother, Manoel, succeeded her husband as king in 1495.

[2] This may have been her brother, the Duke of Bejar, afterwards King Manoel.

Tuesday, 12th of March.

To-day, as he was leaving Llandra to return to the caravel, an esquire of the king arrived, with an offer that if he desired to go to Castille by land, that he should be supplied with lodgings, and beasts, and all that was necessary. When the Admiral took leave of him, he ordered a mule to be supplied to him, and another for his pilot, who was with him, and he says that the pilot received a present of twenty *espadines*. He said this that the Sovereigns might know all that was done. He arrived on board the caravel that night.

Wednesday, 13th of March.

To-day, at 8 o'clock, with the flood tide, and the wind N.N.W., the Admiral got under weigh and made sail for Seville.

Thursday, 14th of March.

Yesterday, after sunset, a southerly course was steered, and before sunrise they were off Cape St. Vincent, which is in Portugal. Afterwards he shaped a course to the east for Saltes, and went on all day with little wind, "until now that the ship is off Furon".

Friday, 15th of March.

Yesterday, after sunset, she went on her course with little wind, and at sunrise she was off Saltes. At noon, with the tide rising, they crossed the bar of Saltes, and reached the port which they had left on the 3rd of August of the year before.[1] The Admiral says that so ends this journal, unless it becomes necessary to go to

---

[1] Having been absent 225 days.

Barcelona by sea, having received news that their High-nesses are in that city, to give an account of all his voyage which our Lord had permitted him to make, and saw fit to set forth in him. For, assuredly, he held with a firm and strong knowledge that his high Majesty made all things good, and that all is good except sin. Nor can he value or think of anything being done without His consent. " I know respecting this voyage", says the Admiral, "that he has miraculously shown his will, as may be seen from this journal, setting forth the numerous miracles that have been displayed in the voyage, and in me who was so long at the court of your Highnesses, working in opposition to and against the opinions of so many chief persons of your household, who were all against me, looking upon this enterprise as folly. But I hope, in our Lord, that it will be a great benefit to Christianity, for so it has ever appeared." These are the final words of the Admiral Don Cristoval Colon respecting his first voyage to the Indies and their discovery.

DOCUMENTS

RELATING TO

THE VOYAGES OF DISCOVERY

OF

JOHN CABOT.

DOCUMENTS

RELATING TO

JOHN CABOT.

LETTERS PATENT GRANTED TO JOHN CABOT AND HIS SONS.[1]

For John Cabot and his sons, touching discovery of unknown land.

Henrie, by the grace of God, King of England and France, and Lord of Ireland, to all to whom these presents shall come greeting.

ET it be known and made manifest 1496, 5 March. that we have given and conceded, and by these presents do give and concede, for us and our heirs, to our well-beloved John Cabottus, citizen of Venice, and to Ludovicus, Sebastianus, and Sanctus, sons of the said John, and to the heirs and assigns of them and each of them and their · deputies, full and free authority, faculty, and power of navigating to all parts, countries, and seas of the east, west, and north, under our banners, flags, and ensigns, with five ships or vessels of what burden or quality soever, and

---

[1] *Rymer*, xii, p. 595.

with as many mariners or men as they will have with them in the said ships, upon their own proper costs and charges : to seek out, discover, and find whatsoever islands, countries, regions, or provinces of heathens or infidels, in whatever part of the world they be, which before this time were unknown to all Christians.

We also concede to them and each of them, and to their heirs and assigns, and their deputies, and we give licence to fly the said our banners and ensigns on whatever towns, cities, camps, islands, or mainlands may be newly found by them.

And the before-named John and his sons, their heirs and assigns, may occupy and possess whatever towns, camps, cities, or islands may be discovered by them, that they may be able to conquer, occupy, and possess, as our vassals and governors, lieutenants or deputies, acquiring for us the dominion, title, and jurisdiction over these towns, camps, cities, islands, and mainlands so discovered. Providing that the said John and his sons, their heirs and assigns, and their deputies, shall be bound and under obligation to us, from all the fruits, profits, emoluments, advantages, gains, and incomes accruing from this voyage, for every their voyage as often as they shall arrive at our port of Bristol (at the which port they shall be bound and holden only to arrive), to deduct a fifth part of the whole capital, whether in goods or in money, for our use.

We give and concede to them, their heirs and assigns, and deputies, that they shall be free from all payments of customs on all and singular the goods and merchandize that they may bring from those newly-discovered places.

And we further give and concede to them, their heirs and assigns, and their deputies, that all mainlands, islands, cities, towns, camps, and other places whatsoever by them discovered, shall not be frequented or visited by any others of our subjects without the licence of the said John and his sons, or of their heirs and assigns, on pain of forfeiting as well the ships or vessels, as all goods whatsoever.

We further will, and strictly command all and singular our subjects, as well by land as by sea, that they shall render good assistance to the aforesaid John, his sons, their heirs and assigns; and that they shall give them all favour and help, as well in arming their ships or vessels, as in supplying them with stores and victuals paid for by their money.

> Witnessed by the King at Westminster, on the 5th day of March, in the eleventh year of his reign.
>
> By the King himself.

NAME OF THE SHIP.

History and Antiquities of Bristol (Bristol, 1789, p. 172), *by W. Barrett.*

"In the year 1497, the 24th of June, on St. John's Day, was Newfoundland found by Bristol men in a ship called the *Matthew*."

FIRST VOYAGE OF JOHN CABOT.

Date of Sailing.

This yeere the King (by meanes of a Venetian which made himselfe very expert and cunning in the Knowledge of the circuit of the worlde, and ilandes of the same, as by a carde and other demonstrations reasonable hee shewed) caused to man and victuall a shippe at Bristow, to search for an ilande, which hee saide hee Knewe well was riche and replenished with riche commodities. Which Ship, thus manned and victualled at the Kinges cost, divers mar- *[In the 13 yere of King Henrie the VII, 1497.]*

chants of London ventured in her small stockes, being in
her as chiefe Patrone, the saide Venetian.   And in the
companie of the saide shippe sayled also out of Bristowe
three or foure small ships fraught with sleight and grosse
merchandizes, as course cloth, Caps, laces, points, and
other trifles, and so departed from Bristowe in the begin-

ning of May : of whom, in this Maiors time, returned no
tidings.[1]

THE LANDFALL OF JOHN CABOT.

Legend on the Map of Sebastian Cabot of 1544.

No. 8.   This land was discovered by Joan Caboto Veneciano, and Sebastian Caboto his son, in the year from the
birth of our Saviour Jesu Christ MCCCCXCIIII,[2] on the 24th
of June in the morning, to which they gave the name of
"*Prima Tierra Vista*", and to a large island which is near
the said land they gave the name of St. John, because it
was discovered the same day.   The natives of it go about
dressed in skins of animals ; in their wars they use bows
and arrows, lances and darts, and clubs of wood, and slings.
This land is very sterile.   There are in it many white

---

[1] From *Hakluyt's Divers Voyages:* "taken out of Fabian's *Chronicle*,
which is in the custodie of John Stowe, Citizen, a diligent searcher
and preserver of antiquities." Also printed in the *Principal Navigations*, where Hakluyt inserted the name of "one John Cabot" before
"a Venetian".

Fabyan died in 1511.   His *Chronicle* was published down to 10
Henry VII, in 1516, and a new edition, with the continuation, was
published by Rastell in 1533.   It does not contain the above entry,
nor any allusion to Cabot.   There is a similar passage in Stow, but
without the date of sailing, and the explorer is not called John, but
" Sebastian Gaboto, a Genoa's sonne borne in Bristow".

[2] This is an obvious error.   It should be 1497.   Mr. Major has
suggested that the first two lines were badly printed in the original,
being slightly separated instead of being joined at the bottom, thus
making "II" instead of "v".

bears, and very large stags, like horses, and many other animals. And in like manner there are immense quantities of fish—soles, salmon, very large cods, and many other kinds of fish. They call the great multitude of them *baccallaos ;* and there are also in this country dark-coloured falcons like crows, eagles, partridges, sandpipers, and many other birds of different kinds.

REWARD FOR JOHN CABOT.

10th Aug. 1497. To hym that founde the new isle, £10.

(*Extract from the Privy Purse Accounts, Henry VII.*)

ACCOUNTS OF THE FIRST VOYAGE OF JOHN CABOT.

Letter from Lòrenzo Pasqualigo to his brothers Alvise and Francesco.[1]

London, 23rd August 1497.

Our Venetian, who went with a small ship from Bristol to find new islands, has come back, and says he has discovered, 700 leagues off, the mainland of the country of the Gran Cam, and that he coasted along it for 300 leagues, and landed, but did not see any person. But he has brought here to the king certain snares spread to take game, and a needle for making nets, and he found some notched trees, from which he judged that there were inhabitants. Being in doubt, he came back to the ship. He has been away three months on the voyage, which is certain, and, in returning, he saw two islands to the right, but he did not wish to land, lest he should lose time, for

---

[1] *Calendar of State Papers* (Venice), i, p. 262, No. 752.

he was in want of provisions. This king has been much pleased. He says that the tides are slack, and do not make currents as they do here. The king has promised for another time, ten armed ships as he desires, and has given him all the prisoners, except such as are confined for high treason, to go with him, as he has requested ; and has granted him money to amuse himself till then. Meanwhile, he is with his Venetian wife and his sons at Bristol. His name is Zuam Talbot,[1] and he is called the Great Admiral, great honour being paid to him, and he goes dressed in silk. The English are ready to go with him, and so are many of our rascals. The discoverer of these things has planted a large cross in the ground with a banner of England, and one of St. Mark, as he is a Venetian ; so that our flag has been hoisted very far away.

First Despatch of Raimondo di Soncino to the Duke of Milan.[2] (*Extract.*)

24th August 1497.

Some months afterwards His Majesty sent a Venetian, who is a distinguished sailor, and who was much skilled in the discovery of new islands, and he has returned safe, and has discovered two very large and fertile islands, having, it would seem, discovered the seven cities 400 leagues from England to the westward. These successes led His Majesty at once to entertain the intention of sending him with fifteen or twenty vessels.

---

[1] A misprint: "T" for "C".
[2] *Calendar of State Papers* (Venice), iii, p. 260, No. 750.

Second Despatch of Raimondo di Soncino to the Duke of Milan.[1]

18th December 1497.

My most illustrious and most excellent Lord,

Perhaps amidst so many occupations of your Excellency it will not be unwelcome to learn how this Majesty has acquired a part of Asia without drawing his sword. In this kingdom there is a certain Venetian named Zoanne Caboto, of gentle disposition, very expert in navigation, who, seeing that the most serene Kings of Portugal and Spain had occupied unknown islands, meditated the achievement of a similar acquisition for the said Majesty. Having obtained royal privileges securing to himself the use of the dominions he might discover, the sovereignty being reserved to the Crown, he entrusted his fortune to a small vessel with a crew of 18 persons, and set out from Bristo, a port in the western part of this kingdom. Having passed Ibernia, which is still further to the west, and then shaped a northerly course, he began to navigate to the eastern part, leaving (during several days) the North Star on the right hand; and having wandered thus for a long time, at length he hit upon land,[2] where he hoisted the royal standard, and took possession for this Highness, and, having obtained various proofs of his discovery, he returned. The said Messer Zoanne, being a foreigner and poor, would not have been believed if the crew, who are nearly all English, and belonging to Bristo, had not

---

[1] *Annuario Scientifico*, Milan, 1866, p. 700 ; *Archiv d'Etat Milan*, reprinted by Harrisse, p. 324, from the *Intorno* of Desimoni, and translated from his text for the Hakluyt Society, with his permission. Also Tarducci, p. 351.   [2] "Terra ferma."

testified that what he said was the truth. This Messer
Zoanne has the description of the world on a chart,
and also on a solid sphere which he has constructed, and
on which he shows where he has been ; and, proceeding
towards the east, he has passed as far as the country
of the Tanais. And they say that there the land is
excellent and (the climate ?) temperate, suggesting that
brasil and silk grow there. They affirm that the sea
is full of fish, which are not only taken with a net, but
also with a basket, a stone being fastened to it in order to
keep it in the water ; and this I have heard stated by the
said Messer Zoanne.

The said Englishmen, his companions, say that they
took so many fish that this kingdom will no longer have
need of Iceland, from which country there is an immense
trade in the fish they call stock-fish. But Messer Zoanne
has set his mind on higher things, for he thinks that, when
that place has been occupied, he will keep on still further
towards the east, where he will be opposite to an island
called Cipango, situated in the equinoctial region, where
he believes that all the spices of the world, as well as the
jewels, are found. He further says that he was once at
Mecca, whither the spices are brought by caravans from
distant countries ; and having inquired from whence they
were brought and where they grow, they answered that
they did not know, but that such merchandize was brought
from distant countries by other caravans to their home ;
and they further say that they are also conveyed from
other remote regions. And he adduced this argument,
that if the eastern people tell those in the south that these
things come from a far distance from them, presupposing
the rotundity of the earth, it must be that the last turn
would be by the north towards the west ; and it is said
that in this way the route would not cost more than it
costs now, and I also believe it. And what is more, this

Majesty, who is wise and not prodigal, reposes such trust in him because of what he has already achieved, that he gives him a good maintenance, as Messer Zoanne has himself told me. And it is said that before long his Majesty will arm some ships for him, and will give him all the malefactors to go to that country and form a colony, so that they hope to establish a greater depot of spices in London than there is in Alexandria. The principal people in the enterprise belong to Bristo. They are great seamen, and, now that they know where to go, they say that the voyage thither will not occupy more than 15 days after leaving Ibernia. I have also spoken with a Burgundian, who was a companion of Messer Zoanne, who affirms all this, and who wishes to return because the Admiral (for so Messer Zoanne is entitled) has given him an island, and has given another to his barber of Castione,[1] who is a Genoese, and both look upon themselves as Counts ; nor do they look upon my Lord the Admiral as less than a Prince. I also believe that some poor Italian friars are going on this voyage, who have all had bishopricks promised to them. And if I had made friends with the Admiral when he was about to sail, I should have got an archbishoprick at least; but I have thought that the benefits reserved for me by your Excellency will be more secure. I would venture to pray that, in the event of a vacancy taking place in my absence, I may be put in possession, and that I may not be superseded by those who, being present, can be more diligent than I, who am reduced in this country to eating at each meal ten or twelve kinds of victuals, and to being three hours at table every day, two for love of your Excellency, to whom I humbly recommend myself.

[1] Perhaps Castiglione, near Chiavari.

London, 18 Dec. 1497, your Excellency's most humble
servant,

RAIMUNDUS.

SECOND LETTERS PATENT GRANTED TO JOHN CABOT.[1]

H. R.

To all men to whom thies presentis shall come send
gretings ; knowe ye that we of our grace especiall and for
dyvers causis us moving, we have given and graunten, and
by thies presentis yeve and graunte to our well-beloved
John Kabotto, Venician, sufficiente auctorite and power
that he by hym, his deputie or deputies, sufficient may
take at his pleasure vi Englisshe shippes in any poorte or
portes or other place within our realme of Ingland or
obeisaunce to that, and if the said shippes be of the bour-
deyn of C C tonnes or under with their apparaill requisite
and necessarie for the safe conduct of the seid shippes, and
theym convey and lede to the Londe and Iles of late
founde by the seid John in oure name and by oure com-
maundemente, payng for theym and every of theym as
and if we should in or for our owen cause paye and
noon otherwise.

And that the seid John by hym, his deputie or deputies,
sufficiente maye take and receyve into the seid shippes and
every of theym all suche maisters, maryners, pages, and
our subjects as of theyr owen free wille woll goo and
passe with hym in the same shippes to the seid Londe
or Iles, withoute any impedymente, lett, or perturbance
of any of our officeis or ministres or subjectes whatso-

-----

[1] Public Record Office, 13 Hen. VII, No. 6.   First discovered and
published by Biddle, pp. 76-77.   Afterwards by Desimoni, p. 56 ; and
Harrisse, p. 328.

evir they be by theym to the seid subjectes or any of
theym passing with the seid John in the seid shippes
to the seid Londe or Iles to be doon or suffer to be doon
or attempted.   Yeving in commaundement to all and
every our officers, ministres, and subjectes seying or
herying thies our lettres patents, withoute anye ferther
commaundement by us to theym or any of theym to
be geven, to perfourme and socour the seid John, his
deputie and all our seid subjectes to passynge with him
according to the tenor of thies our lettres patentis.   Any
statute, acte, or ordenaunce to the contrarye made, or to
be made, in any wise notwithstanding.

———

SPANISH AMBASSADORS ON THE SECOND VOYAGE OF JOHN CABOT.

Despatch from Ruy Gonzales de Puebla to the Catholic Sovereigns.[1]

25th July (?) 1498.

The King of England sent five armed ships with another
Genoese like Columbus to search for the island of Brasil,
and others near it.[2]   They were victualled for a year.
They say that they will be back in September.   By the
direction they take, the land they seek must be the
possession of your Highnesses.   The king has sometimes
spoken to me about it, and seems to take very great
interest in it.   I believe that the distance from here is not
400 leagues.

---

[1] Public Record Office.   Printed in Harrisse's *Cabot*, p. 328.
[2] Desimoni suspects that the true reading is not *vicinidades*, but
septe citades.   (*Intorno a Giovanni Caboto*, Pref., p. 15.)

Despatch from Pedro de Ayala to the Catholic Sovereigns.[1]
(Extract from a long Despatch on several subjects.)

25th July 1498.

I well believe that your Highnesses have heard how the King of England has equipped a fleet to discover certain islands and mainland that certain persons who set out last year for the same have testified that they have found. I have seen the chart which the discoverer has drawn, who is another Genoese like Columbus, and has been in Seville and in Lisbon, procuring to find those who would help him in this enterprise. It is seven years since those of Bristol used to send out, every year, a fleet of two, three, or four *caravels* to go and seek for the isle of Brasil and the seven cities, according to the fancy of this Genoese. The king determined to despatch an expedition, because he had the certainty that they had found land last year. The fleet consisted of 5 ships provisioned for one year. News has come that one, on board of which there was one friar Buil, has returned to Ireland in great distress, having been driven back by a great storm.

The Genoese went on his course. I, having seen the course and distance he takes, think that the land they have found or seek is that which your Highnesses possess, for it is at the end of that which belongs to your Highnesses by the convention with Portugal. It is hoped that they will return by September. I send the knowledge of it to your Highnesses. The King of England has spoken to me about it several times, and he thinks that your Highnesses will take great interest in it. I believe the

---

[1] Public Record Office, *Calendar of State Papers* (Spain), i, p. 176, No 210. The original despatch was in cipher.

distance is not 400 leagues. And I told him that I
thought they were the islands discovered by your Highnesses, and I even gave him a reason; but he would not
hear it. As I believe that your Highnesses now have
intelligence of all, as well as the chart or mappe-monde
that this Genoese has made, I do not send it now, though
I have it here; and to me it seems very false to give
out that they are not the said islands.

ACCOUNT OF SEBASTIAN CABOT.

From the "Decades" of Peter Martyr[1] (published 1516).

These north seas have been searched by one Sebastian Sebastian Cabot.
Cabot, a Venetian borne, whom beyng yet but in maner
an infant,[2] his parentes caryed with them into Englande,
havyng occasion to resort thither for trade of marchandize,
as is the maner of the Venetians, to leave no part of the
worlde unsearched to obtaine rychesse. He therefore
furnished two shyppes in England at his own charges;
and fyrst, with three hundreth men, directed his course so The voyage of Sebastian Cabot from Englande to the frozen sea.
farre towarde the north pole that, even in the moneth of
July, he founde monstrous heapes of Ise swymming on
the sea, and, in maner, continuall daylyght: yet sawe he
lande in that tract free from Ise (whiche had been moulten
by heat of the Sonne[3]). Thus, seeyng suche heapes of
Ise before hym, he was enforced to turne his sayles and
folowe the west, so coastynge styll by the shore, that he
was thereby brought so farre into the south, by reason of
the lande bending so muche southwarde, that it was there

---

[1] From Eden's translation (Willes' ed., 1577, f. 125). *De Orbe
Novo Decades, Dec. III*, Lib. VI.

[2] *Pene infans.* [3] Interpolation.

P

almost equall in latitude with the sea called *Fretum Herculeum,* havyng the north pole elevate in maner the same degree. He sayled lykewyse in this tract so farre towarde the west, that he had the Ilande of Cuba on his left hande, in maner in the same degree of longitude. As he traveyled by the coastes of this great lande (which he named *Baccallaos*), he sayth he founde the lyke course of the waters toward the west, but the same to runne more softly and gentelly, then the swifte waters which the Spanyardes found in their navigations southwarde. Wherefore, it is not onely more lyke to be true, but ought also of necessitie to be concluded, that betwene both the landes hitherto unknowen there shoulde be certayne great open places, wherby the waters should thus continually passe from the east into the west : whiche waters I suppose to be dryven about the globe of the earth by the uncessaunt movyng and impulsion of the heavens, and not to be swalowed up and cast out agayne by the breathyng of *Demogorgon,* as some have imagined, bycause they see the seas by increase and decrease to flow and reflow. Sebastian *Cabot* hymselfe named those landes Baccallaos, bycause that in the seas therabout he founde so great multitudes of certayne bygge fyshes, much like unto Tunnies[1] (which the inhabitants cal *Baccallaos*), that they somtymes stayed his shyppes. He founde also the people of those regions covered with beastes skynnes, yet not without the use of reason. He also sayth there is great plentie of Beares in those regions, whiche use to eate fyshe ; for, plungeing themselves into the water where they perceive a multitude of these fyshes to lye, they fasten theyr clawes in theyr scales, and so drawe them to lande and eate them : so that (as he sayth) the Beares, beyng thus satisfied with fyshe, are not noysome to men. He declareth

Demogorgon is the spirite of the earth.

People covered with beastes skynnes.

---

[1] *Tynnos.*

further that, in many places of these regions, he saw great plentie of laton[1] among the inhabitants. (Cabot is my very frend, whom I use familierlye, and delyte to have hym sometymes keepe me company in my owne house[2]:) so beyng called out of Englande by (commandement of[3]) the catholyque kyng of Castile, after the death of Henry kyng of Englande[4] (the seventh of that name[3]), he was made one of our counsayle (and assistance as touching the affayres of the new Indies[3]), lookyng dayly for shyppes to be furnished for hym to discover this hyd secret of nature. This voyage is appoynted to be begunne in the Marche in the yeere next folowyng, beyng the yeere of Christ 1516. What shall succeede your holynesse shalbe advertysed by my letters, yf God graunt me lyfe.[5] Some of the Spaniardes denye that Cabot was the fyrst fynder of the lande of *Bacallaos*, and affirme that he went not so farre weste-warde : (But it shall suffice to have sayde thus muche of the gulfes and strayghtes, and of Sebastian Cabot[6]).

RAMUSIO'S RECOLLECTION OF A LETTER FROM SEBASTIAN CABOT.

(Vol. iii, Preface, p. 4; ed. 1556.)

It is not yet thoroughly known whether the lande set in fiftie degrees of latitude to the north be separated and divided by the sea as islands, and whether by that way one may goe by Sea unto the Country of Cathaio : as many yeeres past it was written unto me by Sebastian Gabotto,

---

[1] *Orichalcum* (copper ore).

[2] "Familiarem habeo domi Cabottum ipsum et contubernalem interdum."

[3] Interpolation.

[4] "Majoris Britanniæ."

[5] "Modo vivere detur."

[6] "De fascibus et Cabotto jam satis."

our (countrie man[1]) Venetian, man of great experience, and
very rare in the art of Navigation and the knowledge of
Cosmographie, who sayled along and beyond the lande of
Newe Fraunce at the charges of King Henrie the seventh,
King of England.   And he told me that having sayled a
long time West and by North[2] beyonde these Ilands unto
the latitude of 67 degrees and a halfe under the North
Pole, and, at the 11 day of June, finding still open Sea
without any manner of impediment, hee thought verily by
that way to have passed on still the way to Cathaio,
which is in the East, and would have done it, if the
mutinie[3] of the shipmasters and marriners had not rebelled
.and made him to returne homewards from that place.[4]

ACCOUNT OF SEBASTIAN CABOT BY THE ANONYMOUS
GUEST[5] AT THE HOUSE OF HIERONIMUS FRACASTOR.

(*Ramusio*, ed. Ven., 1550-53, i, f. 414.)

During a short pause he turned towards us and said:
" Do you not know, with reference to this business of going
in search of India by the north, what was done[6] by your
Venetian fellow-citizen, who was so learned and experienced
in matters relating to navigation and cosmography that he

[1] Interpolated by Hakluyt.
[2] " Ponente e quarto di Maestro."   [3] " Malignita."
[4] This is the source from which Sir Humphrey Gilbert derived his
very inaccurate information about Sebastian Cabot, in his *Discourse
of a Discoverie of a New Passage to Cataia*.   He also has the date
June 11th, found nowhere else, the latitude 67° 30' and the open sea,
with the mutiny.
[5] Ramusio withholds the name of the guest.   Mr. Harrisse has
shown that it was not the legate Galeatius Butrigarius, as affirmed by
Fox (p. 13) and others : copying Eden.   For Galeas Butrigari had
long been dead (p. 338).
[6] Hakluyt has "as did of late", instead of "what was done by".

has not now his equal in Spain. His attainments have caused him to be preferred to all the pilots who navigate to the western Indies, who are not able to exercise their employments without his licence, and for this reason his title is "Chief Pilot." We answered that we did not know it, and he continued, saying that finding himself in the city of Seville a few years ago,[1] and desiring to know about those navigations of the Castillians, he was told that a distinguished Venetian was there who had knowledge of them, named Sebastian Caboto, who knew how to make marine charts with his own hands, and understood the art of navigation better than anyone else. He soon found himself in company with the Venetian, and said that he was a most gentle and courteous person who was very kind, showing him many things, and, among others, a great mappe-monde with the special navigations as well of the Portuguese as of the Castillians. Caboto said: "My father having left Venice many years, and having come to live in England as a merchant in the city of London, I being then very young, yet had I already learnt the humanities and the sphere. My father died at the time when the news came that the Genoese Christopher Columbus had discovered the coast of the Indies, and it was much discussed by everyone at the court of King Henry VII, who then reigned, saying that it was a thing more divine than human[2] to have found that way never before known to go to the east where the spices grow. In this way a great and heartfelt desire arose in me to achieve some signal enterprise. Knowing by a study of the sphere that if I should navigate to the west I would find a shorter route to the Indies, I quickly made known my thought to his Majesty the King, who was well content, and fitted out

---

[1] Hakluyt has : "being certain years in the city of Seville".
[2] "Dicendosi che era stata cosa piutosto divina che humana."

two caravels for me with everything needful.   This was[1] in
1496, in the commencement of the summer.   I began to
navigate towards the west, expecting not to find land
until I came to Catay, whence I could go on to the
Indies.   But, at the end of some days, I discovered that
the land trended northwards, to my great disappoint-
ment; so I sailed along the coast to see if I could find
some gulf where the land turned, until I reached the
height of 56° under our pole, but, finding that the land
turned eastward, I despaired of finding an opening.   I
turned to the right to examine again to the southward,
always with the object of finding a passage to the Indies,
and I came to that part which is now called Florida.
Being in want of victuals, I was obliged to return thence
to England, where I found great popular tumults among
the rebels, and a war with Scotland.   So that there was
no chance of further navigation to those parts being
considered, and I therefore went to Spain to the Catholic
King and Queen Isabella,[2] who, having heard what I had
done, took me into their service, and provided for me
well, sending me on a voyage of discovery to the coast of
Brazil.   I found a very wide river, now called La Plata,
which I navigated for 200 leagues, always finding it very
beautiful and populous, the people coming to see me full
of wonder.   There were so many rivers that it could
hardly be believed.   I made many other voyages, which
I do not mention, and at last, finding that I was growing
old, I wished to rest, after having instructed so many
practical and valiant young seamen, by whose forwardness
I do rejoice in the fruit of my labour, and rest with the

---

[1] Hakluyt has interpolated : "so farre as I remember".
[2] This cannot be true.   Isabella died in 1504, and Sebastian Cabot
came to Spain in 1512.

charge of this office as you see." This is what I learnt from Sebastian Caboto.[1]

ACCOUNT OF SEBASTIAN CABOT FROM GOMARA.[2]
(1552.)

He who obtained the most news of this land was Sebastian Gaboto, a Venetian. He armed two vessels in England (where he had been brought up from a child) at the cost of King Henry VII, who desired to trade with the spice country like the King of Portugal. Others say that it was at his own cost, and that he promised the King of England to go by the north to Catay, and to bring spices thence in a shorter time than the Portuguese brought them from the south. He also went to ascertain what land of the Indies could be settled. He took 300 men, and went in the direction of Iceland to the cape of Labrador, reaching 58°,[3] although he says much more. He relates how that, in the month of July, it was so cold, and there were such great pieces of ice, that he could get no further, that the days were very long and almost without night, and that the nights were very clear. It is certain that in 60° the days have 18 hours. Considering the cold and the forbidding nature of the country, he turned to the south, and, passing the Baccalaos, he proceeded as far as 38°, returning thence to England.

---

[1] With reference to this conversation, Ramusio says he does not pretend to be able to relate it exactly as he heard it, for that would require a better memory than his, but he will strive briefly to give what he is able to recollect.

[2] *Historia General de las Indias*, Parte I : *Cap. de los Bacallaos.*

[3] "Hasta se poner en 58°."

ACCOUNT OF SEBASTIAN CABOT FROM THE TRATADO OF ANTONIO GALVÃO. 1550.[1]

In the yeere 1496 there was a Venetian in England called John Cabota, who having knowledge of such a new discoverie as this was, and perceiving by the globe that the islands before spoken of stood about in the same latitude with his countrey, and much neerer to England than to Portugall or to the Castile, he acquainted King Henrie the seventh, then King of England, with the same, wherewith the saide king was greatly pleased, and furnished him out with two ships and three hundred men : which departed and set saile in the spring of the yeare, and they sailed westward til they came in sight of land, in 45 degrees of latitude towards the north, and then went straight northwards till they came into sixty degrees of latitude, where the day is 18 howers long, and the night is very cleere and bright.   There they found the aire cold, and great islands of ice, but no ground in seventy, eighty, or hundred fathoms sounding, but found much ice, which alarmed them : and so from thence, putting about, finding the land to turne eastwards, they trended along by it, discovering all the bay and river named Deseado,[2] to see if it passed on the other side ; then they sailed back again till they came to 38 degrees towards the equinoctial line, and from thence returned into England.   There be others which say that he went as far as the Cape of Florida, which standeth in 25 degrees.

---

[1] From the translation published by the Hakluyt Society with the Portuguese text, p. 88.

[2] " Descobrindo toda a baya, rio, enseada."

SEBASTIAN CABOT'S INTRIGUES WITH VENICE.

Despatch of the Council of Ten to Gaspar Contarini.[1]

27th September 1522.

To our Orator near the Cæsarean and Catholic Majesty.

Since the other day one Don Hierolamo di Marin de Bucignolo, a Ragusan, who came before the presence of the Chiefs of our Council of Ten, said that he was sent by one Sebastian Cabotto, who declares that he belongs to this our city, and now resides in Seville, where he has the appointment, from that Cæsarean and Catholic Majesty, of his Chief Pilot for the discovery and navigation of new lands. And in his name he referred to an accompanying deposition as his credential, touching which, although we do not see that we can place much trust in it, yet, as there may be some importance in it, we have not thought fit to reject the offer of the same Sebastian to come to our presence, to say what he has in his mind respecting this matter. Hence we are content that the said Hierolamo should write to him according to the tenor of what you will see in the enclosed. We therefore desire, and we, the said Heads of our Council of Ten, instruct you that, with all diligence but with due caution, you shall take means to find out if the aforesaid Sebastian is in the court or about to come there shortly, in which case you are to procure that he shall come to you, and you are to deliver to him the said letter which we have arranged to send by another way to your very faithful servant, that it may reach you presently. You should endeavour to find out something of

---

[1] This correspondence with the Venetian Ambassador in Spain is preserved at Venice. It was printed by Mr. Harrisse for his work on the Cabots, and it has been translated from his text for the Hakluyt Society, with his permission.

the matter in hand in the event of his being disposed to be open with you, in which case we are well content to leave it to you to ascertain his sentiments. When you see him you should move him with sound reasoning, and encourage him to come here, for we are not only desirous but anxious that he should come to us securely. If he should not be at court, nor about to come, but returned to Seville, take care to send all letters by a safe channel, so that they may reach him. Let him know by whom they are sent, that they come from his own friends here, and under any circumstances report everything to the said Heads of our Council of Ten. Having just received letters from the Captain-General of Candia, with news touching the affairs of Rhodes, we send you a summary, that you may communicate it to that Cæsarean and Catholic Majesty, to the magnificent Grand Chancellor, to the reverend Bishop of Valencia, and to others in your discretion.

> Julianus Gradovico, C. C.
> Andreus Mudesco, C. C.
> Dominicus Capelo, C. C.

Recompense granted to the Ragusan.

1522, September 27. In the college of the Lords the Heads of the most illustrious Council of Ten.

That it may be ordered to the Chamberlain of our Council of Ten that from the moneys of their treasury there be disbursed a gift of 20 ducats to the Lord Hieronimo de Marin, a Ragusan, for good cause.

The order given.

Despatch from Contarini to the Senate of Venice.

Valladolid, 31st December 1522.

Most Serene Prince and most excellent Lords,—

On the third vigil of the Nativity, with due reverence, I received the letter from your Lordships dated the 27th of September; by which is explained to me the proposal of Hieronimo, the Ragusan, in the name of Sebastian Caboto, and I am instructed, if he is at the Court, to give him that letter and to make certain proposals to him, opening the whole business, and exhorting him to come to the feet of your Serenity. In order to execute these instructions, I dexterously ascertained whether he was at the Court, and, this being so, I sent to say that my secretary had to deliver a letter sent by a friend of his, and that, if he wished to receive it, he should come to my lodgings.

He understood this from my servant who went to him, and came on Christmas Eve at the hour of dinner. I withdrew with him, and gave him the letter, which he read, and, in reading it, he lost all colour. Having read it, he put it in his pocket without speaking to me, and looking frightened and amazed. I then said to him that, when he should desire to answer that letter, he should tell me what he wished, and that I would write to those who had sent it, for that I should be prompt in making the business end well. Having been reassured, he spoke to me: "I had already spoken to the Ambassador of the most illustrious Seigneury in England, owing to the affection I have for the fatherland, when those newly-found lands could be made of such great utility to my country; and now, as regards what has been written to me, you ought to know all; but I pray you that it may be kept secret, for it is a matter on which my life depends." I then

told him that I knew all about it very well, and how the
Ragusan was brought before the most excellent Chief
Lords, and that I have received intelligence of all that was
sent in that letter from the most secret magistrate. But,
as some gentlemen were coming to dine with me, it was
not convenient to discuss the business further at that time.
It would be better if he would return in the afternoon,
when we might confer more fully. He then went away
and returned at night, when I received him alone in my
room. He said to me: "Lord Ambassador, to tell you
all, I was born in Venice, but was brought up in England,
and afterwards entered the service of this Catholic King of
Spain, and was made captain by King Ferdinand, with
a salary of 50 m. maravedis. I was then made Chief
Pilot by this King, with another 50 m. maravedis, and, to
help my expenses, was given 25 m. maravedis, making in
all 125 m. maravedis, which may be reckoned at nearly
300 ducats. Having returned to England three years ago,
that most reverend Cardinal wished that I would undertake the command of a fleet of his to discover countries,
which fleet was nearly ready, he being prepared to expend
upon it 30 m. ducats. I replied that, being in the service of
this Majesty, I was not able to undertake it without his
permission. At that time, conversing with a Venetian
friar named Stragliano Collona, with whom I had a great
friendship, he said to me: 'Messer Sebastian, you are
very anxious to do great things for foreigners; do you not
remember your own country? Is it not possible that you
might also be useful to it?' I felt this in my heart at the
time, and replied that I would think over it. Having
returned to him on the following day, I said that I had
a way by which that city might participate in these
voyages, and I showed him a way which would be of
great utility. As by serving the King of England I should
not be able to serve my country, I wrote to the Cæsarean

Majesty that he should not, on any account, give me
permission to serve the King of England, because there
would be great injury to his service, but that he should
recall me. Having returned to Seville, I formed a great
friendship with this Ragusan who now writes to me, telling
me that I ought to transfer my services to Venice. I have
opened myself to him, and I charged him that the affair
should not be made known to anyone but the Heads of the
Ten, and he swore this to me on the sacrament." I answered
him first by praising his affection for his native land, and
then said that the Ragusan had been to the most excellent
Chief Lords, had received letters on the subject, and that now
they should be informed of the details of his plan, and that
the time was come for him to present himself before
your most excellent Lordships in person. But he replied
that as he could not explain his thought to any others than
the most excellent Chief Lords, and that he must therefore proceed to Venice, it would first be necessary to
obtain permission from the Emperor, on the plea that he
wished to recover the dowry of his mother, on which affair
he would speak to the magnificent Chancellor and the
Bishop of Burgos, if I would write in his favour to your
serenity. I answered that, as he wished to go to Venice, I
commended the way in which he proposed to obtain leave.
As I did not wish to expose his scheme, not wishing to do
more than he desired, I thought it well to say this much,
adding that in any deliberation he ought to consider two
things: one was that the proposal should be useful, and the
other that its utility could be secured. But with regard to
the possibility of such an issue I am very doubtful. For I
have some slight knowledge of geography, and, considering
the position of Venice, I can see no way whatever by
which she can undertake these voyages. It would be
necessary to sail in vessels built at Venice, or else they
must be built outside the strait. If they are built at

Venice they will have to pass the Straits of Gibraltar to
reach the ocean, which would not be possible in face of
the opposition of the King of Portugal and the King
of Spain. If they are not built at Venice they can only
be built on the shore of the western ocean ; for they
cannot be constructed in the Red Sea without infinite
trouble. First it would be necessary to make an agreement with the Turk ; and, secondly, the scarcity of timber
would make it impossible to build ships. Even if they
were built, the forts and armed vessels of the Portuguese
would make it impossible to continue that navigation.
Nor can I see any possibility of building ships on the
western ocean, Germany being subject to the Emperor.
So that I can perceive no way whatever by which merchandise could be brought to Venice from those ships, or
from the ships to Venice ; but, being an inexpert person in
such matters, I merely made these observations to him.
He replied that there was much in what I said, and that
truly nothing could be done with vessels built in Venice
or in the Red Sea. But that there was another way, which
was not only possible but easy, by which ships might be
built, and merchandize be carried from the port to Venice,
and from Venice to the port, as well as gold and other
things. He added : " I know, because I have navigated to
all those countries, and am familiar with all. I told you
that I would not undertake the voyage for the King of
England, because that enterprise would in no way benefit
Venice." I shrugged my shoulders, and, although the
thing appeared to me to be impossible, I would not dis-
suade him further, so as not to discourage him from
presenting himself to your Highnesses, and I considered
that the possibilities are much more ample than is often
believed. This man has great renown, and so for the
present we parted. On the day of St. John he came to see
me, to look at some words in the letter of the Ragusan,

doubting whether they might arouse suspicion, and so the letter was rewritten and corrected. He then discussed many geographical points with me, and told me of a method he had observed of finding the distance between two places east and west of each other, by means of the needle. It is a beautiful discovery, never observed by any one else, as he will be able to explain when he comes before your serenity. And reasoning with him on the principal business, I dexterously repeated my objections; but he repeated that the way was easy. "I will go to Venice, at my expense", he said; "they will hear and be pleased with the plan I have devised; I will return at my own expense," and he urged me to keep the matter secret. Such is the arrangement that I have made. Your serenity will hear, and your wisdom will decide on what shall appear best.

Despatch of Contarini to the Senate of Venice.

Valladolid, March 7th, 1523.

Most serene Prince and most excellent Lords,—

That Sebastian Cabot, with whom your Excellencies instructed me to speak on the subject of the spice-countries, and respecting whom I reported, has been to me several times, always giving me to understand that his wish is to come to Venice, and to work in the interests of your Highnesses in that matter of the spiceries. At length he sought me to say that he could not now seek permission to go, doubting whether it might not be suspected that he wished to go to England, and that he would be absent three months. After that he would come to the feet of your most illustrious Lordships, praying that meanwhile a letter might be written in the form of the other that was sent, asking him to come to Venice to expedite his private affairs, thus leave would be more easily obtained. I write to your Highnesses to report what this Sebastian has said, respecting which steps will be taken as seems desirable.

The Council of Ten to Contarini.

Lord Gasparo Contarini, our Orator near the Cæsarean Majesty.

28th April 1523.

We have received, a few days since, your despatches addressed to the Chiefs of our Council of Ten, dated the last of December, in which you report all the intercourse you have had with Sebastian Cabotto on the subject of the spices, and we cannot refrain from highly commending the prudence and judgment with which you have conducted the negotiation. We have also received your despatch of March 7th, from which we learn the resolution of the said Sebastian not to come here for three months; and that he requests a letter may be written on the subject of his own affairs, whereby leave may be more easily obtained. We have therefore caused another letter to be prepared in the name of that Hieronimo de Marino from Ragusa, who came here to make the proposal, and we have ordered that it be placed in the bundle of your circumspect Secretary like the last, to be delivered to the said Caboto, telling him that he should come here in accordance with his promise, as he will always be welcomed by us. Let the said Caboto be informed of this, and, if he is not at Court, the letter should be forwarded to him. Take care that it reaches him. The said Hieronimo Marino is not now to be found here in Venice, nor do we know where he is; but the letters of this Hieronimo arrive here. Receive what we say as your instructions.

ANDREAS FOSCARENUS, C. C.
JACOBUS MICHAEL, C. C.
ANDREAS FOSCULUS, C. C.

Letter from the Ragusan to Cabot.

Venice, April 28th, 1523.

Respectable Master Sebastian,—

It is some months since I came to Venice, and I wrote to you an account of what I had done to inquire where your goods are to be found, that I received good words on all hands, and was given good hope that I should recover the dower of your mother,[1] so that I have no doubt, if you could come, you would obtain all your desires. For the love I bear you, and for your own welfare and benefit, I exhort you not to be false to yourself, but to come here to Venice, where, I doubt not, you will obtain everything ; so do not delay in coming here, for your *ameda* is very old, and failing her there will be very great trouble in recovering your property. Set out as soon as possible ; so no more at present.

I am, always yours,

HIERONIMO DE MARINO.

Despatch of Contarini.

Valladolid, July 26th, 1523.

Most serene Prince and most excellent Lords,—

By the post arrived from Italy, coming by way of Rome, I received with due reverence your letter of April 23rd, in which your serenity informed me of the receipt of my letters reporting the negotiation with Sebastian Cabot ; and adding that other letters have been sent to Sebastian in the name of that Hieronimo of Ragusa with reference to his request. By good luck Sebastian was in Seville when he received the letters, and he returned here on being exhorted to come. He told me that he had no other thought, and with that object he had come ; adding

---

[1] " Et ameda" (?).

that he had sought permission from the Cæsarean Council
to confer with me, and they have also spoken to me in his
commendation. I will advise your serenity of what may
happen next.

Despatch of the Council of Ten to Giacomo Soranzo, Venetian Ambassador in England.[1]

12th September 1551.

By your letters of the 17th of last month to the Heads
of our Council of Ten, we have understood what you have
deemed it necessary to report respecting our most faithful
Sebastian Gaboto, which has been very agreeable to us,
and we approve of your diligence in obtaining special
information respecting his quality and condition. In
reply, we say that you should inform him that this his
offer is most gratifying, using the best words that your
judgment suggests. As to the request that has been made
to you by those Lords, touching the credit he claims and
the recovery of goods, you can reply that we desire to do
all we can to make things agreeable to that Majesty and
to their Lordships ; but, as Gaboto is not known to anyone
here, it will be necessary that he himself should come personally to justify his claim, the matters of which he speaks
being of very old date, and we have now replied to the
magnificent Ambassador of that Majesty in conformity
with your letter ; therefore explain all this to Gaboto. On
this ground he might ask and obtain permission to come,
and you should see that he has the means to come here as
soon as possible. You should endeavour, using the same
method, to gather further information from him respecting
those important particulars that you have been able to
report hitherto, as well as his designs touching this navigation, transmitting full details to the Heads.

---

[1] *Calendar of State Papers* (Venice), v, No. 711, p. 264.

DOCUMENTS

THE VOYAGES

OF

GASPAR CORTE REAL.

DOCUMENTS

RELATING TO

GASPAR CORTE REAL.

From the "Tratado" of Antonio Galvam. 1563.
(Extract.)

N this same year, 1500, it is reported
that Gaspar Corte Real craved a gene-
ral licence of the King Dom Manoel
to go and discover a new land. He
departed from the island of Terceira
with two ships, armed at his own
cost, and went to that region which is under the 50th
degree of north latitude, a land now called by his name.
He returned safely to the city of Lisbon. Taking this
route once more, the ship in which he went was lost, and
the other returned to Portugal. For this cause his brother,
Miguel Corte Real, went in search of him, with three ships,
armed at his own cost. Arrived on that coast, as there
were so many bays and estuaries, each ship entered into
her own port, with this rule, that they should all meet again
on the 20th of August. The two other ships did so; and
seeing that the ship with Miguel Corte Real did not come
at the appointed time, after some time they returned to

this kingdom, and never more had tidings of him, nor did other memory of him abide. The country is called the land of the Corte Reals to this day.

———

From the " Chronica do Felicissimo Rei dom Emanuel",
composita per Damiam de Goes (Lisboa, 1566, fol. 65).

Gaspar Corte Real, son of Joam Vaz Corte Real, was an enterprising man, valorous, and eager to gain honour. He proposed to undertake the discovery of lands towards the north, because many discoveries had been made to the south. Thus he obtained favour for his undertaking from the king, whose servant he was when Duke of Beja, and armed one ship, which was well supplied with men and all necessaries. He sailed from the port of Lisbon in the beginning of the summer of 1500. In this voyage he discovered, in that direction of the north, a land which was very cool and with great woods, as are all lands that lie in that direction. He gave it the name of Green Land.[1] The people are very barbarous and wild, almost like those of the land of Sancta Cruz.[2] At first they are white, but they are so cut up by the cold that they lose their whiteness with age, and remain brown. They are of medium height, very agile, and great archers, using sticks hardened by fire instead of darts, with which they make as good a cast as if it was tipped with fine steel. They dress in the skins of animals which abound in that land. They live in caverns of the rocks and in huts. They believe much in diviners; they practise matrimony, and are very jealous of their women: in which things they resemble the Lapps, who also live in the north from 70 to 85 degrees, fugitives from the Kings of Norway and Sweden, to whom

---

[1] The east coast of Newfoundland.   [2] Brazil.

they pay tribute, always remaining in their heathen state from want of teaching. In the book that treats of the faith, customs, and religion of the Ethiopians, Abexis in the Latin language, dedicated to Pope Paul III, towards the end there is a lamentation, in which it is explained in detail whence so great an evil proceeds. Returning to Gaspar Corte Real, after he had discovered that land, and coasted along a great part of it, he returned to this kingdom. Presently, in the year 1501, being desirous of discovering more of this province, and of becoming better acquainted with its advantages, he departed from Lisbon on the 15th of May; but it is not known what happened to him in this voyage, for he never more appeared, nor were there any tidings of him. The delay and the suspicion that began to arise of his fate caused Miguel Corte Real, Chief Porter of the King, for the great love he bore his brother, to determine to go in search of him. He left Lisbon on the 10th of May 1502 with two ships, but there were never any tidings of them. The king felt the loss of these two brothers very much, and, of his own royal and pious motion, in the year 1503, he ordered two armed ships to be fitted out at his own cost, to go in search of them. But it could never be ascertained how either the one or the other was lost. To that part of the province of Green Land where it was believed that the brothers were lost the name was given of the Land of the Corte Reals. These two brothers, Gaspar and Miguel Corte Real, had another brother, whose name was Vasque Anes Corte Real, who was Controller of the King's Household, of his Council, Captain-Governor of the Islands of St. George and Terceira, and Alcalde Mayor of the city of Tavilla.[1] He was a very good knight and Christian, a man of exemplary life, and one who dispensed many charities, both publicly and

---

[1] Tavira in Algarve.

in secret. His son and heir is Emanuel Corte Real, also of
the King's Council and Captain of the same islands, who
now lives. This Vasque Anes Corte Real, unable to per-
suade himself that his brothers were dead, determined to fit
out ships at his own cost, and go in search of them, in the
year 1503. But, on requesting the king to excuse his
absence, his Majesty could not consent that he should
proceed further in that business, holding that it was
useless, and that all had been done that could be
done.

*A Letter from Alberto Cantino to Hercules d'Este,
Duke of Ferrara. (Extract.)*

Most Illustrious and Most Excellent Prince, and my very
singular good Lord.

Lisbon, October 17th, 1501.

It is now nine months since this most serene king sent
to the northern part two well-armed ships, to ascertain
if it would be possible to discover land or some islands in
that direction. On the 11th of the present month one of
them returned, and has brought people and tidings, which
it appeared to me ought not to pass without the knowledge of your Excellence. Therefore all that was related
by the captain to the king, I being present, is here clearly
written down. First they stated that, after leaving Lisbon,
they always went on that course and towards that pole
for four months, nor during all that time did they see
anything. In the fifth month, still wishing to push on,
they say that they came upon enormous masses of con-
gealed snow floating upon the sea, and moving under the
influence of the waves. Owing to the heat of the sun,
sweet and clear water is melted on their summits, and,

descending by small channels formed by the water itself, it eats away at the base where it falls. The ships now being in want of water, the boats were sent in, and in that way as much was taken as was needed. Fearing to remain in that place by reason of their danger, they intended to turn back ; but they consulted what was their best course, and, aided by hope, they resolved to go forward for some days. Proceeding on the voyage, they arrived at the frozen sea on the second day, and were forced to abandon their intention. So they began to turn towards the north-west and west, and were three months continuing in that direction, always with fine weather. On the first day of the fourth month they came in sight, between these two courses, of a very great country, which they approached with the greatest joy. Many large rivers of fresh water flowed through this region into the sea, one of them sending its waters for perhaps a league from the land. When they landed they found delicious fruits of various kinds, trees and pines of marvellous height and girth, suited for masts of the largest ships that float in the sea. Here there is no corn of any kind, but the men of that country say that they only live by fishing and hunting animals, in which the land abounds. There are very large stags with long hair, the skins of which they use for clothes, and make houses and boats of them. There are also wolves, foxes, tigers, and sables. They affirm that the peregrine falcons are so numerous that it appears to me to be a miracle, like those in our country. I have seen them, and they are very fine. They kidnapped nearly 50 of the men and women of that land by force, and brought them to the king. I have seen them, touched and examined them. Beginning with their size, I say they are bigger than our people, with well-formed limbs to correspond. The hair of the men is long, as we wear it, letting it hang in plaited rings. They have the face marked with great

signs, like those of the Indians. Their eyes incline to
green, and when they look from them it gives a great
fierceness to the whole countenance. Their speech cannot
be understood, but, however, there is no sharpness in it, and
it is altogether human. Their behaviour and gestures are
very gentle ; they laugh a good deal, and show great
delight. So much for the men. The woman has small
breasts and a very beautiful body. She has a very
gentle countenance, and its colour may be said to be more
white than any other tint, but that of the men is much
darker. In fine, except for the fierce look of the men,
they are very like ourselves. They are naked except for
a small covering made of deer-skin. They have no arms
nor iron, but for working or fashioning anything, they use
a very hard and sharp stone, with which there is nothing
so hard as that they cannot cut it. This ship has come
from thence to this place in a month, and they say that
the distance is 2,800 miles. The other consort has decided
to go so far along the coast, with the desire of ascertaining
whether it is an island or mainland. The king awaits the
arrival of the others with much anxiety, and as soon as
they come, bringing news worthy of your Excellency's
attention, I will at once send the particulars.[1]

Servant,

ALBERTO CANTINO.

To the most illustrious Prince and most
excellent Lord Hercules d'Este,
Duke of Ferrara, my most worthy
and singular good Lord.

---

[1] First printed by Mr. Harrisse in his work on Corte Real, p. 204,
from the MS. in the State Archives at Modena. The letter has been
translated from Mr. Harrisse's text for the Hakluyt Society, with
his permission.

Letter from Pietro Pasqualigo to the Seigneury of Venice.

Lisbon, October 18th, 1501.

On the ninth of the present month there arrived here one of the two caravels which the Majesty of the said king sent to discover towards the north-western part in the past year. It has brought seven natives, men, women, and children, from that discovered land. The country is at a distance of 1,800 miles to north and west. These men, in their aspect, figure, and stature, are like gipsies. They are marked on the face in several places, some with more, others with fewer lines. They are dressed in skins of different animals, but chiefly of otters. Their speech is entirely different from any that has ever been heard in this kingdom, and no one understands it. Their limbs are exceedingly well made, and they have very gentle countenances; but their habits are filthy, like wild men. The people of the caravel believe that the above land is the mainland, and that it joins to the other land that, in the previous year, was discovered to the north by another caravel of his Majesty. But they were not able to reach it, because the sea was frozen over with vast quantities of snow like mountains on the land. They also think that it is joined to the Andilie,[1] which were discovered by the Sovereigns of Spain, and with the land of Papagà, lately discovered by the ship of this king when on its way to Calicut.[2] This belief is caused, in the first place, because, having coasted along the said land for a distance of 600 miles and more, they did not come to any termination; also because they report the discovery of many very large rivers which fall into the sea. The other caravel (*Capitana*)

---

[1] Antilles. The Portuguese were the first to give this name to the West Indian Islands.

[2] Brazil visited in 1500 by Cabral, but not discovered. Pinzon had been there in the previous year.

is expected from day to day, from which the quality and condition of the said land will be clearly understood, as she has gone further along that coast, to discover as much as possible. This royal Majesty has derived great satisfaction from the news, because he considers that this land will be very useful to his affairs in many respects, but principally because, being very near to this kingdom, it will be easy, in a short time, to obtain abundant supplies of wood for making the masts and yards of ships, and slaves fit for any work ; for they say that the land is very populous, and also full of pines and other excellent timber. This news has given such pleasure to his Majesty that he has issued orders for ships to go there, and also for the increase of his Indian fleet, to conquer it as quickly as it was discovered ; for there it appears that God is with his Majesty and his works, and favours his designs.[1]

Letter from Pietro Pasqualigo to his Brothers.

Lisbon, October 19th, 1501.

*   *   *   *   *   *   *

On the 8th of the present month there arrived here one of the two caravels which this most serene king sent on a voyage of discovery towards the north in the past year, under Captain Gaspar Corterat (*sic*). It reports having discovered land two thousand miles from here towards the north-west and west, which was before not known to any one. They discovered from 600 to 700 miles of coast-line, without finding the end of it. They, therefore, believe that it is mainland, which is continuous with another land

---

[1] Printed by Mr. Harrisse in his work on Corte Real, p. 209, from the *Diarii di Marino Sanuto*, published at Venice, 1880-1881, in quarto, tom. iv, Fascicule 24, pp. 200-201. The letter has been translated for the Hakluyt Society from Mr. Harrisse's text, with his permission.

discovered in the previous year to the north. The caravel
could not reach the end of the land because the sea was
frozen over with a vast quantity of snow. This is also
believed because of the multitude of very large rivers they
discovered there, for certainly there would not be so many
nor such large ones on an island. They say that this land
is very populous, and the houses of the inhabitants are of
wood, very large, and covered outside with skins of fish.
They have brought here seven of the natives, men, women,
children, and fifty others will come in the other caravel,
which is expected from hour to hour. These are like
gipsies in figure, stature, and appearance, and are dressed
in the skins of divers animals, but chiefly of otters. In
summer they turn the skin inside, and in winter the other
way. These skins are not sewn together in any way, nor
tanned, but are thrown over the shoulders and arms just
as they are taken from the animals. The loins are fastened
with some cord made of the very strong sinews of a fish.
Although they appear to be wild men, yet they are modest
and gentle, and their arms, shoulders, and legs so well
proportioned that I cannot describe them. Their faces
are marked in the fashion of the Indians, some with six,
some with eight, some with no lines. They talk, but they
are not understood by anyone. I believe they have been
addressed in every possible language. They have no iron
in their country, but make knives of some stones, and in
like manner the points for their arrows. They have
brought from thence a piece of a broken sword, gilded,
which was certainly made in Italy. A native boy had two
silver rings in his ears, which without doubt seem to have
been manufactured at Venice.[1] This made me believe
that it was the mainland, because it is not possible that

---

[1] These must have been relics of the expedition of John Cabot in
1498.

a ship could ever have reached that place without having been heard of. There is a very great abundance of salmon, herrings, cod, and similar fish. There is also plenty of wood, and, above all, fine trees for making masts and yards of ships. This most serene king hopes to derive very great profit from the new land, both from the wood for ships, of which they have need, and from the men, who will be excellent for labour, and the best slaves that have hitherto been obtained. It appears to me a matter worthy of being brought to your notice, and if I shall learn more on the arrival of the caravel (*Capitana*), I will let you know.[1]

PAYMENT FOR THE CANTINO MAP.

To the most illustrious and most excellent
Duke and Lord, the Lord Hercules
d'Este, Duke of Ferrara, and my Lord
and most respected benefactor.

Rome, November 19th, 1502.

Most illustrious and most excellent Duke and Lord,—

I understood what your Excellency desired of me, by the letter sent to me in reply to one that I had previously addressed, especially as touching the nautical chart.

By that humble reply I apprised your Excellency that I had left the said chart at Genoa, in the hands of Master Francesco Catanio, who has paid to me 20 ducats (*striti*) that is to say, of three pounds each.

In truth, that chart cost me in Portugal, by contract, 12 golden ducats; but, constrained by need, and having

----

[1] First published in *Paesi Novamente Retrovati* (Vicenza, 1507, cap. cxxvi), and reprinted by Mr Harrisse in his work on Corte Real, p. 211. It has been translated from Mr. Harrisse's text, with his permission.

no one to whom to apply, I was obliged to accept that sum, and to do what I have explained to your Excellency.

The chart is of such a sort that I trust it will be pleasing to your Excellency, and that your Excellency will not regret having disbursed that sum, and that your Excellency will further pay the twelve ducats that the said chart cost me ; it will make me your Excellency's debtor.

Your Excellency will please to advise me what I ought to do in this matter ; meanwhile, holding me to be of the number of the faithful servants

of the most illustrious and most excellent Duke, the undersigned servant,

ALBERTO CANTINO.[1]

———

LEGENDS ON THE CANTINO MAP.

Legend by the Coast of Newfoundland.

Land of the King of Portugal.

This land was discovered by order of the very high and most excellent Prince, the King Dom Manoel, King of Portugal.   It was discovered by Gaspar de Corte Real, Gentleman of the Household of the said king, who, when he had discovered it, sent thence a ship with certain men and women found in that country, and he remained with the other ship, and never more was seen.   It is believed that he perished.   Here there are many masts.[2]

---

[1] Printed by Mr. Harrisse in his work on Corte Real, p. 216, from a manuscript in the Archives of the House of Este at Modena. It has been translated from Mr. Harrisse's text, with his permission.

[2] Trees for making masts (?).

Legend on the East Coast of Greenland between two
Portuguese Flags.

A ponta d: (assia).

This land was discovered by order of the very excellen
Prince Dom Manoel, King of Portugal, which it is believed
is a point of Asia. Those who discovered it did not land,
but they saw very serrated mountains; it is for this reason,
according to the opinion of cosmographers, that it is
believed that this is the extremity of Asia.

INDEX

JOURNAL OF COLUMBUS.

R

INDEX

OF THE

DOCUMENTS RELATING TO THE VOYAGES OF JOHN CABOT AND GASPAR CORTE REAL.

LONDON: CHAS. J. CLARK, 4, LINCOLN'S INN FIELDS, W.C.

𝕳𝖆𝖐𝖑𝖚𝖞𝖙 𝕰𝖉𝖎𝖙𝖎𝖓𝖌.

A CORRECTION.

In 1882 the late Gen. Sir John Henry Lefroy edited for the Hakluyt Society a volume entitled "*The Historye of the Bermudas or Summer Islands*," from MS. 750 of the Sloane Collection at the British Museum. In his introductory remarks our lamented colleague discussed the authorship of this MS., and from internal evidence attributed it to Capt. John Smith, the historian of Virginia.

Ten years have elapsed since the publication of Lefroy's work, and his conclusions have not, as far as I am aware, been questioned. It was only quite recently that Mr. Edward Scott, Keeper of MSS. in the Museum, while cataloguing the Sloane Collection, came upon a MS. in the same handwriting as 750, signed by Nathaniel Butler. This MS., numbered 758, is described by Sir F. Madden in his Catalogue, as follows: "1. Mem^da for 12 heads of Letters written by Capt. Nath. Butler while Governor of the Bermudas [autogr.]. 2. A dialogicall discourse of Marine affairs between the High Admirall and a Captaine att sea, written in six dialogues by Capt. N. Butler in 1634, with a table of contents prefixed. 3. A diary of my personall employments from 10 Feb. 1639 to 2 May 1640, by the same Capt. N. Butler [autogr.]."

A comparison of the two MSS. establishes the fact of the identity of the handwriting, though one is a fair copy, the other a rough draft. Both, however, are written by the same educated hand, and the signature at the end of 758, " Nath. Butler", is genuine.

Had General Lefroy seen the Madden Catalogue he could not have fallen into the error of attributing the *History of the Bermudas* to Capt. John Smith, for Madden expressly states that its author was Butler. But at the time Gen. Lefroy edited his book, the Madden Catalogue, which only went as far as 1100 of the Sloane MSS., had been suppressed. The Ayscough Catalogue, then and still in use, is arranged according to subjects, and our two MSS. fall under separate headings—" Bermuda" and " Butler" occurring in different vols. General Lefroy, basing his arguments on 750, the only MS. known to him, found several passages in his *History of the Bermudas* identical with Smith's *Hist. of Virginia*, Bk. 5, and came to the conclusion that Smith was the author of both books. But Capt. Smith was never at Bermuda, and there is reasonable ground for believing that many of the materials for the Bermuda portion of his work were supplied by Butler. At all events he is mentioned in the list of authorities quoted by that author under his initials N. B., and as he is known to have visited Virginia in 1623, soon after his governor-ship of the Bermudas was at an end, he would most probably have met with Smith, who had returned to New England the previous year to lend his assistance in re-storing the fortunes of that young colony, then at a low ebb. But even more conclusive proof is afforded by the date, for according to Gen. Lefroy, Capt. John Smith died in 1631, while the writer of MS. 758, and consequently of 750, was living in 1640.

It may be worth mentioning that this Captain Nathaniel Butler, who did good service as Governor of Bermuda from 1619 to 1622, and was afterwards (1638-41) Governor of (Old) Providence Island, is one of England's forgotten worthies, being passed over even by the *Dictionary of*

National Biography. He appears, too, to be the individual committed to Newgate in June 1649 by the Council of State for dispersing treasonable and scandalous books (*Cal. of State Papers, Domestic*), by no means a singular instance of the way justice was administered in those days.

E. DELMAR MORGAN,

Hon. Sec. Hakluyt Society.

P.S.—Since the above was written and published in the *Athenæum*, *Academy*, and *Nation* of New York, my attention has been called to the fact that Butler *does* appear in the *Dict. of Nat. Biogr.* under " Boteler". The article is by Prof. J. K. Laughton, who writes me that he hopes for the opportunity of improving it in the *Addenda et Corrigenda.*

Lightning Source UK Ltd.
Milton Keynes UK
UKHW022038010323
417889UK00005B/70

9 781297 922268